ECHOES
IN THE
MIRROR

a memoir of an ordinary woman

Belle A. DeCosta

Visit our website at **www.StillwaterPress.com** for more information.

First Stillwater River Publications Edition

Library of Congress Control Number: 2020905503

ISBN: 978-1-952521-01-0

1 2 3 4 5 6 7 8 9 10
Written by Belle A. DeCosta
Published by Stillwater River Publications, Pawtucket, RI, USA.

*The views and opinions expressed in this book are solely those of the author
and do not necessarily reflect the views and opinions of the publisher.*

I am all the ages I have ever been.
—Anne Lamott

Author's Disclaimer

––––––––––––––

This book is written from memory, and, like most, mine is faulty. The chronology of some dates and events may be out of order, and I took creative liberty with, and at times supplemented, dialogue to fill in the gaps (but never at another's expense).

Admittedly, some conversations and scenes were consolidated and or embellished to enhance the storytelling and to make clear the impact the situation/experience had on me. This is my life's story, recreated in a way to evoke the feelings, meaning, and lessons learned by me, and in that respect, the essence is authentic and genuine.

Also, the names and characteristics of certain individuals were changed to respect their privacy.

Memory is unique to each individual, and each one has its own story to tell. One person's recollection of a conversation or event may vary from another's, depending on the intentions set, the feelings evoked, and the outcome of the experience to that individual. That being said, is this a memoir? Creative non-fiction? Reflections on an autobiography? A novel based on the author's life? I will leave that to you, the individual reader to decide.

I know my intention was to tell my life's story as lived by me and that much I have accomplished. I know what this book is for me. Enjoy.

CONTENTS

PART VII: DESTINATION ME

Introduction

———

"The greatest risk we'll ever take is by far, to stand in the light and be seen as we are..."

—Jordan Smith

S O TRUE.
　　Of course, to be seen as we are, we have to look at where we have been. Study the journey that has helped create the person we are today and will continue to influence who we will become. I say help because we get to decide how that journey ultimately shapes us, how we respond, act upon, and process life's challenges and lessons. It is our choice alone.

Fortunately, so is control of our attitude. To me, attitude is everything. It can find a positive in the direst of circumstance or see a negative in the best of times. It can find hope or crush a dream. Our choice.

What follows is a look at my journey down the yellow brick road. It includes all the potholes, detours, and toll roads along the way. I wouldn't change a single leg of the trip. It has shaped the person I can at last call my best friend: Me.

At sixty-two, I'm finally ready to stand in the light. Wrinkles and all.

Prologue

GREAT, AN ACCIDENT IN THE MIDDLE OF RUSH HOUR TRAF-
fic. On a Friday. Since traffic is moving at a snail's pace, it
can't be a bad one, just an annoyance. Someone must have been
texting or trying to bully their way into a lane. *It's time to find
my patience.* Having had a hard day, this was not a good time
for a long commute to become even longer.

Three of them, in the same nursing home, in the same unit,
all at the same time. Three of my Loveys lost to the darkest place
Alzheimer's and dementia take you to before you finally get to
go home. Just last month, I was still able to engage them in my
class. They were responding to the music and getting a kick out
of the tap slippers I put on their feet. Today they were in Geri
chairs and headed to a better place—after a layover in hell.

When the class ended, I went over to see them. An energy
healer, I asked the universe to send its healing energy through
my touch to comfort them as best I could. When I touched Lila's
face, her eyes popped open.

"Sister, your curls look beautiful," she said.

"That's because you did them for me, Lila," I told her. She
smiled, patted my hand, and closed her eyes. *She's almost there.*

Angie's eyes were open, seeing nothing or everything; only
she could know for sure. I put her hand between the two of mine
and told her I loved her. Without moving her eyes, she brought

our hands to her cheek and leaned into them. *Oh good, she feels the love.*

Edie was shaking and whimpering. Always anxious, they tell me she is now mostly inconsolable if awake. Edie grabbed my hand in a panic and asked if I was there to take her home.

"Please take me home," she begged. I knew which home she meant.

"They will be here soon, Edie." She gave me a beautiful smile, thanked me, and closed her eyes.

Three. Too many all at once for my tired heart to handle.

Next year, I need to schedule more time off. I can't help them if I'm depleted, and right now, I'm running on empty.

I start to think about all the classes I had shared with them in the past. How I loved witnessing the music, rhythm, and movement work their magic and seeing the joy mix with self-satisfaction on their faces. Watching as their bodies sat a little taller with pride at accomplishing things they thought they could no longer do. How much I enjoyed listening while they shared the memories certain songs were bringing out of the fog overtaking their minds. Remembering the bond I had the honor of sharing with them and still share with so many others. As I remember these things, I feel my spirits lift. *That's the reason I do what I do. That's what makes days like today worth it.*

I smile when I realize who extended my commute and why. It made me take the time to process my feelings, to reflect and heal. *Thank you, Angels.*

I finally pull into my driveway an hour late and exhausted. I unlock the front door, and my home immediately wraps its arms around me in a warm embrace. My beautiful boy, JD the dog, greets me at the door with such enthusiasm and happiness, I can't help but match his goofy grin and dance around in circles with him. *What a gift this eighty pounds of light and love is to me!* I turn on my aquarium light and say hello to my water babies before I change into my sweats. I wash the makeup off my face, pour a glass of wine, and collapse on the couch. There is no chance I'm meeting friends later as we had planned, but they'll understand. They are, after all, friends. I mute my cellphone, light my salt lamp, tree of life, and candles, and put my feet up on the coffee table, ankles crossed. JD puts his head in my lap, drapes his legs over mine, and crosses his paws. We are tucked in for the evening. I watch the beautiful water ballet my fish are performing and feel total peace and contentment wash over me. *I bet this is what being in the womb feels like—calm and serene.*

There are two words I never thought I'd use to describe my life. My journey has been many things, but calm and serene? Hardly. I smile, take a sip of wine, and pat myself on the back for getting here in one piece. Well, almost one piece. What a ride it's been.

"You should write it all down," I hear.

Do you mean like a book?

"Yes."

You can't be serious, do you know what that will entail? I'm incredulous.

"Yes, we do. Do it."

No way. That's a lot to relive, a lot to re-feel. It's too much.

"It's a lot, but not too much. Do it. You need to do it," they chorus.

Okay, I'll try.

"Good. It's going to be a long, sometimes painful process, but well worth it."

Are you guys sure?

"Yes. We'll be right here with you, as always."

I certainly hope so. A book? What a crazy, insane idea. A book.

PART I

A PAPER DOLL FAMILY

STAR-CROSSED LOVERS

My father, John Dave Adkins Sr., was born on February 6, 1934, in Amanata, Virginia, located in the heart of Appalachia coal country. He was the eldest son and the third of nine children. His childhood, as he told it, was horrendous.

His father was a hard drinking, womanizing, emotionally "checked out" coal miner and his mother was, to put it politely, unhinged. She was prone to frequent and loud fits of hysteria, crying or raging, depending on her state of mind at the time. She cooked up a storm but never cleaned or did laundry, so they lived in filth. She loved her babies, but once they became toddlers, she passed their care on to their older siblings so she could proceed to have more babies. In addition to the chaos, my father was molested throughout his years at home by an uncle. All the above made a perfect emotional environment of swill for demons to breed, hatch, and fester. Determined to survive, he put himself through college, which delayed the inevitable, but the damage had been done. He never stood a chance.

My mother, Lois Jean Boyle, was born August 26, 1932, in Lincoln, New Hampshire, and moved to Elmira, New York, when she was seven. She was the middle child of three surviving sisters. The childhood she described was the quintessential small-town Americana upbringing. My mother and her sisters shared a deep and loving bond and had two parents who adored them.

Money was tight, but they always managed to make do. In the winter, her father would build an ice-skating rink in the backyard with hay and flood it with a garden hose. When their friends would come over to skate, he would make a fire for them to warm their hands and roast hotdogs. On summer weekends, the family would go blueberry picking or bring a picnic to the lake and spend the afternoon swimming.

I never heard Mom or her sisters say a discouraging word about their childhood. They always felt loved, safe, and secure. My mother's childhood was idyllic; hence, her sunny innocence and incredible capacity to love. And trust. Her reality had always been a positive one, and she was ill-prepared for what a life with my father would bring to the table.

My parents met through a mutual friend while Mom was working as a cashier at Kresge and Dad was in town, participating in the company's management training program. Their long-distance courtship consisted of twelve dates, one a month leading up to their wedding day, June 27, 1955. My mother had never met his family nor had any idea of my father's beginnings. She was blissfully unaware of where she was headed and madly in love.

I genuinely believe it wouldn't have mattered if she had known. My mother managed to remain unaware of the negative happenings throughout most of their life together, and when forced at times to see a harsh reality, possessed an uncanny ability to un-see it. Was it naïveté? Survival? A coping mechanism? My guess is a combination of all three, which allowed her to see through rose-colored glasses. It worked well for her, but did nothing to help or protect her children.

I do know this: Mom loved my brother John and me with every fiber of her being. Her family was her world. Unfortunately, her Prince Charming eventually succumbed to his demons, and she was unable to let go of the fairytale. My brother John and I ended up collateral damage.

BABY STEPS AND TUTUS

I WAS BORN APRIL 16, 1957, IN PERTH AMBOY, NEW JERSEY AND named after both of my grandmothers, Belle and Ann. I've always been grateful to my parents for choosing their middle names and not their first names, or I would be Allie Donalda or Donalda Allie—can't say I'm fond of either one.

When I was a year old, my father fell off the back of a tractor-trailer while unloading merchandise and ruptured several discs in his back. Back surgery is always a crapshoot, but in those days, it rarely went well. His did not. He had to wear a cumbersome metal brace around his torso and was in constant pain for a year. The doctor teased him that obviously, the brace wasn't too awkward, nor the pain too bad because my mom became pregnant with my brother during that time. Where there's a will, there's a way as they say. My guess is this is where his addiction introduced itself, but with a new family he adored, he managed to maintain control and hold it at bay.

Fortunately, after that first year, the excruciating pain subsided, and the brace eventually came off, but his back would prove to be a chronic issue for the rest of his life.

When my brother, John Dave Adkins Jr., was born, I adored him from day one. Mom always teased the only problem she had was I wouldn't leave him alone. I'd stare at him while he

3

slept and would run to get Mom at his first whimper. I would smother John with kisses to the point where he'd cry and then try to kiss his tears away. I would babble to him as only a two-year-old can, even while Mom was trying to get him to sleep. It was love at first sight. My brother was my real live baby doll to cuddle and coddle, and I made sure he got plenty of both.

In those early years, Dad was everything a family man should be. He was so proud of his little family of four and reveled in his role as a husband and father. My father never entered or exited the house without kissing my mom, soundly and proper, and always gave John and me a kiss and a hug. He was our protector and our provider, our rock. Daddy was my hero, and I was his baby girl. I felt safe and loved, and all was right in my world.

One of my first memories—I was around three—is of my father carrying me from my bedroom to the kitchen late one night as Mom hurried out of the nursery, holding John. They threw our coats on as we rushed out the door. Daddy said we were going to camp out in the car and have some fun. I remember us singing songs for about two minutes before I fell back to sleep, all cozy and happy.

It turns out my father had come into my room to check on me, and a rat was eating the silk border of my blanket, which was by my throat. Thankfully, I didn't wake up until Daddy carried me to the kitchen, so I have no memory of my nighttime visitor. When Mom ran to get my brother, she discovered the nipple of his bottle had been chewed off. We had just moved in that day, and there were boxes everywhere, so the critters had plenty of places to hide until we went to bed. The landlord, who ran the motorcycle repair shop below the apartment, had exterminated the garage the week before we moved in, so the rats just moved upstairs and made themselves a new home. Needless to say, we never stepped foot into that apartment again. I smile when I envision my quiet, skinny father, six foot two, 145 pounds, and wearing black-rimmed glasses confronting a buffed, street-hardened biker, but that's how the story goes. Not only did the landlord give back the security deposit and rent, but he covered the cost to have our things gone through with a fine-toothed comb and moved to storage. He also paid the bus fare for Mom, John, and me to Elmira, New York, so we could stay with my grandparents while Dad looked for an apartment. Score one for the home team!

Within a month, Daddy found a rodent-free second-floor apartment, which was not a simple task in Cohoes, New York, at the time. The landlords lived on the first floor and spoke fluent Polish, along with their version of English. They wouldn't let my mother walk to the store, or my brother and I play in the yard, without one of their teenage sons as a chaperone. "Not safe" and "LOVE, LOVE YOUZ!" was the only English they spoke that I could decipher. It didn't matter though, because everything they said and did came from their loving hearts and that I understood perfectly.

They had passed those big hearts on to their children as well. Their twin sons, Mike and Joe never complained about walking the "nice, classy lady from upstairs," to the store or having to hang with John and me in the backyard. They even played tag or Red Light Green Light with us at times. The boys usually had a girlfriend with them, which added to the fun for us. The girls would "ooh" and "ah" over John and me and bring us goodies. We were chick magnets for Mike and Joe, and we loved every minute of it. Luckily they were twins, so the times I'd make the mistake of mentioning one girl in front of another, the boys would just say I had mixed up the brothers. They were handsome and charming, so there were a lot of different girls, which made for lots of candy and ice cream for John and me.

As exciting as all that was, it still wasn't the best part of living there. The landlords' daughter Lynda was my first dance teacher. *My dance teacher lives right downstairs from me!* It doesn't get any better than that for a little girl. I adored her. She was beautiful and had thick black hair that hung below her waist. I would sit and brush it while she studied for the classes she was taking at the community college.

Whenever Miss Lynda heard me practicing tap dance upstairs, she'd come up to praise and encourage me. She often invited me down to her salon (the front porch) to paint my nails and do my hair, and I remember feeling so important when she would ask my opinion on which outfit to wear for her date or how she should wear her hair.

Miss Lynda's studio was around the corner from where we lived, so on Saturdays after my class, I would wait for her while she taught the older girls, and we'd walk home together. How I loved watching those girls dance! I was enthralled by how they moved to the music with such grace and ease. *I'm going to dance like that someday!* Wild horses couldn't have kept me from those Saturdays. I would go home and leap and twirl around the living room until I was exhausted and fell asleep in my tights and leotard.

Miss Lynda was always ladylike and never raised her voice, even while teaching our rambunctious class of four and five-year-olds. So, imagine my shock the first time I heard a screaming banshee downstairs, cursing Joe out for hanging up on her boyfriend.

"Mommy, is that Miss Lynda?!" I asked incredulously.

"No, sweetheart, of course not," Mom quickly replied, "It's her crazy cousin visiting from across town."

That crazy cousin visited often, but never when I was downstairs. When I would cover my ears and say, "I never want to meet that mean lady," my parents would share a smile and say, "Don't worry, Honey, Miss Lynda will make sure you never do." Even the shiniest of coins have two sides.

I'll never forget the day Miss Lynda asked me to be the flower girl at her wedding. We were walking home from the studio, and she asked me if I'd do her a favor, something she couldn't trust anyone else to do.

"Of course!" I said proudly. She needed a beautiful, graceful dancer to walk down the aisle before her, sprinkling a path of rose petals leading to the groom. It had to be done by someone special because they were magical, and if a bride walked down an aisle kissed by the petals, she and the groom would live happily ever after. Miss Lynda had spun the perfect fairytale for a five-year-old, and I was on cloud nine. She had already gotten my mom's permission, of course, and had also asked her to make my dress. Mom could work wonders with a sewing machine, and before I could blink an eye, I had the most beautiful dress I'd ever seen. It was red satin with a big bow and white lace that matched the lace on Miss Lynda's wedding gown. I would put it on every day, and Mom would lay down a white sheet on the living room floor for an aisle. She would sing "Here Comes the Bride" while I practiced strolling and sprinkling petals made of cut-up newspaper from a breadbasket.

By the time the big day arrived, I was a seasoned pro and performed beautifully, not exactly a given for a five-year-old. Had I known the marriage meant Miss Lynda would be leaving the state, I would have flushed the petals down the nearest toilet and kicked the groom in the shins. As if her moving away wasn't bad enough, Joe and Mike got their licenses, and a car became their new chick magnet.

Thankfully, Miss Lynda's assistant continued the Saturday dance class, and I started kindergarten that year, so all was not lost, and I managed to survive.

I was so excited to start school! Mom would put John in the stroller, and we'd start our climb up the long steep hill that the school sat atop. I always waved to the older kids who were waiting for their school bus, but they never waved back. I briefly wondered why they didn't like me, but I was too excited to dwell on it.

After a week or so, I insisted I was old enough to walk to school by myself. Mom reluctantly agreed and, on the first day, stood in the doorway to make sure I got to the top of the hill safely. I did not. I almost made it, but when I waved to the kids at the bus stop, and they saw I was alone, they started taunting me and calling me names. I got so scared I began to run back down the hill, fell face-first to the pavement, and promptly wet my panties. The paperboy, older than my taunters, saw what was happening, turned his bike around, and came to my rescue. He gave my tormentors a few choice words and a threat or two, put me in his massive basket on the front of his bike, and gave me a lift home. At his size and with his deep voice, I should have been more afraid of him than I was of them, but I wasn't. I knew, without a doubt, he was there to help me.

Even at that age, I was determined and still wanted to walk to school like a big girl. The paperboy told my mom not to worry, he would keep an eye out for me and guaranteed I wouldn't have a problem again. And I never did. My new friend always showed up during my walks to and from school, and most times, gave me a lift in his basket. I never knew his real name, but I called him Bear because he was the same color as my favorite brown teddy bear. He called me Snowbelle because I was white, and Belle was my name, he said.

Bear told me he wanted to go to school, but his mom said he was too dumb to learn anything, so he had to deliver newspapers. *That breaks my heart to this day.* I promised I'd teach him to read as soon as I learned, but we moved away before I mastered my first Dick and Jane reader.

When I got older, I realized a couple of things. First of all, those kids at the bus stop weren't that old. They were elementary school age, none over the age of twelve. It was 1962, and busing was taking place. Those kids most likely had to attend a school where they were taunted and called names, and every day was a lesson in social survival. Here I was, with my Barbie lunchbox, skipping into a school they longed to go to and couldn't.

Secondly, my friend Bear had learning disabilities and a tough life. Our friendship was probably the softest thing he had at the time. I would hope such a kind and gentle soul made out okay, but he had the odds stacked against him for sure. At the very least, I hope he found someone who deserved and appreciated all the love he had in his heart. He was, indeed, a gentle giant.

Around this time, I met my first girl friend, Suzy. She and her mom moved into the third-floor apartment some time during my year in kindergarten, and we soon became inseparable. We spent all our time at my apartment because her mom worked nights as a stripper and would sleep during the day.

"What's a stripper?" I asked Suzy.

"A dancer with no clothes on," she replied.

No tutu? Count me out! I'll stick to dancing on Saturday mornings thank you very much.

It took about a week before Mom discovered Suzy had a head full of lice and a derrière loaded with impetigo, both of which she generously shared with John and me. When Mom went up to tell Suzy's mother, her knock on the door got answered with a resounding, "Fuck off! I don't have any money!" I know this because Suzy told me that's how her mom responded to daytime knocks. We weren't even six, so I had no idea what that word meant, and I'm pretty sure at the time my mom didn't either. All she knew was she was not dealing with the anger behind that door.

Super Dad to the rescue! He came home from work with a bag full of lice shampoo and antibiotic cream. The two of them proceeded to put all three of us through the "Car Wash." We picked what color car we wanted to be and went in for the works. My parents managed to make delousing and scraping less traumatic and almost fun. Almost. Not much fun in sanding down the rust spots on the back bumper—just sayin'.

Once they had three clean kids and full washers at the laundromat next door, Mom got busy with a bucket and bleach while Dad went to assess the situation behind the third-floor door. It must not have been pretty because Suzy lived with us until her out-of-town Grandma could come and get her.

It was a two-week-long pajama party! We made a tent with blankets and sat under it with flashlights, eating popcorn while Daddy told us some not so scary ghost stories. Mom taught us how to jump rope, and we baked cookies together, something Suzy had never done.

It didn't occur to me until years later that my little friend never asked for her mom or to go home. Her mom never came to see her even though she had to pass by our door to leave the building. When Suzy's grandmother came to pick her up, she never asked about her daughter, Suzy's mom. So sad. It must not have been the first time this scene had played out for them.

This story also speaks volumes to my parents' hearts and generosity. They not only got involved but took Suzy in as one of their own. When she left, they cried as hard as I did. Suzy and I might have had a brief friendship, but it was my introduction to the special bond that only girl friends can share. I hope things turned out well for her.

John and I never realized we were living in unsavory tenements in less than safe neighborhoods while Daddy paid off his student loans. Mom was too happy to care. It helped that the people surrounding us had integrity and were so kind. They were decent, honest people. The biker landlord who did the right thing. Mike, Joe, and Miss Lynda, who were good teenagers living in a tough neighborhood. Their lives could've turned a much different corner without the set of parents they were blessed to call their own. Bear, who kept a loving heart despite how others treated him. Suzy's grandmother, who had to wait until her next paycheck to take the bus and get her granddaughter, but get her she did. I learned at a very young age not to judge a book by its cover or where it sits on the shelf.

Because of Daddy's job, we moved around and never lived near any relatives, so we were a close-knit little tribe of four. I remember opening up the sleeper sofa on Fridays and all of us piling in to watch Johnny Carson while we munched on snacks in bed. It was the ultimate treat for a seven-year-old. Of course, I'd be sound asleep long before Ed McMahon's, "Heeere's Johnny."

Then there were the peaceful Sundays with my parents reading the paper while John and I pressed Silly Putty on the comics page arguing who was the better artist. The Easter nights on the sleep sofa watching *The Sound of Music* and singing at the top of our lungs. Thanksgiving mornings spent watching the Macy's Parade together, the smell of turkey roasting in the air. Christmas mornings, racing downstairs to a tree full of gifts with my parents already on the couch, a Polaroid camera at the ready and smiles a mile wide. Nights my father would sleep sitting in a rocker with one of us on his lap, sick and wrapped in a ton of blankets. He wouldn't put us down until our fever broke.

I have fond memories of going sledding when we lived in Rutland, Vermont, and my father carrying John back up the hill because the snow was too deep for my brother to walk. I remember visiting Hershey, Pennsylvania, and Sunday drives through the Amish country when we lived in Reading. I laugh when I think of John and me sitting in our kiddie pool on hot days in Jersey, sharing Milk Bones and Kool-Aid with our dog Penny. Yes, she drank Kool-Aid, the grape was her favorite, and, yes, we ate Milk Bones (all colors taste the same). It didn't last long—once Mom caught us, she started closely monitoring the distribution of our poolside cocktails and hors d'oeuvres.

I remember being seven years old and sobbing my heart out because I got the chickenpox first, a light case, and passed them on to my brother, who got them ten times worse. I thought he was going to die, and it was all my fault. It was my father who sat up all night, putting cool cloths on John's body, so my mom could get some sleep. She had her hands full during the day nursing John and trying to keep me from killing him with kindness. Daddy survived on cat naps alone for the duration. *Memories of a loving father.*

That was the same year I made my dance debut, at age seven, in Reading, Pennsylvania. My first recital was in an elementary school cafeteria on a stage about as big as your palm. I thought I was excited, but I had nothing on Daddy. When each of my dances was over, he would give me a standing ovation and yell, "That's my baby girl!" You would have thought I had just performed Swan Lake at the Lincoln Center. *Memories of a proud papa.*

I still chuckle when I remember the long weekend we spent at my Great-Uncle Otis's cabin in New Hampshire. The four of us took a rowboat out on the lake fishing, and after a few hours, we spotted Uncle Otis on shore frantically waving his arms around and pointing to the sky. We turned around and saw black clouds and lightning in the distance. Daddy started rowing like crazy, but we just kept going around in circles. At some point, John asked Mom why there was a rope going down into the water. The anchor. Once my father pulled it up and rowed us safely to shore, we laughed like crazy. That was our first and last fishing trip. *Memories of a healthy, happy family.*

This Daddy was a fun, warm-hearted, strong, and handsome man. He lit up a room when he entered and was loved and respected by everyone who knew him. He was supportive, loving, and would give anyone the shirt off his back. He was by all accounts, a good man. *This Daddy.*

TO GRANDMOTHER'S

HOUSE WE GO

OUR GRANDPARENTS NEVER LIVED NEAR US, SO VACATIONS were, "Over the River and Through the Woods," as the song goes. We saw a lot more of our maternal grandparents, Jim and Anna Boyle, because they were able to come for visits and in the summer would take John and me home with them for a couple of weeks.

Disneyland couldn't hold a candle to those two weeks! It was all about them loving us and us loving them. Consequently, we formed a strong bond, even with the miles between us.

My grandma didn't drive, but she never let that stop our adventures. She'd take us to the public pool even though she hated the water and couldn't take the sun. Patiently, she would sit while we swam and always applauded our cannonballs and handstands. Other times we would walk to the bakery to get a treat, or to the neighbor's house so we could play with their kids.

Grandpa worked second shift, and after he left for work, Grandma would sometimes take us to the amusement park. We were each allowed to ride the merry-go-round and one other ride. I don't know if that was due to money or her fear we'd get hurt, but looking back, I'd say the latter. It was an old amusement park, and the rides were rickety at best. Before going home, the three of us usually got a candied apple, cotton candy, or ice cream for supper, which was way outside of the box for Grandma. Sometimes there would be an outdoor concert at the park, and we would sit on a bench so John and I could join the sing-along.

Oddly, I never heard my grandma sing, even the hymns in church. She seemed to dislike music as much as my grandfather loved it. There is a reason for it, I'm sure, but I never learned why.

Once we got home, and in our PJs, we'd sit on their screened-in porch, and Grandma would teach us how to play Crazy Eights, Old Maid, and Go Fish. As we got older, it was Canasta, Pinochle, Yahtzee, and Cribbage. And, don't think for a minute she ever let us win. Not once. She was one competitive game player. It was the only time being her beloved grandchild got you nowhere. She took no prisoners. If you wanted to win, you had to earn it. A lesson learned at her knee that has served me well.

Much to our delight, my grandparents didn't have a shower. John and I got to take bubble baths in a large clawfoot tub deep enough for us to learn how to float on our backs. After the bubbles disappeared, we would practice the dead man's float. It was like having an indoor pool, with Grandma as our ever-present lifeguard, of course.

One of my favorite things to do was help Grandma with laundry. I loved feeding the clothes through the rollers on the old washing machine then hanging them out to dry in the morning breeze. Even when I got older, and the thrill of being a "big girl" allowed to help wore off, it was still one of my favorite parts of the vacation. I felt so connected to my grandmother, quietly doing that early morning chore together. *Simple times full of love.*

Grandma could knit, crotchet, tat lace, do embroidery, and sew. She tried her best to teach me something, anything, but I didn't have the interest nor the patience to learn. It's tough to knit while you're shuffle ball changing and pirouetting across the porch. As determined as she was, she eventually had to give up—I was hopeless.

I know little about my Grandma's origin other than she was born in Canada to French-Canadian parents, and she moved to New Hampshire as a girl. She was very close to her sisters Rose and Laura, and they knew the Von Trapp children, the family portrayed in the movie *The Sound of Music*. I know this because I was obsessed with the movie, so she thought it was worth sharing with me. It's the only time I remember her even coming close to bragging about anything.

She was a devout Catholic who never missed Sunday Mass and worshipped the Blessed Mother reverently. I vividly remember the crucifix that hung over her bed. To this day, it is still the most moving depiction of Christ's suffering I have ever seen. A work of art that would move a believer to tears. As a child, it scared me.

At the time, I knew nothing about religion. The only time John and I went to church was at my grandparents'. My mother was Catholic but asked to leave the church when she started practicing birth control. My father, raised Southern Baptist, hadn't been to church since leaving home. With both parents disillusioned by their church, John and I had no religious training until John came home one day and asked who Jesus was and what he had to do with Easter. Mom promptly started taking us to a Methodist church and Sunday school. Perhaps they saw it as a happy medium between their two religions? Or maybe it was just the closest church to our house at the time. I don't know, but we never went consistently, and, other than saying grace before dinner, religion wasn't practiced in our home.

By all three of her daughters' accounts, she was the consummate mother, and I can personally attest to her being a superb grandmother. I always sensed a bit of sadness around her, however, even in her happiest moments. I don't believe she ever recovered from the death of her nine-month-old baby Janet, born between my Aunt Violet and Mom, to spinal meningitis. But then again, I don't believe anyone could.

My grandparents had a beautiful built-in china cabinet where they kept the things most precious to them. Souvenirs from trips to see their daughters, china, religious statues, and a Shirley Temple doll. Let me rephrase that: THE SHIRLEY TEMPLE DOLL.

The doll was my Aunt Violet's, who was an avid tap dancer until she entered the convent. Shirley was porcelain and had a crack above her right eye, courtesy of my mom, who threw the doll across the room because her big sister wouldn't let her play with it. Shirley was the Hope Diamond to a little dancer like me.

My grandpa would unlock the cabinet, sit me on the couch, and put the doll in my arms. How special he made me feel, trusting me with something so precious. I was in awe and afraid to move in those early years. *What if I drop her and crack another body part?* I had no idea at the time she was an original and had monetary value. I just knew Grandpa was trusting me with THE something out of THE cabinet.

I felt so grown up and honored the day he gave me Shirley as a gift. I remember thinking he must love me bunches to do that, which of course, he did.

Grandpa was the original tap dancer in our family. His father and uncles were loggers in Lincoln, New Hampshire, and when he was young, he would visit the logging camps on Loon Mountain to clog for money. The loggers, lonely and desperate for entertainment, were very generous to the young Boyle boy. As he told it, he made quite a haul in the summer months. Grandpa also had a beautiful Irish tenor voice and loved to sing Irish ballads. He played a mean piano, mostly ragtime and strictly by ear. To my knowledge, my grandfather had never taken a lesson or learned to read music.

He also loved to eat. I remember him slathering butter on a couple of my grandma's homemade deep-fried donuts for breakfast, followed by half a dozen fried eggs and the better part of a package of bacon. Despite carrying three hundred pounds on a five-foot, eight-inch frame most of his life, he lived into his eighties.

He was the youngest of four children and the only boy, so his mother and sisters spoiled him rotten from birth. Once he married, he expected his wife to continue waiting on him hand and foot, which she did.

My maternal grandparents were kind, loving people who never had a bad word to say to or about anyone; except for each other. They wouldn't fight per se, but boy could they bicker, and they bickered about everything. It was their only form of communication. The one thing they always agreed on was their daughters. They both loved their girls, heart and soul. I don't know what happened during their life together to cause such discord between them. But I do know this; there was also love. Somewhere in their hearts, perhaps buried by a life event they shared with no one, there was still a flicker of love.

My grandfather retired around the same time my father's demons started gaining control. My grandparents' trips to our house became more frequent, and their stays longer, much to my father's chagrin. Daddy would have to ease up on the drinking and tone down the nasty while they were there. My guess is Jim and Anna's actions were intentional. They could spend a couple of weeks with us to assess the situation, and their presence meant their son-in-law had to play nice. Mission accomplished.

MY PATERNAL GRANDPARENTS, DAVE AND ALLIE ADKINS, HAD no means to come to visit, so every couple of years, we'd make the trek to Bishop, West Virginia. My parents would place paint cans on the back floorboard of the car with a piece of plywood atop, then lay cot mattresses over the concoction and the back-seat. Voila! A double bed John and I slept on during the fifteen to twenty-four-hour trip, depending on where we lived at the time.

The last leg of the trip was over the Blue Ridge Mountains, which supposedly is a beautiful scenic drive, but I wouldn't know. My head was always either in a plastic bag throwing up or buried under a pillow out of fear. At that time, there were no guardrails and barely enough space for two cars. The road was one continuous S-curve with no room for error. My father drove like a maniac over those mountains despite my mother's pleas to slow down. He insisted he knew the roads so well he could drive them in his sleep. Between my fear of heights, car sickness, and unease over Mom's concern, I was one green and unhappy camper. Oh, happy day when I was old enough to take Dramamine and sleep through that hellacious rollercoaster ride!

At the foot of a mountain, directly across a narrow street, sat my grandparents' house. They had the most spectacular view from their front porch swing! Unfortunately, that view is the only thing of beauty I remember about Bishop. We had landed in an impoverished, rundown coal mining town in the heart of Appalachia country. Its lifestyle and mindset were so foreign to John and me it was like we had landed on Mars. Luckily, we were pros at adapting to new surroundings, and after all, these Martians were ours. They didn't get to see us often, so when they did, they showered us with all the attention and affection they had stored up since our last visit.

Even if we hadn't been so darn cute and loveable (but too skinny) as Granny used to say, they would have adored us. We were J.D.'s children, and that made us royalty. J.D., as my dad was called down-home, was revered, surpassed only by Jesus Christ himself. He was the firstborn son and the first Adkins to get out of the mines and work his way through college. He had a career way up north and married a classy, pretty little filly who "bore him two babes," as Granddaddy used to say.

My father's younger siblings adored him. He held all the answers to their questions about life beyond the mountains and had stories galore to tell. They also appreciated they had school clothes, shoes, and a present under the Christmas tree because J.D. regularly sent money home.

The first adjustment I remember having to make in Bishop was the bathroom; there wasn't one. They had an outhouse instead, fully stocked with an ungodly smell, flies, spiders, and the occasional poisonous snake. Oh, and plenty of magazines and newspapers with which to wipe yourself. God bless Mom and her endless supply of tissues.

When we were young, Mom would have to hold us up while we did our business, or we would have fallen through the hole, probably as big a fear for her as it was for us. No sane person headed out there after dark without a gun. There were skunks, mountain lions, bears, and drunken coal miners. Since neither one of my parents knew how to shoot, we would use a porcelain pot in our room at night. John thought that was the greatest thing ever and drank everything he could get his hands on after supper. Me, not so much. Between the outhouse and the pot, I drank as little as possible. It's a wonder I never got dehydrated or had a bowel blockage.

As an aside, my grandparents finally got a bathroom when I was around eleven, and I was just as excited about the tub as I was the toilet. The summertime heat and humidity in West Virginia are second to none, and it creates some very nasty body odors, mine included. The tub made being hugged to the bosom a much more pleasant experience.

There was also a new language to learn. On the first visit I can remember, Granny was holding my brother on her lap, cooing, "Chile, you so sweet, Granny's gonna eat you up young 'un!" I told Daddy we were going to have chilled young 'un for supper 'cause they were sweet, and Granny loved them. I can still hear his belly laugh in my heart sometimes.

Not all of the new language was so heartwarming, however. Some of it was born of ignorance and hate. I was sitting on the porch with my granddaddy one day when a black man came walking down our side of the road. The second he saw us, he lowered his eyes and quickly crossed to the other side. When I waved and hollered hello to him, Granddaddy had a fit. "Them niggers are mean dumb animals, chile. Theys either running from trouble or heading to trouble. You mind yourself like a lady." As hard as I looked, I didn't see any mean animals, dumb or otherwise. I just saw a nervous man whose skin was the same color as my friend Bear's.

Then there was the day I found out where my grandparents got their meat. Granny told one of my uncles to get a chicken for dinner, and thinking he was going to the store, I tagged along. Until that is, I saw him go towards the pen where we fed the animals. I might've been young, but I figured out in a flash what was happening and started running back to the house. I didn't see the slaughter, but I heard it and got hysterical. Up to that point, the only animals I had ever tended to were pets. In my world, my uncle had just murdered a pet to cook for dinner—a dinner I didn't eat, I might add. I never fed the animals again after that. Applying a six-year-old's logic, I figured the skinnier they were, the longer they'd live.

On that same visit, I was sitting on the porch swing at dusk with Granddaddy, him with his quart of Schaefer's and me with my glass bottle of Coke. All of a sudden, we saw a mountain lion walk stealthily through the treeline at the foot of the mountain. The animal was magnificent! I remember being in awe and terrified at the same time. Granddaddy admired him for a moment, grabbed his shotgun from under the swing, and told me to git inside. He said he had to take care of it before it got to the pens. *He must be going to use that weird stick to shoo him away.* When I heard the shot, I thought someone had set off a firecracker. I didn't even know what a gun was, much less what it sounded like when fired. Thankfully it was years before I found out Grandad had killed it.

It was a lot to take in all at once, and I was one culture-shocked little girl that year. No bathroom, learning a new language, being introduced to an ugly animal called blind hate, killing pets for dinner, zoo animals across the street and not in the zoo, and loaded shotguns on the porch. I am eternally grateful for not being raised on Mars. Mom must've been exhausted by the time we headed home. I can't imagine having to decipher and then explain all of this to your young children in a way they would understand it, but not accept it, and yet embrace and love their clan. Somehow, she managed to do it. My guess is love.

As I got a little older, I learned to appreciate southern dishes and my granny's talent for cooking. She could work magic with a cast iron fry pan and a coal stove. Her milk gravy, biscuits, and fried chicken were second to none. Her southern kidney beans and green beans, made with fatback and bacon, were mouth-watering. I never liked collards or dandelion greens (too bitter), but I would have sweet dreams about her rhubarb pie and apple cake. She loved cooking for her family, and that love came through in every bite.

One day I was helping her bake her famous apple cake and asked her how much flour I needed. She picked up a fist full out of a burlap sack, threw it in the bowl, then added a little more. When I asked why she didn't use a measuring cup, she laughed and said, "Lord chile, that ain't how you cook." For the most part, it worked for her. Except for coffee—coffee needs to be measured. Granny would throw a bunch of grounds into the bottom of an old tin coffee pot, fill it with water, and it would sit on the coal stove all day. When it dried up, she'd add some more water. It was a muddy mess, but exactly how Granddaddy liked it. He would pour a third of a cup of coffee, fill it to the brim with moonshine, crack a raw egg into it, and stir like crazy so the egg wouldn't cook before he drank it down. That was Grandad's breakfast of champions.

Here's a little of Granddaddy's history as passed down to me: He was born in a time and place where it wasn't unheard of for sisters to bear their brother's babies, moonshine was more plentiful than water, and food was scarce. Children were taught to shoot before they learned the alphabet. Some didn't survive, and most that did ended up poaching or mining at a very young age. The lucky ones got to graduate sixth grade.

Granddaddy was one of the lucky ones. He could read a little, write some, and add even less. He was spared the mines until the ripe old age of twelve and mined until he developed symptoms of black lung. By then, his brood of nine was older, and some had moved out of the house. He managed to support the rest by running the most productive moonshine still in the hills and being the perfect hire for deputy sheriff—he hated blacks and could turn a blind eye. I want to vomit when I think of what that probably meant.

He was hard-living, hard-drinking, hard-loving, and hard-hating—a womanizer whose children went without shoes to pay for his vices. He lived as he had learned.

I know very little about Granny's beginnings. As told to me, she was the daughter of a strict, fire and brimstone preacher of English descent, and a Native American mother. Her daddy saw Grandad as the devil himself, which only stoked the passion Granny felt towards him. They ran off together in her very young teens (how young I do not know). As it turned out, my great-grandfather wasn't far from wrong about Grandaddy. It didn't matter to Granny though, devil or not she worshipped her man. Years later, at Grandad's gravesite, she tried to throw herself on top of his coffin to go with him. Dramatic yes, but sadly true.

MY TWO SETS OF GRANDPARENTS WERE FROM VERY DIFFERENT cultural and social worlds. Grandma and Grandpa had both been born into loving, moralistic families and raised in a safe, close-knit community. Clean living personified. They, in turn, provided the same environment for their children. The lifestyle they led had an air of wholesomeness to it, with an added touch of innocence. They lived a simple, quiet life, worked hard, and had little, but were always thankful and satisfied with their lot. They thanked God for providing what they had and blamed no one for what they lacked. The thought of taking money from their girls once they left home and started their own lives would have never occurred to them.

Granny and Grandad did not have as fortunate a start. They were both born into much harsher homes—cruel environments where survival of the fittest was the first lesson learned. As horrible as the upbringing they provided for their children was, it was still a step up from where they had started. Barely. Perhaps they chose to stay tucked into the discontentment, anger, and mistrust they had known since birth because it was comfortable and familiar. Or maybe it was so ingrained into the fiber of their being as to be part of who they were. As an adult, I can see they took no responsibility for their lot in life and blamed everything and everyone else for their troubles. Once their children left, they were expected to send money home to support them, which they did at a cost to their own young families.

Two different worlds. Two different moral compasses. Both my blood.

A DARK CLOUD

ON A SUNNY DAY

As I've said, my father was able to manage his addiction for nearly a decade. Because we moved so often, it was easy for him to get prescriptions: a new town, new doctor, the next town, next doctor. There was never just one medical professional keeping track of his pain meds. Even so, he managed to function normally at work and home.

The real trouble began in Boston, where we lived for three years. The same town, same doctor, not enough scripts. Enter alcohol. I had never seen my father have a beer, much less a shot, but now the combo became his after-dinner dessert, and he usually went back for seconds.

Dad had finally reached the goal he worked ten years to achieve, and got promoted to manager for Kresge. We lived in Randolph, south of Boston, and the store was in Dorchester, an unsavory area at the time. He always quipped more merchandise got stolen than bought. Add the brutal, traffic infested commute, and it was a stressful time for my father.

One afternoon he was chasing two teenagers he caught stealing. They ran out of the store, shoving the door back at my father so hard he went through the glass and ended up hanging over the metal bar by his waist. He needed hundreds of stitches on his face, hands, and legs. It also threw his back out bad enough that he needed the metal brace again. So much pain and not enough pills equated to more alcohol use. Shots and beers became his evening pastime. Add in the onset of extreme anxiety and Librium, and things got ugly fast. His demons (depression and childhood abuse) saw the opening they'd been waiting for and, with the addition of a new beast—full-blown addiction—wasted no time taking over. My father would never be the same again.

On the sunnier side of this time in life, I received excellent dance training in Boston, which solidified my love for the art. Master Charles ran one of the most respected dance studios in Boston, and also groomed apprentices for the Boston Ballet and The School of Theatre Arts. It wasn't unusual to see professional dancers taking one of his classes as well when they were in town to perform.

Master Charles was strict, demanding, and a stickler for technique. He was also a fantastic motivator. It didn't matter if you were a novice or a seasoned dancer, a professional or a child, in your prime or past it; he inspired all dancers to be better than they were. Which, of course, made them better. Trust me when I tell you, he didn't do it through excessive praise or hand-holding. He did it by working you hard, and by challenging you to challenge yourself both physically and mentally. He also offered a lot of criticism, always constructive, but still criticism. *Have I mentioned criticism?* If he did praise you or give you one of his rare nods of approval, you knew you had met the challenge within yourself and had improved.

He looked like Woody Allen and carried a big stick—literally. He would move around the massive studio banging out counts on the floor and also used it for corrections (gently, of course). Dancers dreaded that rod's appearance by their side. When Master Charles was dissatisfied with your foot's turn out, the stick would give it a little nudge. When your split was not satisfactory, you'd feel the rod placed on your shoulder. If your tap technique was a bit off, the stick would appear right next to you, tapping out the tempo. How he found the tapper a fraction of a beat off in an advanced class of fifteen students, I'll never know. But he always did.

One day after class, Master Charles asked to speak to my friend Penny's mom as well as mine. *Uh oh.* We had both had a few visits from the stick in class and thought we were dropping down a level.

Au contraire! We were moving up. He wanted to make sure our moms would be comfortable with us dancing alongside much older students. Master Charles also wanted to offer us a semi-private tap class because he felt we were exceptional for our age (which was nine). It was Christmas in July for Penny and me! Master Charles thought we were worthy of dancing with the student teachers AND having a semi-private class as well. He reminded us it would mean more afternoons, longer hours, and even harder work. Like that was going to be a buzzkill for two obsessed young dancers. While we were jumping around in celebration, my mom asked to speak with him alone.

I found out later she had thanked him but said we couldn't afford more classes. Master Charles forfeited the money. "You get her here, and it will be my pleasure to work with her." He had a teacher's heart.

You would think teenage dancers in an elite studio would have resented two little twerps in their dance classes, but it was quite the opposite. The training was much harder than either Penny or I anticipated, and when the student teachers saw us struggling with something, one or more of them would help us during class breaks.

Mom was right there for every class, taking notes and writing steps down so I could practice at home, which I did endlessly. My brother John didn't mind spending so much time at the studio because Penny's brother was his age, and they got along well. Another plus was the studio was on the second floor over a drugstore, where the two boys could get all the candy and soda needed to keep them quiet. And they always made sure it took plenty.

My favorite class was our semi-private tap class. It was also the most grueling and demanding. It was supposed to be an hour and a half long but always ran longer. Master Charles would work us until our legs felt like rubber and then work us some more. He would drill us endlessly on combinations and techniques until finally, that stick would bang the floor, and he would say, "Excellent." Just when we'd let out a sigh of relief, he would add, "Now let's make it even better." I loved every minute of it. He was training my mind and body to work together and create something beyond what I thought I was capable of doing.

There was a girl, Betty, who danced in the tap class right before ours. Her mother used to harass Master Charles endlessly to let Betty tap with us. Betty's forte was ballet, and she could dance circles around most of us in the studio en pointe (she became an apprentice for the Boston Ballet a few years later). But for whatever reason, her mother wouldn't rest until she tap danced with Penny and me. Finally, in the third year, Master Charles relented.

Betty hated the class. It was a constant struggle for her, and she was in tears at the end of most sessions. As I've said, Master Charles was tough: you kept up, or you heard about it. On top of that, Betty's stage mom was even tougher on her.

After a particularly intense class, Betty told us she was quitting. She didn't want to ruin our upcoming audition for a chance to perform at the John Hancock Center. No way Penny and I were letting that happen. Betty and Penny started coming to my house on Sundays, so we could practice without her mother critiquing her every move. Betty's improvement was immediate. Once she realized her mom was the problem and found her self-confidence, her feet were on fire. There were no more tears after class.

Master Charles had a yearly dance recital that allowed all of his students to perform a routine in every discipline they studied. It was a festive atmosphere and great fun, an excellent chance for us to showcase our accomplishments to our family and friends.

His concerts, however, were something completely different. Representatives from ballet companies, known choreographers, innovative dance troops, and off-Broadway show producers attended those performances scouting for up and coming talent.

For apprentices, students in a theatre arts school, and semi-professional dancers, these concerts were their chance at the big leagues. There were also plenty of guest dancers, professionals who performed to show their support and appreciation for Master Charles.

Every concert, Master Charles would handpick a few studio dancers to audition for one of the coveted spots left in the program. Penny, Betty, and I were so proud and honored when we got the nod!

Concert dress rehearsals ran like clockwork. There were no do-overs for personal mistakes, only for production mishaps. Our little tap trio's rehearsal performance was a DISASTER. It could not have gone worse for us. We entered stage right instead of stage left, which meant we either had to reverse the entire dance or turn our backs to the audience and perform for the backdrop. We did the best we could, but it was ugly. When we finished, you could hear a pin drop in the auditorium. Master Charles, watching from the front row, rose to his feet and, with a sweep of his arm, dismissed us from the stage. He never said a word, but his disapproval and disappointment were palpable. We were stunned and ashamed, devastated. How could we make such a mistake?

That rehearsal is the first memory I have of letting myself and others down; the first time I tasted humble pie. It shook me to my core. I couldn't keep water down, much less food. Forget sleeping that night—I was too busy beating myself up. Had it been anything other than that dance, I don't think it would have been such a tragedy for me. But that dance lived inside of me. I was that dance. If I couldn't figure out how to get on stage, how could I trust myself to remember the intricate steps? I had practiced that routine a thousand times, and it was as natural as walking for me. But that night, lying in bed, I went over it countless times in my head and never got it right. Not once. All I could see was Master Charles's disappointment in us. All I could feel was my disappointment in myself. It was a lot for a just turned twelve-year-old to process in one day. Anxiety rapidly replaced my self-confidence and overtook my ego.

By morning I had worked myself into quite a tither. Convinced all my hard work was for naught, and I was a lousy dancer, I was dreading a performance that I had dreamed about for years. I promised myself that after this concert, I would never go through this again.

When I arrived at the John Hancock Center on the day of the performance, Betty and Penny were already there. Our moms left us at the backstage door, and we went through hair and makeup together without a word. The makeup artist gave up putting makeup on Betty because her silent tears kept turning her face into a melted mess. Even with all the foundation and rogue they caked onto Penny's face, she still looked gray. I kept licking my lips, trying to produce enough saliva to be able to swallow, so my lips were white, and my teeth were bright red. We looked like the cast from a B-rated horror flick—a zombie, a ghost, and a vampire.

After we donned our costumes, we huddled together in the corner like three little wounded birds waiting for a hawk to swoop in and carry us to our death. What happened instead was a beautiful white dove fluttered over to our corner and with kind eyes whispered something in a language we didn't understand. It was evident our dove was a professional ballerina by the graceful way she moved and the elegant way in which she carried herself. It was apparent she was a prima ballerina by the way the sea of dancers parted to let her pass.

She led us to an empty hallway and faced us in a specific direction. She clapped her hands once; the universal way a dance master says begin. We just stared at her and shook our heads no. She stuck her chin in the air, stamped her foot and clapped again. We danced—we were afraid not to. There was no music, and no countdown. Just the three of us, our hearts, and steps totally in sync, doing and sharing what we loved most in an empty hallway. When we finished, she opened her arms for a hug and got bowled over by three ecstatic girls. She then faced the direction she had had us dance in and did a deep curtsy, turned, and faced the opposite way and mimed sitting and applauding. Then she walked to stage left and, in her exquisite white tutu and pointe shoes, gave a silly impression of a tap dancer entering the stage. She blew us a kiss and ran off, leaving us in a fit of giggles with our confidence and enthusiasm restored.

Our performance got a standing ovation that night. Even better, Master Charles, standing in the infamous stage right-wing, bowed to us. Not just one of his rare nods but a bow. He might have even smiled.

When the three of us talked about it later, we agreed that as well as we did on stage, it didn't even come close to the magic we achieved in that hallway. We never found out who our beautiful white dove was, but we knew without her, given our age and nerves, our performance would have been as disastrous as our rehearsal. She had insisted we not give up, that we believe, and when we did, it was magical. She had restored our faith in ourselves. Without her intervention, I would have quit dance that night, which would have altered my life's path dramatically. She was an inspiring gift, but not the only one I received through my Boston dance training.

I learned so much more than dance during my time at Master Charles's studio:

I learned stern and strict did not equate to mean and uncaring.

I learned how to accept constructive criticism from others and myself and use it to improve instead of harboring resentment or feeling defeated.

I learned the harder you work, the sweeter the reward.

I learned that when you're in over your head, you dig a little deeper, work a little harder, and keep putting one foot in front of the other. You might not end up where you want to be, but you'll end up further along.

I learned that success is not a synonym for perfection.

I learned the true meaning of teamwork.

I learned the value of resilience and tenacity when facing a challenge.

I learned my inner voice could wreak havoc if I didn't keep it in check.

I learned the profound effect the kindness of a stranger could have on someone.

I learned when hearts and real friendship bond together, incredible, magical things can be accomplished.

I learned success is sweeter when shared.

I learned a bow beats a nod any day of the week.

Of course, it was years before I fully realized all I'd learned in those three years, but the knowledge was there nonetheless to help a young girl navigate through the next eight years of her life. Difficult years, at best.

My father's issues had begun to affect his job performance, so the company sent someone from corporate to check out what was happening with their one-time rising star. Fortunately? Unfortunately? It turned out to be the same mutual friend who had introduced my parents. My father convinced him he was fine, he just needed to get out of the inner-city store, and he'd be able to get his head back together.

That infamous transfer began an endless cycle of enabling. I lived in too many places to count in the sixteen years I lived with my parents. Boston was the longest at three years, but some were as short as five months. It all depended on how well and long my father could control his demons' behavior.

His corporate angel managed to keep Daddy one step ahead of the firing squad (pun intended) for many years. He accomplished it by transferring my father before his employees caught on, or it started to show on his store's bottom line. The question is, why? Was it because of the friend's loyalty to Dad, or was the Kresge corporation afraid he would sue them over the truck accident? My guess is it was a little of both, but they had nothing to fear. My father was a company man through and through.

The move from Boston was the first move I resented, the first time I had to sacrifice something so important to me: my training with Master Charles.

Sadly, it would not be the last.

HICCUPS AND HORMONES

———

My father's transfer from Boston to Center City, New Jersey, happened two weeks after my twelfth birthday. John and I stayed in Boston with Mom for a few weeks to acquire enough days in school to pass the year. There would only be one other time I would start and complete a grade in the same school.

Because the owners of the house my father rented in Center City sold it, we had to move out the same summer we moved in. John and I hadn't started school yet and only knew a few kids in the neighborhood, so it wasn't as stressful a move as most. We relocated to a nearby town, Mantua, New Jersey.

By this time, my father had started washing down his pills with vodka most mornings, and my mother was tucked safely into her denial. The more there was to see, the more she chose not to see. To preserve her fairytale, Mom put on her rose-colored glasses, and at the ripe old age of twelve, I started to take on an adult role in some circumstances.

I had sprained my foot that summer and was on crutches for the first day of school. I begged my mother to drive me to school instead of putting me on the school bus. It wasn't my first time as the new kid, and I knew what was probably coming.

"Don't be silly, Belle, everything will be fine, you'll see," she answered. Because as long as I got on that bus, she could pretend everything was okay. So, I had to take one for the team.

After having my crutches thrown to the back of the bus and my lunch stolen by a kid offering to carry it for me, my new teacher called Mom and pointed out why the bus was not a good idea.

Meanwhile, John was not off to a great start with his fourth grade teacher. The teacher mistook John's quietness and mumbling as a sign of rudeness or disinterest and quickly labeled him a problem student. The more he picked on John, the more my brother withdrew.

After a parent-teacher conference, Mom came home and lectured John on his bad attitude, which was something a teacher had never accused him of before. She didn't ask John if anything was bothering him, or wrong, and poo-pooed the idea the teacher was picking on him.

I was the one who asked my brother what was going on, and his answer made perfect sense for a fourth-grader. When we moved from Trenton to Boston, John's first grade teacher put him in a speech therapy class. It didn't take the therapist long to figure out he didn't have a problem; it was just his Jersey accent. Now that we were back in Jersey, he was afraid his Boston accent would land him in speech therapy again. John figured the less the teacher heard him say, the better his chances were of avoiding that embarrassment. The fact he had witnessed the other kids teasing a girl with a lisp only added to his anxiety. *Somebody has to help him!*

Determined to help, and no longer the typical twelve-year-old, I walked John to class the next day, and we explained the situation to the teacher. Such a simple solution to relieve my brother's angst and to diffuse a bad situation. Once the teacher was aware of the problem, he took my brother under his wing, and things improved quickly. Mom thought her lecture had straightened my brother out, and that's why his grades had improved. She was proud of his turnaround and happy it had all worked out.

I am pretty sure that if we hadn't talked to the teacher, John would've flunked fourth grade.

I was so excited when my foot healed, and I could finally get back to dance. I was surprised when Mom pulled up to a house in the middle of the boondocks and announced, "Here we are," but I trusted her. After all, she had found Master Charles so she must know what she's doing.

I will never forget that first lesson with Miss Dana. Her studio was a finished area of her basement so small I could barely dance. The ceiling was too low to do overhead port de bras (ballet arm movements) in proper form, so the barre work was minimal. My ballet lesson was on demi because my head hit the ceiling en pointe. The dance area was too small to perform jazz combos, so Miss Dana had me pace them out in place. There was no tap lesson that first night. The lesson plan Miss Dana ordered from a catalog hadn't arrived on time, and she had never taught tap above Level One. *A catalog lesson? Level one?*

Just a few short months ago, I was training with Master Charles. Now, I was taking dance in a studio built for munchkins with an instructor who needed instructions on how to teach tap. *YIKES!* I couldn't wait to get out of there and talk to Mom about checking out other studios in the area. So, imagine my shock when Miss Dana said, "See you next week," and my mom answered, "We'll be here, thank you." *WHAT?!*

We were barely in the car when I got started. "Mom, you can't be serious! You saw what happened in there! There's not even enough room for me to dance, and she can't teach tap. I doubt she's ever taught anyone other than little kids in there or anywhere else for that matter!" I was in a full-blown twelve-year-old snit.

"Don't be disrespectful, Belle Ann." Mom continued, "It was the first lesson, and you need to give her a chance. Don't be so quick to judge. And it wasn't THAT small. You're exaggerating." She was there. She had seen the entire lesson and had witnessed all the issues. But my mother had already convinced herself it wasn't so bad because that fit best into her box.

"I'm not going back there again, Mom," I said, and began to cry.

"You dance with Miss Dana, or you don't dance at all." *Well, that just took all the fight out of me.*

"How did you find her?" I asked through my tears.

"In the phonebook," was her devastating reply.

The phonebook. Mom knew how much I loved to dance, and the vital role it played in my life. She also knew what level of training I had received at Master Charles and how difficult leaving his studio was for me. This move was the first time she hadn't visited a studio in advance, and it was the worst time to have let me down. *The phonebook.*

"It will all work out just fine, Belle. You'll see." *Those bloody rose-colored glasses again.*

I stayed with Miss Dana, and before long, the two of us came to an unspoken agreement. I went to the studio once a week, and she would teach me the individual steps. Then I would take copies of the dances home so I could "practice." Practice is in quotations because that's when I was able to put the dances together. Home is where I put my ballet routines en pointe and added port de bras. It was where I could do more than a couple of jazz steps at a time.

Since Miss Dana didn't choreograph, and all her routines came from catalogs, I started taking liberties. I'd change a step here, add an arm or throw in a leap there. Pretty brazen for a twelve-year-old student. When I showed her the changes I'd made, she would always be encouraging but made corrections and added her opinion, which I would respectfully adhere to (sometimes begrudgingly).

Miss Dana, however, gave me free rein when it came to the tap routines. Sometimes when I showed her the rhythm combinations I had choreographed she would want to learn them. That was when I discovered how much I loved teaching and sharing dance.

My lessons were 8:00-10:30 p.m. on a school night, so the only other student I knew was Lucy, whose private class was right before mine. She was a year or two older than me and took only ballet.

Because Lucy was so petite, she was able to string a couple of steps together in the small studio. Her body was so expressive when she danced, even without the space to let go. I instinctively knew her passion wasn't born at Miss Dana's, and I was right. Lucy had trained with a teacher in Philadelphia, Miss Annette. She was at Miss Dana's because, like me, her family had moved. I had no idea why—it's not like I was ever going to Philadelphia—but I felt compelled to ask Lucy for Miss Annette's address and phone number. I wrote them down and tucked the paper into my dance bag.

Miss Dana's recital was at the end of March. I was so preoccupied with my newfound love, choreography, I hadn't even asked where it would be. I wasn't surprised when I found out it was in an elementary school cafeteria. At the dress rehearsal, I learned the studio consisted of Lucy, me, and a few students under the age of eight.

Lucy and I couldn't perform on the small stage, and on the night of recital, the folding chairs had to be set up halfway back to the kitchen so we could dance on the floor. It didn't matter; with so few students, there were still plenty of seats. I was intrigued by Lucy's dances. I had never seen lyrical ballet before, and the way she used her body to tell the music's story appealed to me. I decided to add that dance discipline to my repertoire and made a mental note to sign up for lessons.

As for me, I barely noticed that I was back in a dinky cafeteria. I was performing dances that were my creations, and I didn't care where I was or who was there. I danced my heart out that night, and for the first time, I danced for an audience of one. Me. As far as I was concerned, I was the only one there. It was such an exhilarating, freeing experience! It was a defining moment for me as a dancer and as a young girl. I had discovered the joy of, and the need for, celebrating my accomplishments within myself—such an important discovery to make.

It's worth noting there was no Daddy in this cafeteria, giving me a standing ovation and yelling, "That's my baby girl!" Just a disengaged man who was trying hard to look focused.

During my brief time at Miss Dana's, I discovered choreographing and teaching, two aspects of dance I might not have otherwise explored. I went on to develop a real love for both, but especially for teaching.

I found teaching Miss Dana the tap rhythms just as exciting as learning them myself. It took a special lady to admit her limitations and be willing to learn from a student. Not to mention allowing Lucy and me to alter our routines. Miss Dana allowed us to grow at our own pace instead of holding us back. My mom was right that first lesson; I had been too quick to judge. I realized if you keep an open mind, there is something to learn from everyone.

There was another major event that happened to me in Mantua. I discovered boys, or, more accurately, a boy. My first crush was Dougie, the son of a preacher man. Yep, my minister's firstborn.

When Dougie and I shared our first slow dance at the church's youth group dance, he couldn't quite figure out where to place his hands. On my back? My waist? My shoulders? His palms were sweating so bad I could feel them dampen my dress.

Meanwhile, I was having some issues of my own. I was shaking like a leaf, and my heart was beating so fast I was afraid I'd pass out. *Should I put my head or my chin on his shoulder? Maybe I'll just keep my head on my shoulders—should I look over his shoulder or at him?* I must've looked like a bobblehead doll.

We were stumbling over one another's feet, and I'm sure my face was just as red as his. We both let out a sigh of relief when it was finally over.

It didn't deter us from trying again, however, and the second time was the charm. Prince Charming and Cinderella had nothing on our second spin around the floor. Whenever I hear Mel Carter's "Hold Me, Thrill Me, Kiss Me," I remember that dance and staring into Dougie's big green eyes. Or were they blue? Fifty years is a long time.

Being twelve, neither one of us had ever REALLY kissed. We decided to wait and have our first kiss on Confirmation Day because that's when we'd be adults. Such anticipation and excitement! I'm not ashamed to say I even practiced on a pillow; I was determined to put in a better performance than I had for the first dance. The kiss never came to fruition. We moved in late April before the big event.

MOVING WAS BEGINNING TO TAKE A REAL TOLL ON JOHN AND me. We didn't have a childhood home, a hometown, or long-term friends. We never really got to know anyone, and no one ever got to know the "real" us. Socially, we were always the new kids, the outsiders. I learned early on how to morph myself to fit the new norm and became a full-fledged chameleon at school. Style, music, slang, food, what classes I liked, do I read, smoke, drink, swear; all of it depended on where I lived at the time and what the quickest route was to being accepted, because I didn't have much time before I had to start all over again.

The one constant thing I had in life was my dance. It didn't matter to me where we lived, how good or bad my instructor du jour was, or if I performed at the John Hancock Center or in a school cafeteria. Dance was in me, a part of me, and therefore always with me. It was there to comfort and console me—to accept the real me. It was the one thing that grounded me in the emotional tornado that became my adolescence. I have always wished my brother John could have found his niche, a passion able to help him through the storm, but unfortunately, he never did.

On top of all the social issues to deal with, there were academic problems to navigate as well. I would be bored to tears in honor classes in one state, we would move, and I'd need tutors to pull C's in the new one. Move again, and I'd be high honors. John won a reading award he was so proud of, but when we moved, the new school told him he was reading a level below and needed extra help.

You can imagine what an effect all of this had on our self-esteem and confidence. It would have been incredibly hard even with a stable home environment. But with my father's behavior escalating and my mother's head burrowing ever deeper into the sand, it was fast becoming unbearable.

FRAYED APRON STRINGS,

AN ASTRONAUT, AND AN UNCLE

My father transferred to Erdenheim, a suburb of Philadelphia, and we moved days after my thirteenth birthday. It would be the third house I lived in and the second school district I attended that year.

Having to leave my first crush Dougie behind was heartbreaking, but departing before THE KISS took place was tragic for a girl my age. To make matters worse, I had less than two months in the new school to make friends before the summer break, and thirteen-year-old girls aren't exactly eager to befriend an outsider.

One morning, Mom caught me crying, and I confided in her. I told her about my feelings for Dougie, the missed kiss, and how hard it was to make friends in a new junior high school.

Her reaction was, "Thank goodness that's all it is; I was afraid it was something drastic. Now, stop acting silly and help me unpack these boxes. There will be plenty more Dougies in your lifetime, and you'll have friends before you know it."

Talk about dismissing a young girl's feelings! Acting silly is not the best way to address an adolescent who has just poured her heart out to you. It was, however, a typical response for a mother to make in the 1960s. Parenting in those days was all about the "You'll live, and it's not the end of the world" strategies.

What was not typical, however, was sharing the story at the dinner table with my father and brother. I saw that as a betrayal. My father quipped I was becoming a drama queen and unkindly nicknamed me Liz Taylor. I made a mental note not to confide in my mom again, and I didn't until I was an adult. I don't think she even noticed, but if she did, she was probably relieved. It made it easier for her to pretend all was right in my world.

That was a very lonely summer for me. It was void of sleepovers, parties, and Saturdays at the mall. Liz Taylor spent a lot of time in her room and was told at least once a day to stop moping around. *Thank goodness dance is starting soon!*

At supper one night, Mom mentioned she wasn't keen on driving into the city for my dance lessons and was going to look for another studio. "No! If you won't drive me, I'll take the bus," I yelled. I just knew I had to go to Lucy's Miss Annette's after the crazy way I got her number and landed in Philly. I was awarded a slap across the face for sassing my mother and sent to my room. My mother's betrayal at one supper and now a slap at this one. The dinner table was fast becoming a place I wanted to avoid at our house.

Mom eventually agreed to drive into the city as long as I took Saturday classes. When I called to register for classes, I learned Miss Annette only taught modern and freestyle ballet. *Oh well, I have to go through with it now after the stand I took at dinner a few nights ago. Besides, I still have this overwhelming sense I need to dance there.*

The studio was a humongous space in an old warehouse; it echoed it was so big. Miss Annette, on the other hand, was as tiny as a sparrow. She never walked but would scurry and flutter around on her toes in perpetual motion. Miss Annette was much older than I expected, given her chosen dance discipline, but possessed more energy than a woman half her age. Her hair was dyed bright red, she wore heavy stage makeup, and was always barefoot. She was artistic, innovative, and a free spirit. The woman was also, and I mean this in the kindest possible way, batshit crazy. She was fond of long, flowing scarves and always wore one somewhere on her person. She would flit through the studio, waving it around as we danced, telling us, "Be the scarf darlings, float and flow with the air!"

I remember one class we laid curled up on the floor while she covered us with tarps to simulate oppression. She then started playing "music" that sounded like a combination of metal shrieking, pots banging, and glass breaking. We were to break the bonds of oppression and set our spirits free through our creative movement. I mean, I got the concept, it just wasn't for me. When Miss Annette decided to have us dance in the parking lot during a rainstorm, "to cleanse our creativity of inhibitions," I decided I'd had enough. As my classmates filed out into the downpour, I sat in the warehouse entry space to await the end of class.

Now what am I going to do? How could my intuition have been so wrong? Lucy trained here?! As I sat there feeling sorry for myself, I noticed a group of dancers come in and head towards the stairs. I waved, and one of the girls asked why I was sitting there. When I explained my predicament and that I was now a dance orphan, she smiled and told me to follow them. "Miss Rose won't mind one more student in today's class—she loves meeting new dancers." *There's another studio in this building? Who knew?*

The minute I walked into Miss Rose's studio, I knew I belonged there. *Now, this is more like it!* This studio would nurture and develop my dance and take it to a new level. I felt that truth just as sure as I breathed, and I was right. There was even a carpool so Mom wouldn't have to drive into the city all the time. As I said, it was meant to be.

I now had my explanation for why I felt compelled to get Miss Annette's number from Lucy.

Miss Rose was gregarious, fun, unconventional, and blunt. Very blunt. She also had a thick New York accent and rarely completed a sentence without swearing. My guess is that was one of the reasons she only accepted students thirteen and older.

The official reason she always cited was, "Young students require patience and finesse, and I'm fresh out of both." She was a former Rockette and was, "in many a Broadway chorus line back in the day," as she was fond of saying. Picture a young, sober Liza Minnelli, and you'll have the perfect visual of my mentor.

Naturally, Miss Rose taught all the tap and theatrical jazz classes, but she chose to hire instructors (only the best) to teach ballet. Her take on classical ballet was, "That s#*t is too formal and restricting for me to spend my day doing, but it is beautiful." Lyrical? "So free-flowing and interpretative, but all that drama and emotion wears me down."

Miss Rose wasn't fooling anyone. She excelled in all dance techniques as we witnessed when she would take over an occasional ballet class.

In one such pointe class, Miss Rose stopped me in the middle of a combination and asked me what the heck (my word, not hers) I was doing? My blank look let her know I had no idea why she was upset. She proceeded to dress me down in her not-so-subtle fashion.

"Why, with the talent you possess in other dance disciplines, do you insist on clunking around in those frapping (again, my word) shoes like a cow?" I should've been insulted, but I wasn't; she was right.

I defiantly stuck my chin in the air and stated, "Because I want to be a dance instructor, and I need to know how to dance en pointe."

She surprised me by doubling over in laughter. "Thank God! Is that why? Thank God! I was afraid you were passionate about it, and I was gonna have to kill your unicorn. Have you ever seen me in those little pink ribboned torture chambers? No, and you never will. But here I am, teaching some of the best and brightest."

"Being a good dance instructor is about what you know, not about what you can do. It's about taking that knowledge and developing your students' skills. Now let's get you and your flat feet out of those shoes and into an instructor training program where you belong."

As I unlaced my shoes, she reiterated that I sucked en pointe.

"Yeah, I know," I said out loud and then, under my breath, "Way to be encouraging."

"You expected me to lie? Toughen up kitten—it's a dog eat dog world out there," she said with a wink.

I loved her.

Miss Rose's studio was always in a state of organized chaos. She rented the entire second floor of the warehouse, so there were usually two or three different lessons happening at the same time. The only thing dividing the classes were partitions on wheels, eight feet tall and twelve wide that we moved around as needed. They did nothing for the noise level, but that didn't seem to distract any of us, and added to the festive atmosphere.

Miss Rose didn't have recitals or performances. Her focus was on technique, strengthening, and creativity. She was all about developing your skills. If you were into costumes and applause, you were dancing at the wrong studio. Her focus was on helping dancers prep for professional auditions or to get their teaching certification. She also had cut-throat competition squads, which, frankly, I found out of character for her. They always practiced at the far end of the studio and kept to themselves. I watched beautiful dancers get accepted to a squad, only to quit dance entirely defeated a few months later. It was brutal.

If you gained a couple of pounds, you were out. If you missed a practice, you were gone. If you got injured, you danced through it or they replaced you. I never understood the attraction or the need to make a squad. To me, they drained all the joy and heart out of dance and replaced it with naked competitiveness and mean-spiritedness. I witnessed a lot of eating disorders, lifelong injuries, and emotional scars as a result of those squads. *It was total craziness.*

In the meantime, school started back up, and Mom was right, I did make friends. I also started dating in that "early teen fashion." Walking to class and eating lunch together, going to school dances, or the mall on Friday nights and hours-long phone calls. Jimmy was my first kiss (uneventful), Dan was the first one to try and cop a feel (he failed), and Ronnie was the first to say I love you (he didn't). I caught him kissing Jane at her locker one day and was relieved because I wanted to go to the semi-formal with Tom. Such was the love life of eighth and ninth graders in those days.

I came home from school one afternoon to find Uncle Willie, one of my father's brothers, on the couch. He was in town for a couple of nights on his way to somewhere; I don't remember where. My father got home shortly after me, and the two of them started in on the Jack Daniels. *Excellent, just what Dad needs, an in-house drinking buddy.* By suppertime, they were both obnoxious, and later when they started crying and slurring stories about their childhood, Mom, John, and I went to bed.

We lived in a Cape style house, so the bedrooms were upstairs. At the top of the stairs, there was a landing maybe five feet wide and no longer than eight feet long. Directly across from the stairs was the bathroom, and my brother's room was to the right. My parents' room was the first room on the left, and my room was next to theirs, directly across from John's.

I woke up sometime during the night, (*or am I dreaming?*), to a commotion on the landing, (*or is that John's room?*) I tried to see what was going on, but a gigantic astronaut was floating at the foot of my bed. I couldn't see his face through his helmet, but I could feel his eyes bore into mine. The air hose, attached to his suit, hissed so loudly it hurt my ears. When I looked up, it didn't connect to anything above; it just floated towards the ceiling. Every time I moved so I could see around him, he would block my view, and paralyze me with his stare that I could feel but not see. He would not allow me to witness what was happening on the landing (*or was it in John's room?*) I tried to hear what was going on, but his airhose was too loud. When I went to get out of bed to find out what in the world was happening, I saw my floor covered in snakes. Terrified of snakes, I had to stay put.

As abruptly as the commotion started, it ended. Suddenly, the lights were out, and everything was quiet. The astronaut and snakes disappeared, and I closed my eyes *(or were they already closed?)*. Just as I drifted off to sleep *(or did the dream end?)*, I heard someone crying.

My first thought when I woke up in the morning was the awful nightmare I'd had the previous night. It had felt so real, but of course, it couldn't have been *(could it?)*. *Nah, seriously, snakes and an astronaut ghost—get a grip of yourself, girl.*

My second thought was, is that Mom yelling at Dad? *About damn time.* I sat on the top of the stairs to listen, and sure enough, she was letting him have it. His brother was to leave immediately.

"Wake him up and get him out, now!" she demanded. It seems Uncle Willie had climbed into bed with Mom and Dad the night before, naked as a jaybird, and proposed a threesome. Mom had not been amused. "I have a young daughter in this house, and I don't want that pervert anywhere near her. Get him out NOW!" Mom was adamant. For the first time in my life, I heard my mother put her foot down, and it rendered my father speechless. Uncle Willie was shown the door before his morning coffee, never to be seen or heard from again. I can't say that I missed him.

Not until decades later was it revealed it hadn't been me in harm's way that night.

Around this time, I started suffering from terrible menstrual cramps. One morning they were particularly bad, and I asked Mom if I could stay home from school. She told me no, periods were a fact of life, all girls got them, and I needed to get used to it. She assured me I'd feel better once I got up and at 'em. Once again, a typical response from a 1960s mom.

Well, I knew that was the reality she needed to believe, but all girls didn't suffer like I was, and I knew from experience moving around wasn't going to help. But I went off to school without another peep because I knew the school nurse was my best shot at getting any relief, and I was right. When the nurse called Mom to come to pick me up, she strongly recommended my mother take me to see a doctor, which she did.

As the doctor examined me, Mom said something like, "She needs to get used to periods." He put her hand on my abdomen. "Feel that? Those are the same contractions you get in early labor. Your daughter is in real pain." He suggested I go on the pill to help with the cramping and clotting and wrote a prescription.

On the ride home, I begged Mom to PLEASE not discuss the doctor's visit at the dinner table, and she did as I asked. My bad. By the time she talked to my father later that night, he had ingested too many drinks and one too many Librium. The wrong Daddy showed up.

"No daughter of mine is going on the pill to be able to have sex right and left without a care in the world," he bellowed. "Use your head, Lois. Do you want her to end up a little whore?" *Whore? Sex? Geez, all I want to do is stop the pain and keep from bleeding to death.*

My mother went to the drugstore that night, but not to fill the prescription. When she got home, she handed me a new hot water bottle and a heating pad, making it crystal clear to me where her allegiance lay. She never said another word to him or me about the situation.

By now, there were only brief appearances made by my real daddy. In his place was a verbally and emotionally abusive man that lashed out at us, his children. His new nicknames for John were dumb-ass and mama's boy. He had stopped calling me his baby girl and labeled me a little whore in what felt like a heartbeat. He didn't physically beat us, but boy did his angry words and degradation leave open wounds and lifelong scars. John and I could do nothing right and a whole lot wrong. We walked around on eggshells when he was home because his mood would turn on a dime. Oh, how I resented him. The anger I felt towards him. How I longed to have my daddy back!

Where was Mom, you ask? She was singing in the kitchen, making dinner, downstairs doing laundry, or at the sewing machine making clothes. Anywhere, but in the truth. I believe it was because to see the truth, she would've had to acknowledge it and therefore do something about it. It would have taken a strength I don't think she possessed. At the very least, her fairy-tale would have ended.

Strangely enough, at that time, I never felt any real resentment or anger towards my mother. Frustration and exasperation, for sure, but always love. I had this overwhelming urge to protect her and her innocence. I so envied her innocence!

My father transferred to Seekonk, Massachusetts, in March of my freshman year. By that time, I had earned my certification to teach from the Dance Masters of America and was teaching classes for Miss Rose. I had increased my knowledge of choreography and music interpretation and was learning how to use both to best showcase dancers' individual strengths.

Dance had taken on a different role in my life. I still enjoyed taking classes, but I loved teaching even more. I had little interest in performing but couldn't wait to see my students bring my choreography to life. A transformation that started at Miss Dana's had evolved under Miss Rose's tutelage. I was, first and foremost, a dance instructor. Little did I know it would be over ten years before I taught again.

As for leaving school in Erdenheim, I didn't have any significant issues. I hadn't developed any close friendships, and there wasn't a special boy. Although there was a lot more angst of being the new kid again because this time, I was entering high school.

DEAR DIARY

WE SPENT THE REMAINDER OF MY FRESHMAN YEAR AND most of my sophomore year in Seekonk. It was the first time I ever felt immediately comfortable in my school surroundings. From day one, I never ate lunch alone, walked to class alone, or had to introduce myself to a teacher. There was always someone around showing me the ropes, including me in the study hall note passing, and making sure I knew which boys to avoid (one of whom I married, but that's a different chapter). In no time at all, I was a member of the telephone grapevine and included in all the need to know info. Within a month, I had a date to the sophomore semi-formal with the president of the sophomore class. No small feat for a freshman AND a newbie. By the end of the school year, I was included in summer parties, sleepovers, and had a steady boyfriend, Bernie.

It was a small school in a small town, and within no time, I felt at home. The real me, not a Belle I had to morph into to be accepted. Being able to be myself was huge, considering it was also the first high school I was attending. It gave me a confidence I had previously only felt with my dance.

My brother John was also thriving. He had a best friend, Mickey, and was dating his first girlfriend, Betsy, who was Mickey's sister. He was doing great in school and had taken up playing the trumpet. Where I had always been outgoing and involved thanks to dance, John was usually quiet and shy. It was good to see him so happy and engaged.

But then there was home…

We were having supper one night, and John got up to answer the phone in the kitchen. My father, drunk, flipped out because he hadn't asked to be excused first and told John to go upstairs, he'd be up in a minute to teach him some manners.

John screamed, "NOOOOO!!" and was more upset and angry than I'd ever seen him, but he went. I couldn't believe my father was punishing John over nothing, and my mother was remaining silent, so I came to my brother's defense. Dad threatened to keep me home from the dance on Friday night if I didn't watch my mouth, so I shut up.

After dinner, my father staggered upstairs, and Mom and I went to do dishes. When I asked her why she hadn't intervened, she said, "Because, parents have to present a united front."

"Not always, Mom. Sometimes mamas need to protect their young," I told her, and went to do my homework.

One Saturday soon after, I was helping Mom collect the laundry and drycleaning. She had started working full time, and laundry was one of my chores. While getting my father's suits ready for the cleaners, she found a handful of pills in a pocket and mumbled something about him always losing his prescription bottles.

I decided to give it a shot. "Are you kidding Mom? You can't believe he's getting those pills from a doctor!" I said.

Her reply was, "Of course, he is Belle Ann. Where else would he get them?"

Ahhh, the art of unseeing, of being unaware. Fairytale kept intact. Innocence preserved. View still looking rosy. Clouding up a little maybe—hopefully? Nope. Not yet.

I was so excited to have a group of friends and a social life that, for the first time, dance moved down on my list of priorities. I took a few pick-up classes here and there but nothing steady. I was too busy having teenage fun. Football games, school dances, dating. Not to mention doing all the "what not to do" things that teenagers of the early 1970s discovered and somehow managed to live through. Things like riding around country roads on Friday nights drinking Boone's Farm Apple and Strawberry Hill wines. Having parties when someone's parents were out of town believing the neighbors weren't going to tell, or doing donuts in the Speedway parking lot in Gremlins and Pintos during snowstorms. A bunch of us smoking pot in Bill's attic room while listening to Led Zepplin and Hendrix or watching a great new show called *Saturday Night Live.*

Some time in the late fall of my sophomore year, I caught the eye of Dave. He was a senior, and drop-dead gorgeous with the most incredible, hypnotizing blue eyes. Eyes that he knew how to use. He was fun, played the drums, drove a sports car, and had charisma to spare. Dave was the perfect package to steal a teenage girl's heart, and mine was one of them. I honestly don't remember how or where we met, but all of a sudden, there we were. We hung out together in a group, but I don't recall us ever having a one-on-one date. It's a good thing too because I was completely gaga over this boy. I mean, I couldn't form sentences around him, couldn't focus, could barely put one foot in front of the other when I was with him. All I could do was stare at him in awe. I was a puddle of goo. Add in the hormones that start rocking and rolling in a girl that age, and I doubt I would've remembered how to say the word no. Luckily, or unluckily, depending on how you look at it, the opportunity never presented itself. We ended up moving a few months later—again.

I had started keeping a diary to record my social life, but also found it helped me deal with my feelings towards my father. I could leave my anger on the page instead of carrying it around with me. When the journal went missing, my first thought was my brother, but he swore he didn't even know I had a diary. *Yeah, right.* I went to rat him out to my mother, and she told me she was the one who took it.

I went ballistic. "YOU READ MY DIARY? HOW DARE YOU? HOW COULD YOU? THOSE ARE MY PRIVATE

THOUGHTS!" (Like she was the first mom to have ever read her teenage daughter's diary.)

What upset me even more was the content that bothered her. It wasn't reading about Dave and the turmoil of new feelings starting to stir inside me. Or the discovery of my drinking, smoking pot, the secret parties, or the lies I told her about where I was at times. It was the angry and resentful entries about my father and the toll his behavior was taking on John and me that she couldn't tolerate. I guess seeing it in writing had finally clouded her rosy view. When I asked for the diary back, she told me she had thrown it out. She had thrown my innermost thoughts and feelings in the trash. *If you can't see it, it's not there.* "It's not healthy for you to write about your father with such anger and bitterness. Diaries are for recording nice memories," was her defense.

"Throwing it out won't change the facts or what was in it," I fumed and stormed up to my room.

Once again, in early March, John and I were told we were moving. Destination, Alexandria, Virginia. This time I was not going quietly and tried to reason with Mom.

"Mom, tell him you won't move again until he gets help; he needs rehab."

"I can't do that, Belle Ann." *Well, at least she didn't deny it.*

"Why not?" I asked. No reply.

"I know you're aware of how all this is affecting John and me; you read my diary. You can't pretend everything's okay anymore."

"Oh, you were just overly dramatic, Belle," she tried. *Not this time, Mom, that won't work this time.*

"No. No, I wasn't, and you know it," I calmly replied. "He's emotionally and verbally abusive to us, his behavior is worsening, and I can't let you pretend otherwise any longer."

"Make him get help Mom, please! You can't keep uprooting your children and continue to follow an addict all over the universe. We need some stability," I begged.

"I can't threaten to leave him, he'll hurt himself," she whispered.

"I didn't say leave him, I said to make him get help, Mom—there's a difference," I countered.

"He'll take it to mean the same thing, and I'm afraid he will kill himself." She wasn't going to budge.

"If you don't do something, he will kill your children one day at a time," I replied.

I turned out to be quite the little prophet. The move from Seekonk in the spring of my sophomore year was devastating for me. It also marked the end of what little normalcy our life had left.

The Armageddon that awaited us in Alexandria was our family's undoing.

PART II

TEENAGE TWILIGHT ZONE

ARMAGEDDON

MOM COULD NO LONGER AVOID THE FACT HER PRINCE HAD some real issues. My father had been falling off his white horse for years but had always managed to climb back in the saddle. It had gotten to the point where sometimes he couldn't get back up, and most times, he didn't even bother to try.

No longer spared her children's reality, Mom became crushed. God forgive me—and he has—part of me was glad she was finally joining our little club. Now my mother would have to see, have to be aware, would have to do something. She did, and she was, but it didn't matter. Mom still did nothing. The only change was now that Dad had alienated his last believer, his one fan left on the home team, his behavior worsened. He managed to remain a functioning addict at work, but it took all the control he had. There was nothing left by the time he got home. As if that wasn't bad enough, John and I were barely surviving in our new school.

Mount Vernon was a state-of-the-art high school, a complex that offered students everything under the sun. College prep courses, business degrees and a host of vocational degrees, various levels of honors classes, a college-worthy library, open classroom concept; it had it all. These things are commonplace in schools nowadays, but in the early 1970s, Mount Vernon was ahead of its time. It resembled a small college campus, but in reality, it was a war zone in the middle of the suburbs.

The student body, four times the size of Seekonk High, was a mixture of the "elite brat pack," whose parents worked at the Pentagon or in DC, and kids from upper and lower-middle-class areas. John and I enrolled in March of the school's inaugural year, and tension between the social classes was already boiling over. Bullying, name-calling, fistfights. The Haves vs. the Have-Nots. The Haves were infinitely crueler and usually the instigators.

Students were unruly, and classes lacked discipline. My Greek Mythology teacher, in her first year of teaching, set the chalk down one day and, without a word, left the classroom, never to return.

I loved French and was an A student at Seekonk High, so I was surprised to find how far behind I was at Mount Vernon. The teacher spoke only French once the bell rang. When I tried to explain my problem in the first class, he shrugged and told me to take my seat. He continued the session in French and repeatedly called on me to answer questions, knowing I didn't understand. He started speaking to me very slowly and loudly, which made the class laugh. You don't need to understand a language to know when you're being humiliated. I collected my things, walked out of class, and quit French.

It didn't pay to try to eat in the cafeteria. Most times, someone would grab your tray, and thank you for buying their lunch. Ditto if you brown-bagged it. Sometimes a member of the elite brat pack would walk by and knock your food on the floor with a snicker, just for kicks and giggles.

The school had a fenced-in outdoor area called the smoking cage (not unusual in the 1970s), where students were allowed to smoke during breaks. One day, I saw a young boy beaten unconscious because he wouldn't give a group of guys his pack of Marlboros.

I walked into a bathroom one afternoon and was slammed up against the wall by three girls. They were so close to my face that I could smell what they had eaten for lunch on their breath. They told me they would mark my face if I ever tried to use one of their bathrooms again. Since I had no idea which bathrooms were theirs, I developed the bladder of a camel.

As traumatic as school was, it didn't hold a candle to the discovery I made a week before my sixteenth birthday.

Walking home from school one afternoon, I remember feeling especially drained. I couldn't wait to get home and have a couple of hours to myself before my parents got in from work. When I saw my father's car in the driveway, I remembered Ben, a family friend, was supposed to stay with us for a few days. *So much for my time out.*

My disappointment was instantly replaced with shock and disbelief when I opened the door. There sat my father and Ben, wearing nothing but their tightie-whities, drunk, drinking a beer, and watching TV. I have no idea what they were watching, but gay porn would have been fitting for the atmosphere I entered. It didn't take much to figure out what had just happened. The room reeked of sweat, they were sitting unnaturally close, and both had that dreamy post-coital look on their faces. Right in the family room, in the middle of the afternoon, for all to see. *Am I really seeing this?! How can this be happening?!*

They showed no shame or embarrassment that my father's teenage daughter had walked in on their afterglow. They were so cavalier about the whole thing they waved to me and asked me how my day went. *I can't deal with this! Can I? I have to. How should I handle it? Should I even react? No. No, he's drunk, it won't go well for me. Think girl! You need to think, not panic.*

I turned off the TV, told them to put on some clothes before John came home, and went to do a load of laundry.

Once I was in the laundry room, I let the shock of what I'd just seen wash over me. While I was still reeling, the realization of what I had barely missed seeing smacked into my psyche, and I started to cry.

I was alone and friendless in a strange place. I had no family or mentor close enough to confide in, and I had a little brother to protect. *Oh my God, John!* I was going to have to tell my mother.

"*You can't—it will kill her!*" said Protective Me.

"*Could I even find the right words to say it out loud?*" asked Confused Me.

"*She probably won't believe you, and you'll just make things worse,*" said Scared Me.

"*Don't even bother; it won't make any difference. Nothing will change,*" said Defeated Me.

Defeated Me won, and with that victory, I became dinner for a soul-eating depression. I shut down completely. I was nothing but an empty shell.

One morning, soon after I saw the vision I couldn't unsee, my father was sitting at the kitchen table, and I was rummaging around in the fridge when I felt an object hit me in the back. He had thrown his English muffin at me. He must've been lecturing me about my attitude, and I had him tuned out—part of my new survival plan.

"You look at me when I talk to you! I'm sick and tired of your disrespect," he growled.

I walked over, took a big gulp of his orange juice, which was ninety percent vodka, looked him in the eye and said, "I'll respect you when there's something to respect." It was about time he knew his 7:00 a.m. glass of OJ wasn't fooling anyone.

"Oh, and while we're on the subject of respect, looks like I'm not the family whore after all, am I Daddy?" *Holy crap, did I say that out loud?*

Yes, I did. For all the times he called me a whore because I kissed a boy goodnight one too many times in our driveway, or missed curfew by fifteen minutes, or for wearing my jeans too tight: such age-appropriate and innocent things. At that moment, all the damage and hurt his words had caused me over the years banded together and gave me strength. I wanted him to know I understood what I had walked in on.

He brought his hand back to hit me, and I didn't even flinch. I just stared him down and he looked away first. I would hope some of it was due to shame at never addressing what I had walked in on with me, but I could also smell his fear.

Please talk to me! Don't I matter to you? Explain things to me. Don't make your secret my burden; help me!

He must've been scared of the combination of raw anger and fear he could see in my eyes. He should have been. I know I was. My father said nothing; did nothing. Mom? She was making the beds, blissfully unaware of what was going on in the kitchen or, on occasion, happening in the family room. Nothing like a cozy family breakfast to start the day. *How in the world has this become my life?*

Some days I could keep my head down and get through the school day, and other times I could not. On those days, I would go to the nurse's office to get dismissed. When Mom picked me up on one of those many days, she suggested we take the afternoon to find a dance studio. "No thanks, I just want to go to bed," I said. *Empty shells can't dance.* And with that, I let go of the only lifeline I had at the time: dance. She never asked again.

My biology teacher, an older, soft-spoken gentleman, had hatched baby chicks in an incubator and also kept a snapping turtle in an aquarium. One day, when he stepped out to the hall for a minute, some of the students opened the incubator over the aquarium. "NOOOOO! Please, no," I screamed.

They laughed as the turtle attacked and tore apart the helpless chicks—the elite brat pack's idea of entertainment. The teacher came in when he heard all the racket, picked up the remains of his babies, and openly cried, which made them laugh even harder. He could not believe the cruelty. Neither could I. I went out into the hall, threw up on the floor, and walked away.

I had been to the nurse's office so many times I was no longer allowed to go there, so I went directly to the guidance office.

Being the early 1970s, and decades before the mental health awareness campaign, my thoughts are school officials didn't receive training to spot adolescent depression because it was unheard of at the time. Teenagers who exhibited the type of behaviors I was were labeled as problem students, and they dealt with us as such.

My counselor, Mr. Callus, said I was overreacting about the chicks, and he was not sending me home. I replied that anyone with a conscience and a heart would be reacting the same way, and I was not going back to class with those monsters. So, I just sat there then sat there some more until I wore him down and he called my parents. My father staggered in, the perfect package of dilated pupils and slurred words. *Good, now my guidance counselor will see. I mean, he's trained to spot substance abuse, right? Maybe now he will question why an exemplary student has suddenly become nothing more than a walking checked-out attitude.*

How naïve of me. Like a counselor, working in a school from hell, diffusing God knows what daily, had time to look at a transfer student's records. Without knowing my history, all he had to go on was the girl he saw at Mount Vernon, and she was a disengaged mess. *I'm a problem student. Me. How has this become my life?*

Mr. Callus barely acknowledged my father's presence, much less his condition. He had him sign the release paper and said something about my bad attitude, to which my father readily agreed. I left the office and walked home. There was no way I was getting in the car with my father driving in his inebriated condition.

He never said a word to me about that day. He was either afraid of what I would say if we were alone or he didn't remember I was supposed to be in the car. Either way, it spoke volumes to me at the time. *I don't matter to him; he doesn't care. I am on my own.*

The monsters who murdered the chicks didn't even get suspended. The biology teacher took a medical leave of absence, and I crawled further into my black hole. By the end of the year, there was a security presence on campus, monitors in the bathrooms, and graffiti on some hallway walls.

I barely passed. The only thing that saved me was my first two semesters in Seekonk. In three short months, my world had transformed into utter and complete chaos.

THE CORNER TREE

---

*S*UMMER—*FINALLY!* MY PARENTS LET ME TAKE A TRIP TO Seekonk and stay with my friend Donna for a couple of weeks. I think Mom was hoping it would snap me out of my funk. I was upset when I found out drop dead gorgeous Dave was driving cross-country and wouldn't be around, but I didn't dwell on it—this was time for celebrating, not for sadness. Within a couple of days of being back in the fold of my friends, I felt myself starting to crawl out of the hole.

There was a street corner where we all congregated, "just about supper time," as the song says, and it was there I first took notice of Steven Pierce. He was sitting up in a tree, whittling on a stick, and for some reason, that tickled me. He caught me giggling, smiled, and said, "Hey, come on up," and I did. The rest, as they say, is history.

Steven was quiet and gentle, a creative soul who won my heart with his kindness and tenderness. Oh, and his kiss. He kissed me the same way he listened, treated, talked to, and looked at me: with a protective tenderness and an all-in love I desperately needed at the time. We shared our secrets and our wounds with the kind of trust that only the young possess. Mind you, he was not without his issues. We were virtually two peas in a pod full of issues.

Steven was a free spirit, albeit a pessimistic one. His opinion of all things and people that required him to show structure, conformity, or deference to authority was dark. I mean, pitch-black dark. Since it's impossible to grow up or live in a society without adhering to any of the above, he would mentally check out. Often, and from the time he was eleven as I understood it. Barbiturates were his drug of choice, and lots of them. At the time we got together, he was under a doctor's care, at his parents' insistence, trying to get clean (or so they thought). It wasn't long before I also became a mellow way for him to check out, and he got his drug use somewhat under control—key word being somewhat.

Although I realized Steven had the same issue as my father, he was kind and loving towards me, where my father was not. At the time, that was enough for me to view their addictions through two different lenses.

Music was everything to our corner gang, the common thread that reinforced the bonds that were already there. I was a lifelong dancer, and Steven had an incredible ear, worked magic with a soundboard, and could find his way around a drum set. The rest of the gang consisted of guitarists, bass players, and drummers. They could all sing, and a couple of them were song-writers. Jimmy, an incredible guitarist, lived in the house next to the corner, and many a night was spent in his basement while the guys jammed, picked each others' brains, and kept getting better. When they put a band together, there was no one else in the area that even came close. Eventually, they parted ways and started playing with others or solo. I'm not sure when they broke up or why, but I'm pretty sure they remained friends.

In a flash, my vacation was almost over, and I called home to beg for more time. My parents agreed to two more weeks, but that was it. Because Donna's family was leaving on vacation, I moved to Billy's house. With all the time our group spent in Billy's attic, I had gotten to know his parents well. They already knew about my father's drinking and also how devastating the move to Alexandria had been for me. During my stay with them, I filled them in on good ole Mount Vernon High, but not the secret. I only shared the secret with Steven. They were sympathetic and supportive, and it was great being in a healthy home environment.

When my time was up, they called my parents and asked if I could stay the rest of the summer, which, of course, was an emphatic NO. Mom did agree to a few more days, but I was to be home by the weekend.

Having been forced to age, in some ways, well beyond my teenage years, my stay in Seekonk helped me heal enough to realize some crucial things:

As long as my life remained status quo, I would have to live in the dark hole to survive.

My inner light, my essence, was still burning (admittedly much dimmer), and that meant I was worth saving.

I was the only one I could count on to do the saving.

I needed a plan fast.

Billy's parents were generous people and more than a little concerned about me. Desperately I asked, and they agreed to let me come back and live with them during the school year. I could help around the house for my room and board, and I planned to get a part-time job after school to pay for my other expenses. Of course, everything hinged on my parents' consent, which was a significant roadblock. If Mom and Dad weren't willing to let me finish out the summer in Seekonk, there was little to no chance they would agree to a school year. I was determined to stay out of the hole, however, and knew I couldn't do it living in Armageddon. *I will convince them to agree; I have no other choice.* Steven insisted on coming to Virginia with me. He, like everyone but me, knew this cockamamie idea wasn't going to fly.

I called my parents and asked them if I could bring a friend back with me for a visit. I wanted them to think it was a girlfriend, and they did. I should note that when my family was living in Seekonk, Steven wasn't part of my inner circle, so my parents had never met him.

Having now raised a daughter of my own, I can better appreciate the angst my parents felt when they saw whose hand I was holding getting off the plane. As I've said, Steven was a free spirit. His hair hung past his shoulders, with a bandanna tied around his forehead, and he wore a ripped T-shirt. A pair of old jeans and dirty moccasins completed his ensemble. As you can imagine, it was not a warm and fuzzy welcome.

My father greeted Steven with, "You are NOT staying at our house, and you better be on a plane back to Seekonk by tomorrow night."

Steven looked him straight in the eye and said in his quiet way, "No problem, I'll stay at a motel. But I'm not leaving. Not until she tells me she's okay." *Well, aren't we off to a splendid start.*

My parents wouldn't even hear me out, much less listen to what I was saying. My place was with them. Period. The so-called plan never stood a chance anyway, but adding Steven into the mix sealed its fate. When he was trying to calm me down after my failed presentation, Steven told me he knew they would never go for it. I asked him how when he had never met them.

"Your mom, because you're her rock and she can't lose you. Your dad, because without you to blame, he would have to own the mess. I came to keep you from going into another tailspin and shutting down again."

I remember feeling so safe and comforted at that moment. *He understands, he gets it. He cares.* To this day, I still believe he was the only one who knew how close I was to the edge. How hard I was fighting for myself; to save myself from the dark hole. I still can't bring myself to think my parents knew and did nothing; Dad because of guilt and Mom out of habit.

I needed a plan B and boy, did I come up with a doozy. Steven and I would run away. There are no limits to what a desperate sixteen-year-old will do to have her voice heard, and I needed my parents to listen to me.

There was no hitchhiking, going hungry, or sleeping in cardboard boxes. We ran in style. I had saved money from an after-school job at a shoe store, so Steven and I pooled our resources and hopped a plane back to Seekonk. I needed to show my parents this was real for me, and things could not remain the same as they had been. Running away was a cry for help. I never intended to disappear, and I didn't. After a couple of days, Steven took me to Billy's parents' house, and I called home.

After many tears between Mom and me, and an agreement from my father to hear me out and discuss some changes, I flew back to Virginia alone. Steven had recently turned eighteen, and I was afraid my father would have him thrown in jail. I was right.

The minute I de-planed, my father started in on me. *So much for discussion, listening, and changes.* His initial plan was to have Steven charged with statutory rape. Problematic since I was still a virgin. Undeterred, he switched to "I'm having the S.O.B. charged with taking a minor across state lines." That one was legit, and it frightened me. He had me in check. *Think Belle, think.*

Trying to diffuse the situation, Mom asked me if I had a good flight. *Bingo!* I told her it was fine. "Oh, and there was a guy on the plane that looked so much like Ben I said hi before I realized it wasn't him. I thought maybe he was coming back for another visit." *Checkmate Daddy.*

Welcome back to Armageddon, baby girl.

Soon after I returned, my father announced we were going for family counseling. I was tearing the family apart, and the time had come to do something about it. Steven had pegged him to a tee, and by running away, I had given him the perfect opportunity to put it all on me.

So much for my cry for help.

SHHH...

COUNSELING? YES, PLEASE! MOM AND JOHN WERE JUST AS excited as I was about it. Surely a professional would see what was going on and help. We soon discovered my father had gone a few times on his own to give Dr. Phyllis some background and to share his concerns. The dear doctor had already started forming her opinion, based on Dad's charm and falsehoods, before ever meeting the rest of us.

She scheduled appointments to see Mom, John, and myself on separate visits (one apiece). We then had what turned out to be our first and last family session.

Here's a summary of Dr. Phyllis' initial analysis: John and I were spoiled and able to act out due to our mother's overindulgence. We all blamed my father for our unhappiness and pain when, in fact, we were causing our problems and his with our selfish behavior. Being disciplined or told something we didn't want to hear did not constitute verbal or emotional abuse. *She hasn't heard us at all! Didn't she listen to the language he uses, the name-calling, the degradation? What about his drinking? The pills?* Although the three of us talked at length about his substance abuse, she saw no indication of it during her previous visits with him. He took a prescription drug for anxiety and an occasional pain pill when his back acted up. Dr. Phyllis didn't consider stopping for a drink once in a while an alcohol problem. *Is she kidding?! Prescribed? Occasional? Once in a while? Her name should be Dr. P.H. Dipstick.*

My mom's jaw hit the floor, John laughed out loud, and of course, I had a comment. "You've been played by a con man, Doc." She ignored our reactions. We were to go home and discuss ways we could come together as a family. She also wanted each of us to keep a journal of our feelings to share at the next session. It would help build trust. Feeling vindicated, Dad dropped us off at home "to think about what she had said," and supposedly went back to work.

When Mom got up to use the bathroom in the wee hours of the morning, she found my father passed out in the driveway with the car still running. It must have been one of those once-in-a-while nights.

I didn't tell Dr. Phyllis what I had walked in on, what I now knew, because I didn't want her to focus on that. I wanted her to focus on my father's substance abuse. That's what had eaten our family alive, and that's what she needed to address. I knew I was struggling with what I had learned and my father's silence on the matter. He must've known the impact it had on me, and his dismissiveness was devastating. I also knew I was in over my head carrying the secret and confusion all alone, but I would deal with that as best I could. I needed Dr. Phyllis to save the family, and that meant ending his addictions. At sixteen, it didn't occur to me that hiding his true self was one of the demons causing his drinking and pills.

Demons. I might've been dealing with Dad and his demons, but thirty years later, I found out John had suffered at the hands of the devil himself. My brother had made a much bigger sacrifice than me to try and save our so-called family. It is inconceivable to me that he managed to stay mute about such horror.

I can't say if I would've confided in Dr. Phyllis had she been more competent and less quick to jump to conclusions, and I certainly can't speak for my brother. Maybe she could've eventually gained our trust—I don't know. I do know this: John and I are a testament to the great length children will go to save their family, even a dysfunctional harmful one.

The next weekend my father jumped a guardrail, flipped his car over in a ditch, and smashed into a tree. He was brought to the hospital but had only minor injuries, probably because he was so intoxicated he didn't react on impact. They arrested him after treatment, and that's when he called his wife.

Before the police released him, they sat Mom down and talked to her. My father was known to them, something she hadn't realized. There had been pull-overs, fender-benders, and some courtesy calls from bartenders to follow him home (not unheard of in those days). But this time they couldn't look the other way. The accident was a different story, and they were charging him. On top of being drunk, they had found loose pills in his pocket. They also believed that the accident was most likely a suicide attempt. He was traveling at a high rate of speed and headed directly for the tree. If he had cleared the ditch, he would've succeeded.

Not knowing where else to turn, Mom immediately called Dr. Phyllis when she got home. My mother told her how she'd found him in the driveway the night of our session, then detailed the accident. The doctor admitted she might have missed some things, but, after all, she was a family counselor, and substance abuse was not her field of expertise. *So maybe you shouldn't have been so quick to dismiss a potential problem.* She gave my mother suicide warning signs to watch for and gave her the name of a colleague to call on Monday. She wished Mom luck and promptly mailed out a hefty bill for a two-hour weekend phone session. Dr. P.H. Dipstick, such a poor representative of her profession.

The accident should have meant my father's gig was up, but it did not. He found the right lawyer, who lined the right pockets, got him off, and kept it out of the papers. All of which kept him out of jail and saved his so-called career. I can only imagine what a fortune it must have cost, and my parents had nothing. I have no idea where he got the money, nor do I want to know. Ever.

Of course, according to him, the cops were crazy. "Suicide? Where do they get suicide? Some guy cut me off for Christ's sake. And why are you harping on me about my drinking again? A shrink told you I don't have a problem. Why can't you people accept that?"

Why, indeed.

THE PROVERBIAL LAST STRAW

SOME TIME IN THE EARLY FALL OF 1973, MY FATHER GOT A call at work that Granddaddy was dying. He came home totally out of his mind, full of toxins and emotion, and insisted he was driving to Bishop, West Virginia immediately. Mom tried to calm him down and wait until morning when we would all go. Dad was so crazed he didn't hear her and continued screaming like a rabid animal.

He pulled down the attic stairs to get a suitcase and, after a couple of tries, realized he was too intoxicated to climb. Yelling something incoherent, he grabbed John by the hair and shoved him into the ladder to do it for him. Terrified, John was shaking so badly he couldn't move, so my father slapped his face and brought a fist back to hit him.

That's when I lost it. With a battle cry, I put myself between the two of them and gave my father a shove that landed him flat on his back, not hard to do in his condition. I screamed for John to get in the attic and stay there, no matter what. I knew he would be Dad's target of choice if he could find him.

As I grabbed a nearby table lamp, I started screaming. "Get out! Get out! Leave now, or I'm calling the cops! I swear I'll have you locked up!"

It was a time before cellphones, and there was no way I could hold him at bay and reach my bedroom phone to call the cops.

"Mom!" I yelled. She was in my room and could make the call. "Mom!"

That's when I first heard my mother, lying on my bed, sobbing.

"Don't call the cops! I love him! I don't want him to leave! Please don't make him leave! I love him!"

And just like that, it was out. What her truth had always been and what it had meant for her children's reality. Mom loved us but had given her heart to him first.

The fact she was willing to put us in physical danger to keep him meant she loved him more. That's how, as a wounded sixteen-year-old, I saw it. It instantly untethered me into the perfect storm, and I was lost at sea.

I had paid a high price for the last year and a half to shield her from a truth that would have killed her, and here she was committing the ultimate betrayal. She was sacrificing her babies.

My mother, like many parents of her generation, held the belief that kids would always bounce back, would be okay no matter what. They were wrong. Children, when pulled too taut for too long, will snap like a rubber band, and that is what happened to me at that moment.

By the time my father got to his feet, I was as furious as he was crazed. If he had taken a swing at me, I would've killed him with the lamp, and we both knew it.

I demanded he get into his bedroom and stay there until morning and was surprised when he did. I wedged a chair under the knob and tried to catch my breath. I climbed the attic stairs and told John it was safe to come down, then went in to confront my mother. I had never felt so betrayed.

I told her since she was the one who insisted he stay in the house in his crazed state, she needed to go in there with him and make sure he stayed put. When my mother, still crying, started to say something, I cut her off in a voice soft and thick with emotion.

"He's in a total rage, out of control and for the first time, tried to beat one us. He's crazier than he's ever been, and all you heard was me telling him to get out." *What about us?! What about your babies?!*

"You love him? You want him?" *My God, how could you, still?* "Then, you go keep him under control. We'll take care of ourselves." *From here on out.*

To this day, I don't know if she was going to say she was sorry, stick up for him, or tell me I didn't understand. With the damage irreversibly done at the time, I didn't care.

What I did know was how devastated and scared I felt. I was afraid of the amount of anger I felt towards my mother. All the havoc, chaos, and hurt we suffered at the hands of my father was second nature to me by this point. But her betrayal and abandonment were unfathomable to me.

I put the chair back under the knob after she entered the bedroom and went to comfort John. I couldn't stop shaking that night. I was more afraid of my reaction to my father's escalating behavior than I was of him. If he had come back after John or me, I would've brought that lamp down on his skull without hesitation. The fact I was capable of that kind of thing terrified me. *What have I become?*

Now that the feelings of anger and abandonment towards my mother were in the mix, would I remain this angry, cornered animal? Yes. In my heart, I knew the answer was yes. Blind rage and fear had taken over the darkness.

I called Steven the next morning and had all I could do to stop him from coming down to Virginia with a lamp of his own.

"Marry me," he said. "Yes," I said.

Steven had provided me with a plan.

That evening, I sat down with my parents, ready to fight for my life. I told them if they refused to sign for me to get married and take John, I would call family services, report them, and have us placed with Grandma and Grandpa. I had no idea if that was even possible at the time, but neither one of them called my bluff. I went on to say something akin to, my father's behavior had reached the point of physical violence, and my mother made it clear she was with him no matter what that meant for her children.

The little girl in me was hoping they would fight for us. They would tell me I didn't have to do this! Daddy would get help this time, and I was wrong about Mommy.

Sixteen-year-old me knew better.

Neither one of them said a word.

My parents agreed to sign. My father because I think he just wanted me gone. It would be so much easier without me home. I kept making him accountable for his actions and the chaos he caused. And there was that secret I knew. Always having to worry; would I tell now, ever? My father must've been so, so tired. I want to think he felt some guilt and remorse for the way he had handled, or more appropriately didn't handle the secret with me, but I will never know.

I've always felt my mother signed for three reasons; guilt, fear, and love. She had blurted out her truth, saw the damage it caused, and knew there was no taking it back. She was also afraid I'd run again and this time disappear for good. Finally, I think Mom realized the consequences of her inaction all those years and the price her children had paid.

At that time in Virginia, you had to be sixteen and a half to get married, even with parental consent, so Steven and I had to wait three months until December. I went to school and to work, and Steven traveled back and forth from Seekonk to Alexandria whenever he could.

About a month before the wedding, I got a phone call from my father's infamous corporate angel, the so-called family-friend. He had the unmitigated gall to lecture me on my upcoming nuptials. I was being selfish, ruining my life, and breaking my parents' hearts, blah, blah, blah…

I stopped listening to him. He hadn't had anything to do with our family, other than my father, for years. I knew he was well aware of my father's condition because he was the one who always transferred Dad in the nick of time. He had to know things weren't going any better at home than they were at work and chose to stay away instead of being a friend. In my opinion, he had forfeited his right to add his two cents worth years ago. But I bit my tongue until I thought it would bleed because I didn't want to do anything to jeopardize the papers getting signed.

I didn't bite it hard enough. When the lecture ended, I said, "Does this mean you won't be coming to the wedding?" I guess he didn't appreciate my sarcasm because he called my father, and I got grounded for being disrespectful. One month before my wedding, I was still young enough to get grounded. Craziness.

Just as crazy, Steven was visiting at the time, so my father was forcing us to stay home alone together. It was during this time I lost my virginity. Hey, we couldn't go anywhere, you can only play cards for so long, and TV was nothing but reruns.

I have to say the first time was a disappointment. I couldn't believe this was what the big deal was all about. It was messy, it hurt, and I wasn't looking forward to a lifetime of it. Later in the day, during an *Andy Griffith* rerun, we gave it another try, and I realized, in grand fashion, why it was such a big deal. *Now I get it!* We laughed ourselves silly when Gomer Pyle let go with his signature "Go-o-o-o-lliee" soon after my first awakening.

Being grounded wasn't so bad, after all.

A CHILD BRIDE

———

O N DECEMBER 30, 1973, I BECAME MRS. STEVEN ROGER
Pierce. Our wedding party was so young we resembled
the cast of a school play. At fourteen, his younger sister Nancy
was my "child of honor," and my brother John was his "best
boy." Now that I think about it, others must have signed as
witnesses because they weren't of legal age. I wore no makeup
at the time, which made me look even younger than I was, and I
asked Steven to cut his hair chin length so it wouldn't be longer
than mine. We looked exactly like the babies we were.

A few weeks before the wedding, I found a simple wedding
gown and veil at the mall that wouldn't make me look like I
was playing dress-up. When I tried it on, it fit perfectly (even the
length was right). A discontinued style, it was only $100.00, and
the shop threw in a blue garter for free—sold. I had a pair of
white fabric shoes I hadn't dyed for a prom because we'd moved
away, and that completed my ensemble.

I don't remember picking out or ordering flowers, but I must
have because we had bouquets and boutonnières. Mom made
the wedding cake, and his mom made the maid of honor's gown.
In the early 1970s, teen marriages were still commonplace in the
south, so finding a minister to marry a young couple was not a
problem.

The wedding was an intimate candlelight service in a quaint
chapel beautifully decorated for Christmas. There were poinsettias,

evergreen roping, and prince's pine and cranberry wreaths. Disney couldn't have created a more enchanting setting.

The small reception at my parents' house was a simple home-cooked buffet and was supposed to be alcohol-free after the toast. We should have known there was no chance of that happening with my father hosting his worst nightmare come true. He ended up down and dirty drunk and made lewd and inappropriate remarks about Steven and me. Humiliated, I looked around my wedding reception, consisting of my brother's and parents' guests, and saw my only friend there, my groom. Steven, grinning ear to ear, was holding up a set of keys, and he gave me a wink. We escaped to his parents' camper parked in the driveway and left the mess behind.

The first thing we did was consummate the marriage (a couple of times as I fondly recall). Afterward, as we snuggled in our sleeping bag for two, my groom fell asleep while I mentally reviewed the last eight months of my life, March through December 1973.

I had to leave the first school I was ever comfortable in and landed in a school of turmoil. I discovered my father was bisexual in a most disturbing way and was left on my own to process it. I fell into a depression so deep I couldn't dance and fell from high honors to problem student status. I ran away as a desperate plea for help. I kept my father's secret in counseling to protect my mother and to try and save our family. I discovered my anger towards my father ran so deep I was capable of doing him great harm if cornered. I felt abandoned by my mother now that I knew her truth. I essentially blackmailed my parents with the threat of the Department of Children, Youth & Families to marry a boy I started dating five short months ago.

A boy I knew had a drug problem barely under control and married him anyway because he offered me hope where there was none at home. *Geez Louise, no wonder I'm so tired. That's a lot of life in a short amount of time.*

Tucked into that sleeping bag with Steven, I felt safe for the first time since moving to Alexandria, and I slept like a baby. I had saved myself. I had done what was necessary to pull myself out of the black hole, and I had survived.

The next morning, Steven and I headed north with my new in-laws and our shiny wedding rings. I was happy and scared to death, all at the same time. I was also apprehensive about my brother because he was going to bear the entire brunt of it now. As hard as I tried, I never got John to agree to come with me. He wouldn't leave our mother there alone.

And I was sad for my mother. As angry as I felt at her betrayal, I still mourned her sadness. In a few short months, she had been forced to see the ugly truth and had to own the damage her role as an enabler had caused her children. She also had, in a moment of unchecked emotion, blurted out where her deepest feelings lay, and she was now paying a heavy price. She was letting her daughter go, too young, in hopes of saving her girl.

Mom was crying too hard that morning to come out and say goodbye. My brother later told me she had stayed in my room for two days.

PLAYING HOUSE

MY IN-LAW'S HOUSE HAD A STUDIO APARTMENT IN THE basement that had been empty for years. Steven and I cleaned it up, tucked in, and started our life together.

I tried going back to school, but to be honest, I never gave it a real chance. There was something strange about kissing my husband goodbye and getting on the school bus. Also, I had missed so much school in Armageddon that I was struggling to catch up. My heart wasn't in it.

Money was another issue. Two people couldn't live on Steven's minimum wage job. I couldn't get an after-school job because we only had one car and lived in the country (no buses). Steven ran a press at a medical supply factory, and he got me a full-time job inspecting plastic bedpans and IV tubing. Without a second thought, and as dumb as it was, I quit school. Every morning we'd cross our fingers the 1969 Roadrunner would start so we could pick up two other people and ride to work together. Neither one of them had cars, and we couldn't afford gas without them, so it was mutually beneficial.

Despite the lousy jobs, having next to nothing, and even less privacy, we were happy. The fun nights in Jimmy's basement continued, listening to the guys jam and talking with their girlfriends. I loved going to the band's gigs and was so proud of them and their gifted soundman, my hubby.

On Saturday nights, Steven and I would go to his sister Sharon's house and play Hi-Lo Jack or go to the dog track with his dad, Edmond where we'd place our big two dollar bets. His mom, Betty, taught me how to can vegetables and put up preserves. We lived on a small farm where I helped deliver a calf and learned how to drive a tractor. When the family would go camping in Maine, Steven and I would sleep under the stars by the fire while his parents and younger sister slept in the camper. If all this sounds like, "What I did on my summer vacation," it's because that's the way it felt to me. It was years since the tribe of four had done anything together, and I was enjoying being part of a family again.

Not to mention we were two teenagers with no one to answer to and no restrictions. I remember waking up mornings to the rooster crowing, Steven spooning behind me snoring, and feeling so safe and happy. We were two kids playing house.

All of this AND I had dance in my heart again! There was no money for lessons, but I would push the furniture against the wall and turn our one-room apartment into a dance studio. It felt so amazing to be wrapped in the comfort of my dance and creativity again. It was like being enfolded in an angel's wings. I was one content young lady, loving life.

I should clarify that my in-laws were no Ward and June Cleaver. Quite the opposite. They were tough, stubborn Swedes who lived on the cranky side of life. Their glass was always at least half empty, if not bone dry, and they blamed everyone but themselves. It seemed to me Betty and Edmond didn't like most people, and that included each other. They held grudges and could be mean spirited. It wasn't unusual for Edmond to be mumbling about cutting one of their kids out of the will because of some perceived slight. They were disgruntled with their lives and pretty much everyone in them. My in-laws were, however, always kind to me during this time. Perhaps they credited me for the improvement in their son, which made adding another teenager (me) into the mix worth their while.

John came to visit us that first summer and was so happy and relaxed while there, I hoped he might stay permanently. He reunited with his girlfriend, Betsy, and her brother Mickey and the three of them were inseparable once again. John would help them work their father's farm during the day, and then they'd ride their bikes over to our place once we got home from work. All was well until Edmond found out who their father was. His property abutted my in-law's, connected by some wooded acreage. Years earlier, there had been a fight over the installation of an electric fence. Edmond accused their father of coming too close to his property line. I don't know the outcome, but my father-in-law still held a considerable grudge, which surprised no one.

After my father in-law's discovery, any little thing Mickey, Betsy, and John did was a problem. He complained about their bicycles in the driveway and their loud voices and laughter late at night, which was seven thirty since they had to be home by eight. Fortunately, Edmond didn't realize their origins until near the end of my brother's visit, but the writing was on the wall as far as I was concerned. It was time for Steven and me to move out.

We found a three-room apartment in a not so safe part of Pawtucket, Rhode Island. Moving from the country to the inner city was a shock, but finding out how much utilities and buying food cost was a huge reality check. *Welcome to the real world Barbie and Ken.*

I had spent my life making adjustments and just set about making some more. I clipped coupons and learned to cook and make lunches on a shoestring budget. I became a pro at spotting furniture on the curb worth taking home to refinish or paint.

Steven, on the other hand, was not adjusting quite as well. Our life together was starting to look like that structured, conforming, responsibility thing he so hated. I was becoming less of a safe-haven and more like the dark side of reality. Hence, his barbiturate use started to increase.

After a year or so, Steven took a job at a car parts store, and I got a better paying position at the factory. With money not so tight, we were able to get an apartment back in the country, and with life more comfortable our relationship improved. I decided it was a good time to start nudging my husband back on track about his drug use before it became an insurmountable problem. It only took me a couple of months to figure out I was too late. Steven had already replaced me with his barbiturates and was pushing me to the dark side as one of "them." I was still determined to give it everything I had to turn him back around, though. I had to, for the baby's sake.

I had just found out I was pregnant.

THE THREE I'S

MY BABY. I KNOW THE EXACT DATE I BECAME PREGNANT. IT was October 9, 1975. The instant I conceived, I felt a light hand on my lower abdomen, and a loving warmth spread throughout my body. From that moment on, my entire focus shifted to that little being. I became fiercely protective since I knew I was going to be the baby's best shot at a normal life, whatever the hell that looked like.

As I've said, I tried to get Steven straightened out, but he was already tucked into the safety of his drug induced la-la land and didn't hear any of it. The minute I told him I was pregnant, I saw the fear creep into his eyes. Let's face it, a man-boy who had to get high to handle the responsibility of paying bills and going to work wasn't about to face parenthood with anything less than terror. There was no doubt in my mind; providing stability in this baby's life was going to be up to me, and I was determined not to drop the ball.

Don't you worry, baby, Mommy's here.

By this time I had somewhat come to terms with my inner feelings towards mom. My mother and I had never addressed that fateful night. I still harbored feelings of betrayal, but time and distance had eased some of the pain. I was removed from the daily chaos of my family's life and had moved on, but I hadn't forgiven her. Not yet. However, the miles between us made it easier for me to pretend, so as far as she knew, everything was fine. That's the face I showed to her and the world.

My mom was over the moon when she heard I was expecting. She got to work sewing my maternity clothes and countless onesies for her grandchild-to-be. My grandma knitted and crocheted enough sweater sets to last a year, my sisters-in-law threw me a shower, and one of the people Steven worked with gave us like-new baby necessities. Thank goodness for everyone's generosity because we didn't have two nickels to rub together. Strange as it may sound, I wasn't worried at all. I **INTUITIVELY** knew it was meant to be, and it would all work out. I wasn't even concerned when Steven and his barbiturate use started to escalate. I figured it would happen, and had mentally prepared for it. I had hoped he would be able to man-up but knew better than to count on it. After all, he wasn't the first addict to ever let me down.

I had been well aware of the parallel between my father and Steven from the beginning. Addiction is addiction, no matter whose battle it is. The big difference between them for me? I saw my father as too far gone, which he was, and Steven as a candidate for a full recovery, which he was not. That said, if I had to do it all over again, given the same set of circumstances, I would make the same choice. To this day, I'm confident I made the right decision to marry and leave Armaggedon. At the time, it was the only option I had to save myself.

The more drugs Steven took, the less use I had for him. The less use I had for him, the more drugs he ingested. He came home late one night, higher than high, and extra pessimistic.

"I'm afraid of how far we've grown apart and scared for our baby. We're bringing a baby into a world of cruelty, destruction, and empty people."

Oh, for Pete's sake, seriously? I was more than a little **IRRITATED**, and it was time we had a chat, or more accurately for me to dress him down.

"We've grown apart because you're too high too often. You're a walking zombie most of the time. The baby will thrive in this world as long as we provide a safe and loving home, which won't happen with an addict for a father." I knew that all too well.

"You need to knock off the drugs, and the doom and gloom attitude or our baby WILL be born into your ugly version of the world, and it will be you that created it."

He was still the same Steven I had met in the tree on the corner, but I wasn't the same Belle. I had grown up.

Don't you worry, baby, Mommy's here.

My pregnancy was an easy one, just occasional morning sickness and leg cramps. I remember my tears of wonder the first time I felt a flutter in my belly. It was over in an instant, but it was awe-inspiring and very emotional for me. A confirmation this baby was real, a life in the making. Feeling the baby move never got old for me. When I was seven or eight months along, I was lying on the couch watching TV with a bowl of ice cream balanced on my belly. All of a sudden, this little foot swept across my considerable girth and sent the dish toppling to the floor, which made me laugh. *That was a beautiful fan-kick little one!*

I'll admit there were times in the ninth month when all of that moving around wasn't so magical.

One night, Steven and I went Seekonk Speedway to watch the stock car races. We had pit passes, and when the racer's started their engines, so did the baby. I mean non-stop kicking and thrashing. I had to leave right away. Being so young, I didn't realize the noise and vibrations would affect the baby. When I got to the parking lot, and in the car, the little one started to calm down, which made one of us. I had to stop crying before I could drive us home. I was sure the baby was now deaf or had oatmeal for brains, and it was all my fault. Once I got my hormones under control, and we were underway, I smiled and patted my belly—*excellent tap-dancing sweetie.*

Then there were the times when it felt like two tiny hands were holding my ribs, like chains on a swing, and little legs would pump with all their might to go higher and higher. Or when I was trying to sleep propped up due to indigestion and couldn't because, in that position, there just wasn't enough room in there for my stomach and a comfortable baby. The baby would start moving around until I either threw up or laid flat. *Okay, little one, I love you, but you've outgrown the facilities, and we need to move this along.*

We did. My labor was short, five hours (still too long if you ask me), and the birth was trouble-free. At 8:10 p.m. on July 26, 1976, I gave birth to Jean Elizabeth Pierce. She was six pounds, seven ounces, nineteen inches long, and the most beautiful baby ever born. She looked up at me with her huge dark eyes, and I swear I saw a little smirk. An instant bond formed between us.

My daughter, my Saving Grace.

1976 was a time before drive-by births, and the typical stay was three days, but Jean and I had to stay five. Jean because she was jaundiced (not because of deafness or oatmeal brain) and me because of a migraine from the epidural. The day we were discharged, Providence, Rhode Island was hit with the remnants of Hurricane Belle, a befitting sign of what was to come that still makes me chuckle.

Mom, now living in Buffalo, New York, came to help me out, but Jeannie was such a good baby, it was more like a visit. My mom was in her glory. It was a thing of beauty to watch her with my daughter. Seeing such pure, unconditional love between the two of them dissipated the resentment I was hiding towards my mother. It was a reminder of the mom she was in my early childhood before our world fell apart. My heart broke for them when she had to leave.

After Mom returned to Buffalo, Steven, Jean, and I settled into a routine. I would feed Jean, get Steven off to work, shower, and then we'd have snuggle time before taking off for the day. Our second-floor apartment was hot as an oven by midday, so Jeannie and I would spend the afternoons at my in-laws', the park, or running errands. She was an adaptable baby, and when it was time to eat or sleep, she would do it anywhere.

During this time, Steven started working weekdays until the store closed at eight and wouldn't get home until after nine. I didn't believe that was where he was every night, but he was bringing home more money, and I figured the other times he was out partying. Honestly, by then, I didn't care. Until one night I had to—my blissful **IGNORANCE** was coming to an end.

RUDE AWAKENINGS

———

ONE NIGHT IN SEPTEMBER 1976, I AWOKE SUDDENLY, FULLY alert, and heard Steven talking in his sleep. He never even mumbled in his sleep, much less talked.

Steven laughed and said as plain as day, "The guys put a bell under the seat in the van to bust on me. Yeah, it rings when I hit a bump—a little reminder they said."

I'm going out to check. Sure enough, there was a bell under the driver's seat along with a dealer's stash of drugs (and I don't mean pot). I also recognized an overpowering, distinctive scent.

No, not perfume. It was the body odor of a female individual, Etta, (known as Hippiette in my mind). She was a girl Steven's older brother brought back for a visit from California—why I'll never know.

The few times I was in her presence, she was a total space cadet, and dirty. I realize I sound vindictive and catty, but it's all true. She didn't practice hygiene, feminine or otherwise, hence her potent odor. It was apparent Hippiette didn't shave because she had tufts of hair sticking out from under her arms, and her legs needed a good combing. She had very long bushy hair that was a tangled, unkempt mess in desperate need of a brush. I don't imagine her oral hygiene was any better, but I can't say for sure because she never talked to me—only mumbled. How and when had she made the jump from the brother to my husband, I never found out. I was just relieved, Steven, and I hadn't had sex since she had come to town, so I knew I was clean. *Okay, that was catty.*

I admit, the girl was a blow to my ego. But our marriage had already crumbled, and our love lay in a pile on the floor. The stash was a different story. The stash was a deal-breaker. Now that he was dealing drugs, I knew it was just a matter of time before the baby and I were in harm's way. Jean and I were so out of there, but to where?

I was nineteen, uneducated with no money, no job, and a new baby. I certainly wasn't going to my in-laws. My friends were all teenagers living at home, and I hadn't seen Billy or his parents since I'd run away over three years ago. The only place left to go was home sweet home. Armageddon. I had to think, and Jean and I needed a roof over our heads until I came up with a plan. I was returning to the very environment I had worked so hard to escape. I felt so defeated until I sensed a hand on my shoulder and the same loving warmth as when I conceived Jean. All of a sudden, I knew we were going to be alright.

Don't you worry, little girl, Mommy's got this.

My father had been transferred from Virginia to the snow belt region of Buffalo, New York. It was his last chance with the Kmart Corporation (previously Kresge). He either cleaned up his act, or he was out. Dad bought their first home, a large house they couldn't afford, filled it with expensive furniture, and purchased a new Buick Riviera. My guess is, he knew it would be his last chance ever to do so, and he went for it. They ended up losing it all, but for our brief time there, Jeannie and I lived in style.

Once in Buffalo, I was pleasantly surprised to see the calming effect Jean had on her grandpa's demons. He adored her, which improved his behavior immensely during our stay, and all the loving attention my daughter received from her Grandma, Grandpa, and Uncle John allowed me the time and energy I needed to think clearly. I already knew two things for sure: I would raise her in the Seekonk area, and there would be a divorce unless Steven went into rehab and got completely clean. Jeannie's childhood was NOT going to include living with an addict. Period. I was determined to break my family's cycle.

The first dilemma I had to solve was getting a job with no education. To me, the clear solution was Kmart. I asked my father to call the head of human resources in the Seekonk store to get me a job. When he did, she reminded him the company didn't hire full-time help without a high school diploma and apologized but said she couldn't help. *No problem.*

"Have your corporate buddy call her dad."

"I can't ask him to override policy," he said.

"Okay then, I will," I countered. No way my father was letting that happen. He contacted his corporate angel, who made the call and okayed the hire. I had a job! It was an entry-level job paying minimum wage, but I knew I'd work my way up. All I needed was a foot in the door. I was to start in a month.

The next hurdle was childcare. I figured if Steven refused rehab and it was over, he'd have to pay child support, and I could use that to pay for a sitter. It would be tough going until I started making more money, but doable.

I tried to reach Steven to tell him Jean and I would be coming back and needed the apartment, but he would never answer the house phone. When I tried to call him at work, his co-workers always told me he was on the road. I finally called his parents and informed them I would be back within ten days, and their son needed to be out of the apartment. I certainly didn't have the money or time to rent someplace new, and besides, this apartment was three miles from where I'd be working. They said they would make sure he was gone.

Yes, I had a plan!

For the first time in almost two months, I could breathe again. Being so occupied with trying to figure things out, I hadn't realized how much weight I'd lost. I'm five foot five and was down to ninety-five pounds. When I finally noticed my skeleton in the mirror, I gave it a talking to in no uncertain terms. *Time to bulk*

up lady, you're going to have to be strong enough for two now.
I started eating everything in sight, even though it made me gag
at first. I was on a mission. I had a daughter to raise and come
hell or high water I was going to do right by her.

Jeannie, on the other hand, was thriving during our stay in
Buffalo. She was living with an uncle and two grandparents who
doted on her endlessly. And her mom was always within her
sight, a baby's utopia. The only thing her life was missing was a
unicorn—and a father.

Mom planned to travel to Seekonk with me to help us get settled and give me time to find a babysitter. But, John, was a senior
in high school and working, and had to stay home. I had noticed
a change in my brother during our stay; a new confidence about
him, and he seemed more relaxed. When I mentioned it to him,
John smiled and said there had been significant changes in his life
since moving to Buffalo. He didn't offer what they were, and I
respected his privacy, which in hindsight, I regret having done.
I was just happy to see him finally comfortable in his skin.

While Mom and I were packing for our trip back, Steven
called and said he was sorry. He knew how badly he'd screwed
up and wanted a second chance. *Second? More like a hundredth.*
I told him only if he agreed to in-house rehab.

"I'll do anything you ask, just please come home," my husband said. With that, I made my decision to say yes. Steven said
he'd drive up the next day to bring his family home.

I spent all night on an emotional roller coaster ride, arguing
with myself.

You can't possibly think he'll get clean, do you?

Not really—well, maybe.

Do you honestly believe he's grown up enough in this short
amount of time to handle being a husband and a father?

*No, of course not—well, possibly. Maybe it took losing us
to wake him up.*

Yeah, right. Will you ever be able to trust him again?

No. Well, perhaps in time.

No, you won't, ever.

I know.

Do you still love him?

No. Well, maybe a little—I don't know!

Then, why put yourself through this?

Because he's Jean's father—I have to try.

Yes, yes, you do.

Steven never showed. When I called to find out why, his father told me he had been out all night and was presently passed out on his boyhood bed. That told me everything I needed to know.

I'd have to find a sitter AND a lawyer when I got home.

A PAPER MOON

———

After our long drive from Buffalo to Seekonk, all Mom and I wanted was some food, a shower, and sleep. Instead, I unlocked the door of my home and we stepped into a dumpster. The place was disgusting. There were dog feces and urine, cigarette butts, and rotten food scraps everywhere. It also reeked of Eau de Hippiette. The tub had dried vomit in it, and I won't even attempt to describe the toilet.

Tiki! Why hasn't the dog come to greet me? I knew she couldn't be with Steven at his parents' house because she didn't get along with their dogs. I found the poor girl cowering and shaking under the kitchen table with a crazed look in her eyes. It was plain to see she was scared and neglected, but she also looked like she had ingested drugs. There was no sign of the dog's food or water bowl, so heaven only knew the last time she was fed and watered.

I had flown to my parents' house and left Tiki with Steven. Because he loved the dog, it never occurred to me he wouldn't take care of her. The fact he hadn't was proof of how far he had fallen.

I finally got the dog to eat and drink and coaxed her out from under the table, but it was weeks before she stopped cowering and shaking.

I kept Tiki until she died of a heart attack eight years later, but she never did lose all her crazy, and I never lost my guilt for leaving her behind. There are some pictures forever seared in your mind, and the vision of poor Tiki under the table is still with me.

But I digress. While I tended to the dog, Mom left to pick up a pizza and purchase every cleaning and disinfectant product known to man. Once we ate, she started scrubbing the nursery while I tackled the bathroom. We needed a clean place to sleep, and I wasn't leaving Tiki again, so a motel was out of the question.

Hours later, we took showers and dried off with paper towels. I got the sleeping bags down out of the attic, laid them on the nursery floor, and finally, in the wee hours of the morning, Mom, and I got some sleep.

We were lucky Jeannie was so easy-going because we cleaned non-stop for a week. She was perfectly content to sit in her swing or tote seat and watch the action. We threw out the carpets, bedding, linens, towels, and pillows. We steam cleaned the mattress, flipped it, and steamed it again, then tackled all of the furniture and curtains. Mom and I scrubbed the woodwork and walls in every room, and by the time our cleaning crew of two finished, it was sterile enough to perform surgery on any surface in the place. Thankfully it was a small apartment, and Mom had a credit card.

I soon realized Steven wasn't giving me a dime until a court ordered it, which meant no money for childcare. My parents were in over their heads financially, and I had already put a balance on Mom's credit card. I wasn't about to ask them for more money, and I refused to ask my in-laws. They never called while we were in Buffalo to ask about Jeannie and hadn't been over to see their granddaughter since our return.

On top of that, I was sure they were aware of the deplorable condition their son left the apartment in and hadn't told me. They weren't in my good graces, to say the least. That left me with only one option, and boy did I hate the very thought of it: welfare. I had no choice. I needed assistance to pay for a babysitter so that I could work.

When I went to apply, I left Jeannie at home with my mom so she wouldn't see what was happening. Overkill I know, since she was only months old, but that's how awful I felt about the whole thing. I don't know how the system works today, but here's my experience with the welfare office over forty-two years ago: you took a number, sat down, and waited, then waited some more for them to call your name. The waiting area was chaotic, with kids running everywhere, babies crying, and people arguing in different languages all at once. The noise level was deafening, and the décor was drab and dirty. The air was heavy with a sense of defeat, and I swear I could smell the depression. I had never felt so ashamed and got up to leave many times but never made it to the door. I had a little girl depending on me.

After what felt like forty days and forty nights, I heard my name called. Without even looking up from her paperwork, a cranky beast of a woman pointed to a metal folding chair and told me to sit.

She immediately started to growl at me, "Name? Citizen? Social Security Number?" I gave her proof of all the above.

"Married?" she asked.

"Well, kind of, I'm filing for divorce," I replied.

"So, married. The number of dependents?"

She still hadn't looked at me.

"Including me?" I asked.

"You plan on eating?" she responded.

I needed to dial back her rudeness if I was going to make it through the interview without breaking down.

"Would you please look at me and listen to why I'm here?" I asked.

She did look up then and said oh so smugly, "Welfare. You're here for welfare." *OUCH.*

"Yes, but just to pay for childcare while I'm at work." I was having a hard time keeping it together but made myself maintain eye contact.

She paused. "While you're where?" she asked. She laughed, then informed me, "That's not how this works, Sugar. It's all or nothing."

I was astounded.

"You're telling me to get any help at all, I have to take the whole package and not work?"

She was getting crankier by the minute. "Yes," was her reply. "Now, do you want to apply or not?"

Still convinced she didn't understand me, I tried one more time.

"But I have a job and medical, and I'll make it work for rent and food. All I need is help with childcare for a couple of months!"

She sighed, and asked me again if I wanted to apply, "Yes or no? People are waiting."

I got up and left without saying another word.

My answer was no, a definite, emphatic NO.

When I got back to my car, I let all the anger, shame, fear, and frustration take over for a while and had quite the pity party for myself. Once the partying was out of my system, I dried my eyes and started choking down large portions of my pride because this wasn't about me.

I drove directly to my in-laws prepared to kowtow or go into battle, whichever was needed. It turned out neither one was necessary. I explained my situation, and they agreed to help. I didn't know if it was out of guilt or an effort to make up for their son's behavior, nor did I care. His mother said she'd watch Jeannie five days a week until I could find a sitter for two or three of those days, depending on my finances. Betty would then continue to cover the off days until I got on my feet. Edmond had an old station wagon he got running and offered to let me use it. I was back on track.

Maybe I do have this, after all.

Asking Edmond and Betty for help seemed inconceivable to me a day earlier, but compared to the welfare office, it was a walk in the park. Sometimes, there are no good choices, and you have to choose the lesser of two evils. Pick one, live with it, and keep moving forward.

Just as the dust started to settle, Steven showed up one night, yelling and pounding on the door. He said he needed to pick up the rest of his things. He was high as a kite, so I told him to come back in the morning.

If you've never seen someone high on barbiturates, picture a disjointed sleepwalker trying to find his footing on a cloud. They also speak in a slow, slurred mumble that only us experienced listeners can understand. They are very passive in their high because, well, they are over-tranquilized.

The yelling and aggressiveness were out of the norm, and I was frightened. There was no way I was letting him through the door, but I had to stop the racket, or the landlady downstairs would call the police. So, I grabbed a cast iron frying pan, unlocked my second floor apartment door, and went to smack him in the face with it. I didn't even have to hit him. The shock of me standing ready to do battle with a weapon in hand, coupled with his condition, was enough to send him tumbling down the stairs.

Once I saw him land in the first-floor foyer, I quickly locked the door and engaged the deadbolt. I was so angry I threw the few things he had left in the apartment out the window and onto the front lawn. I figured he could pick them up if and when he regained consciousness. *Mama bears are fiercely protective.*

Later that night, I was awakened by what I assumed was one of Steven's customers. He was in the front yard yelling for Steven and throwing rocks at the bedroom window. I got up, opened the window, and told him Steven didn't live here anymore, and if he didn't get off the property I was calling the cops. He threw another rock, this time at me, and said he wasn't leaving until the S.O.B. settled up with him. I suggested he look through the stuff strewn on the front lawn and slammed the window shut. I turned out the light, sat down on the floor, and with the frying pan in hand, waited for whatever was coming next. *Jesus—what a night! How in the world has this become my life?*

I guess the dissatisfied customer found what he was looking for because he left. So very brave of me, you say? More like pissed off all the way to stupid—Yikes! I didn't call the cops because I figured they were both there to pick up drugs. Even though Mom and I hadn't found any during our cleaning frenzy, until I could search my humble abode and make sure it was clean, I was afraid to involve the law. Now that I think about it, maybe that's the stash Tiki had found and eaten.

Before I got back into bed, I tiptoed down the stairs to make sure I hadn't killed my soon to be ex-husband—either that or to finish him off. I'm still not sure which. He was snoring, none of his limbs were at an odd angle, and he wasn't bleeding from his ears or mouth, so I assumed he would live. I took his keys to all the entryways and a wad of money out of his pocket. I figured a month's rent was a small price for him to pay for putting us in harm's way. I then kissed my middle finger and graciously gave it to him as I climbed the stairs.

Don't you worry, little girl, Mommy's got this.

Once I started divorce proceedings, things got weird with my in-laws. His dad no longer offered to help with car repairs, although he did let me keep the car, and his mother was suddenly too tired to watch Jeannie two days a week. I had heard through the grapevine they thought that now I was getting the court-ordered twenty-five dollars a week in child support, I should be making it on my own. They felt I was taking advantage of them. Ah, the cranky side of life; I had forgotten about that. So, I added two more days of childcare a week, a quart of oil every time I got gas and a once a month car repair (if I was lucky) to an already overstretched budget. I had been borrowing from Peter to pay Paul for a while, and the dog and I were living on Campbell's soup and a lot of saltines because Jeannie was still on baby food. There was no room to cut back there. Yep, that twenty-five dollars was going to save the day for sure. *HA!*

What did save the day for me was Jeannie sitting on my belly and using word salad (aka baby babble) to tell me all about her day. Or watching her crawl around in circles laughing hysterically with the dog chasing its tail. The two of us would cuddle up on the couch, me watching *Starsky and Hutch* and Jeannie peeking to make sure I wasn't catching her putting her thumb in her mouth. When she was tired, I'd pretend not to see, but most times, it was a game of "gotcha" that made both of us giggle. My favorite was when she'd put my face between her little hands and bounce my head side to side singing "Ma Ma Ma Ma" until I would sing "Loves her Jeannie Jeannie Beans" and we'd laugh at our silliness and hug all our love.

I was nineteen, alone, and had nothing to guide me as a mother but my intuition, my North Star. Still, I was determined we'd make it.

Yeah, we've got this little girl.

"It's only a paper moon, sailing over a cardboard sea, but it wouldn't be make-believe if you'd believe with me."
                                                              –Nat King Cole

PART III
MY NORTH STAR

AN ADULT IN THE ROOM

I WAS FORTUNATE TO FIND A BABYSITTER WHO WAS TERRIFIC with Jean and lived right down the street from Kmart. She even took her on the two nights a week I had to work until ten. I felt horrible having to wake Jeannie up at the sitter's house and put her in an ice-cold car to take her home, but I had no choice. By the time we got settled in, it would be almost eleven. We would snuggle until she fell back to sleep only to wake up at six and start all over again.

Still, Jeannie was always easy going and smiling unless she was teething. Then she would be sick with fever and projectile vomiting and continuously cry in pain. We didn't have to rise and shine on those days because we'd still be up. The sitter was gracious enough to come to our house when Jeannie was sick so I could still work, but between worrying and no sleep, I was a walking zombie until the tooth finally made an appearance.

I remember when Jeannie was around nine months old and going through the "I'm not going to sleep" stage all babies go through. It was only day five but felt more like day five hundred. Being the 1970s, the pediatrician told me that as long as I knew she was okay, let her cry it out. He said every time I went in to check on her, I only reinforced the behavior.

One night, after an hour of Jeannie screaming and crying to the point where she had the hiccups, I could no longer tell if she was okay. What I did know for sure, however, is I was not.

I went storming into the nursery, screaming and crying right along with her. Jeannie was so worked up; it took her a second to realize what was happening. When she did, she just stood in her crib and looked at me like I was a She-devil. I saw the look on her face and realized, with horror, my baby was afraid of me. *Crap, why am I so bloody young and immature?* Sometimes I felt so tired and too young and so overwhelmed (but always blessed).

I picked Jean up, hugged her rigid little body, and kept telling her I loved her over and over again. After we both stopped sobbing, I told her she needed to go to sleep and stop all the crazy. She did, and from that day until she was two years old, she went to sleep without a peep.

Was it out of fear the She-devil would show up again? That question bothered me for a long time. I had learned a valuable lesson. From then on, I always tried to let my own crazy out elsewhere, like screaming into a pillow or talking to myself before approaching Jean.

I managed to keep my finances afloat for most of that first year, but when $$ is coming in, and $$$ is going out, it's bound to catch up with you. I received a small promotion with a raise and was getting the whopping twenty-five dollars a week child support, but it just wasn't enough. Things were coming to a head moneywise, and I needed to find a solution. Fast.

One day a new employee at Kmart, Cathy, and I were talking about how neither one of us was making it financially. I blurted out I had an apartment close by and was looking for a roommate. *I am… who knew?* Cathy was only a few years older than me, in her early twenties, and we barely knew each other, so I wanted to be clear about things. I explained I had a daughter, so there couldn't be any unannounced parties, and casual sleepover dates had to leave before morning. There could be absolutely no drugs and no excessive drinking. She agreed, and I soon realized I had nothing to worry about. Cathy moved in before Jean's first birthday and instantly bonded with my daughter. An Auntie was born.

The apartment proved to be too small for all of us, so we moved shortly after Jeannie's first birthday. Cathy and I rented a ranch in Seekonk from my ex-sister-in-law, Sharon. It was a great house with one major drawback—it was right next door to Steven's parents. It was not one of my smarter moves. I think part of me hoped they would start spending time with Jean, but knowing them as well as I did, I should have known better. What they spent their time doing instead was staring out their windows, spying on me, and I couldn't wait for the lease to be up.

Our next move was to a townhouse in Riverside, Rhode Island, with a great layout. The street-level door opened onto a landing where you went up a few stairs to the primary level or down a few to the basement level bedrooms. It had a bathroom on each floor, and sliding glass doors in the kitchen that opened onto a beautiful deck.

It also had a ghost. Yes, you read that correctly, and I don't mean Casper, the friendly ghost. This spirit was not happy about her new roommates and started letting us know soon after we arrived. She tried being subtle at first, but when we weren't taking the hint, she kicked it up a notch or three.

Two feet of gravel encompassed the perimeter of the townhouse. From the first night we lived there, we would hear someone walking on the gravel late at night but never saw any feet pass by our basement bedroom windows. It was bizarre. After a couple of nights, Cathy and I started sleeping with baseball bats by our beds.

When, unpacking, I opened the storage area under the stairs, I got hit with a blast of ice-cold air, and the light in the unit went out. I changed the bulb, and it immediately blew out again. But when the landlord sent an electrician over to fix the problem, he couldn't find anything wrong. That light in the storage area never worked again. *It's no big deal. It's stuff we don't use anyway.*

One day Cathy and I came home from work and found our perfectly healthy parakeet dead. We bought another one right away so Jeannie wouldn't notice and found that one dead the next day. The downstairs bathroom mirror would fog over even when no one had showered. The nighttime gravel walking became louder and went on longer. When I mentioned it to the guy I was dating at the time, he said he'd take care of it. He waited by the door one night with a bat in hand, and when the walking started, flung the door open, ready to do battle. There was no one there, yet the three of us were still hearing the footsteps in the gravel.

We were finally catching on and knew it was time to find another place ASAP. Within a couple of days, we found a house in Bristol and filled out a rental application. In the week we were waiting to be approved, the downstairs bathroom mirror stayed permanently fogged. I went into the kitchen one morning to find the sliders wide open with the stick to jam them shut still in place and no footprints on the frost-covered deck.

When we still weren't leaving quick enough for our not so friendly ghost, she decided to make herself abundantly clear one night. My bedroom was an immediate right at the foot of the stairs, directly across from the storage door, and Jeannie's room was to the right of mine. Cathy's bedroom was on the other side of the storage area towards the front of the house. Once the lights were out and we were quiet, rustling and whispering started coming from the storage area. Cathy and I both grabbed our bats and raced to the hallway. The rustling became thrashing, and the whispering became a very clear "Get out, Get Out, GET OUT, GET OUT!"

The whole downstairs suddenly became so cold we could see our breath. I screamed, Cathy turned on all the lights, I ran in to get Jeannie, and the three of us and our two baseball bats huddled together upstairs until morning. With the gravel walker making his rounds, there was no way we were going outside. Come morning, we packed a few essentials and promptly got out. Our first stop was to see the landlord, who was renting the Bristol house. He stood in front of us hemming and hawing as to why he hadn't given us an answer yet when his phone rang.

While he took the call, Cathy whispered to me, "He thinks we're gay. That's why he doesn't want to rent to us." *Yes! Perfect! A plan.*

When he came back to find us still there, I casually mentioned I hoped he wasn't discriminating against us because it would be such a messy, expensive process for all. We got the house.

The move from Riverside to Bristol was the only time we used a moving company to relocate. No way we were going back into that townhouse, never mind the storage area. We later heard that years earlier, they'd found the body of a woman strangled to death hidden in the storage space. *Well, that explains why the rent was so cheap.*

We lived in the Bristol house from the time Jeannie was three until the summer before she started first grade. Oh, and we never had a problem with the landlord. *Hey, whatever works.*

Bristol is also where I did some growing up as a parent.

I tried to apply the She-devil lesson I had learned at all times, but some situations needed addressing in the moment, and I would overreact.

One morning when Jeannie was three or four, she got up before I did. The house only had two bedrooms, so Jeannie and I slept together in the same bed. She was an active sleeper and had been extra busy the night before, so I hadn't gotten any sleep. I was trying to catch forty winks when this little voice kept whispering Mommy over and over again in my ear.

We both ran out of patience at the same time and chorused, "MOMMY!" and "WHAT?!" in unison. The two of us jumped a mile, and the Cheerios box she had in her hand went flying. The poor kid just wanted breakfast! It would have been nice to have an adult in the room to get it for her. *Oh wait, that's supposed to be me.* Speaking of not being an adult...

I was into racquetball for a while, and a few friends and I played most Sunday mornings. The club had a supervised playroom where Jean stayed while I played my matches. One Sunday, after I showered and got Jean, some of us grabbed a table in the snack area to have a cup of coffee. I looked up, and "what to my wondering eyes should appear," but Dave, THE Dave from high school. The unfinished business, drop dead gorgeous, drown in those deep blue eyes, charming Dave—that one. As he and his buddy sat down to join us, I could tell my daughter wasn't feeling well but was having trouble seeing anything but the way Dave was looking at me. *He feels it too!*

After an hour or so, I went to put her coat on to leave and realized she had a fever. The minute we got home, I changed her into her PJ's and saw her little torso covered in chickenpox. She must've been in pain and so uncomfortable at the club, but never said a word. I was beside myself—What kind of mother was I for Pete's Sake? By that evening, pox covered her body, and her fever had spiked to 104. I spent most of the night in a tub of lukewarm water and Aveeno with Jeannie stretched out on top of me. It was the only thing that gave her any relief. As she dozed on and off, I sat in that tub, crying, shivering, and growing up. I got a healthy dose of guilt that day, precisely what I needed, and it worked. By morning I was a much more mature parent, albeit a prune-skinned one.

There were some downsides to living in Bristol. Its location meant a long drive to work and earlier mornings. Neither Jean nor I were early birds, and 5:30 was barely doable for us. Let's just say the mornings weren't always pleasant at our house.

Cathy and I would drop Jean off at preschool in Seekonk at 7:30 a.m. and pick her up after work at around 5:30 p.m., something I hated, but I had no choice. It was a long day for a little girl. By the time we got home, had dinner and a bath, it would be Jeannie's bedtime. Never wanting to miss out on the action, she would stall as long as possible. Not having time with her during the day, I wanted to hang with her at night, so I indulged her. Once again, there was no adult in the room, and consequently, Jean rarely got enough sleep.

The other Bristol drawback was expenses. The increase in rent and gas, having to go back to using a laundromat, and the outrageous heating bills (the house wasn't properly insulated) put a squeeze on the budget. We made the necessary adjustments, however, and moved along. Jeannie knew if she had a Twinkie after supper, there wouldn't be one in her lunch the next day. I knew if we went to McDonald's for supper, the laundry wouldn't get done that week. We watched TV snuggled in sleeping bags and quilts to keep the heating bill down. Our circumstances might not have been optimal, but everybody's belly was full (including the dogs), and we could make rent every month. If I started to get down about things, I'd remind myself of a time, not so long ago, when that wasn't the case. It always righted my internal compass and put my attitude back on the right track.

Yeah, I've got this.

A VILLAGE

———

IN AUGUST 1979, MY FATHER GOT DIAGNOSED WITH STAGE four small cell lung cancer that had metastasized to his lymph nodes. By that time, Dad had lost everything but his wife. Their house, cars, and financial stability were gone. Kmart had demoted him to assistant manager after his employees found him passed out on the floor.

When Mom called me with his diagnosis, I drove up to Buffalo for the weekend. My father and I had so much we needed to say to one another that we ended up saying nothing at all. He hugged me as I was leaving and wouldn't let go until I hugged him back. As I got into my car, he kept saying, "I love you, Belle." I could only look at him. My hurt and anger were still too raw to say it back to him, and he started to cry. I backed out of the parking space and left my father waving, sobbing, and dying on the back stoop. It was the last time I saw him alive. Another vision forever seared in my mind.

"You cannot travel back in time to fix your mistakes, but you can learn from them and forgive yourself for not knowing better."

—Leon Brown

As Mom left the hospital on the evening of November 8, she kissed Dad and said she would see him in the morning. "Not if I can find that rope and climb to glory," he said. On November 9, 1979, at age forty-six, my father grabbed his rope and climbed to join Grandad and Granny.

My father was a tortured soul who suffered from depression and numbed that disease with another one—addiction. His life became a vicious circle. Depression that led to substance abuse, that allowed horrible behavior, which led to guilt and remorse that caused more profound distress, requiring increased substance abuse and allowing worse behavior. Eventually, the circle got out of control and became an emotional tornado he couldn't control. It took me years after he died to understand this and forgive him, but I eventually did.

Mom wasted no time leaving the frozen landscape by Lake Erie and moved to Seekonk. With the insurance money from my father's death, she bought a small five-room bungalow, found a job she loved, and settled into her new life.

With our mom safely tucked in near me, John felt he could finally move on with his life. He went to the Boston recruitment center and joined the Air Force. I can still see the mixture of relief, excitement, and fear on his face when we dropped him off at the train station for boot camp. He never looked back, even with all of us shouting we loved him and missed him already. When I asked him about it in a phone call, all he said was, "I don't do goodbyes." My baby brother, the lone wolf.

In the middle of all this change, my sweet grandma got sick. Between her heart and her sugar, her body just got too tired. She and Grandpa stayed with my aunt in Southern New Hampshire for a short time until she passed. When we took her home to Woodstock, New Hampshire to bury her, my grandfather broke down and cried. He kept repeating he didn't know what he had until she was gone, a mistake so many people make. He was so distraught he never entered their home again. Grandpa stayed with his sister, who lived down the street, while his three girls cleared out the house.

Now came the question of what to do about his living arrangements. Grandpa had never lived alone a day in his life and couldn't even operate a toaster. His sister was elderly and not well, one of my aunts was a nun, and the other was married with a house full of her own. Mom was the logical choice, and she brought him home to Seekonk to live with her.

It wouldn't be long before we filled that little house to the rafters with people, dogs, love, and laughter. Lots of love and laughter.

Less than a year after Grandpa moved into Mom's, Jeannie started kindergarten at the same facility where she had attended daycare and preschool. However, come September, I would have to live in town for her to enroll in Seekonk's school system for first grade. At the time, it was the best public school system in the area, and I was adamant Jean would get her education there. The problem was, there wasn't any place for rent in Seekonk we could afford. I needed a plan.

My solution? We all piled into Mom's house, Cathy included, just for a year so we could save some money. Five small rooms, three women, one older man, one kid, and eventually, three dogs. I don't know how it worked, but it did. There was one bathroom the size of a small closet, and we ladies had to sleep on trundle beds (Grandpa had a room of his own). With the trundles pulled out, you couldn't get to the dressers, the closets, or even walk into the rooms without stepping on a bed. There was no place to put dirty laundry or wet towels, so laundry was done daily.

On top of everybody who lived there, the house was always full of friends, young and old, guest dogs, and, on occasion, overnight relatives. All the love and laughter went a long way to make up for zero privacy and no peace and quiet. It was a left of center village for sure, but oh what a marvelous tribe for my daughter!

Grammy Crackers: Grammy Crackers and her little Miss Magee. I can't remember where they found their unique names for one another, but I do know they shared an incredible bond. Many years later, when my daughter spoke at my mother's funeral service, she said, "My grandmother put the magic in my childhood," and she so did.

There was always a note in Jeannie's lunchbox or a picture of female stick people, one tall and one short, holding hands and standing on cloud nine with xoxo. Mom would read Jeannie the same book as many times as she wanted to hear it, and listened intently to all of Jeannie's stories, word for word (and they could get looong). She made Jean elaborate birthday cakes that took her all day to carve and frost and sewed Jeannie fancy Halloween costumes and beautiful clothes. Grammy Crackers always stopped whatever she was doing if her Miss Magee wanted to play or asked for her attention. She taught Jeannie how to sew, worked jigsaw puzzles with her, and loved helping with school projects. My mom took Jean on her yearly vacations to see John, stationed in Florida, and those trips usually included a jaunt to Disney and Sea World.

What I don't think my daughter realizes is how much magic she put into her grandmother's life. She provided my mom the opportunity to be her loving, nurturing, caring self without having to deal with the angst and pain my father caused. Mom got a real chance to shine with her Miss Magee, and she did.

Mom never contradicted or undermined me in any way with Jean. I was Jeannie's mom, and she respected my rules and my wishes without fail, even if she didn't agree with some of them or her Miss Magee didn't like them. I admired her for that. It couldn't have been easy, especially with us all living under the same roof. It showcased her love and respect for me.

My mom's love for Jean and the relationship they shared enabled me to let go of any residual feelings of anger and abandonment I had towards her. It showed me her pure heart once again—the one that mothered me before Daddy's demons took control of our lives.

Also, she selflessly took us all into her sanctuary, the first home that had offered her any peace, and let us turn it into a zoo. That is something that takes a real commitment to family and love.

Gramps: That's what Jeannie called him, and boy did he adore her! When she was in the first grade, he walked her to and from school strutting like a peacock and proudly announcing to everyone she was his great-granddaughter. My grandmother's engagement ring was his most prized possession, and he couldn't wait until Jean was old enough to wear it. Gramps would take it out and show it to her all the time, and Jeannie always rewarded him with the proper enthusiasm. He escorted Jeannie to her first sweetheart dance and was so honored to be asked. They never lost patience with one another, and always treated each other with love, respect, and kindness.

My grandfather was the first male heart Jeannie was exposed to, and he didn't let her down. I'm so grateful they were able to have their time together.

Auntie Cathy: Dia and Beans were their nicknames for each other. Cathy loved my daughter like she was her own and treated her as such. She moved in before Jean's first birthday, and we were roomies until the summer of Jeannie's junior year of high school. Cathy was there the times I couldn't be and was Jeannie's ear when I was THAT MOM. She picked up the ball when I dropped it and, yes, sometimes overstepped her bounds. I let her because she loved us both unconditionally.

Many people thought Cathy and I were gay. We were not. Having moved so often, I was an adult before I experienced real friendship, and Cathy was my first true friend, the kind who stands by you no matter what. She saw the best and the absolute worst of me, and her loyalty never wavered. Because of that, I trusted her with the most cherished piece of my heart: Jean. She never let either one of us down.

Cathy was assertive and outspoken, took no prisoners, and put up with zero nonsense. She was also incredibly loyal, generous to a fault, and had a caring heart she readily shared with those she could trust.

The universe knew what it was doing when it put us together in that Kmart breakroom.

Fur Babies: We were all dog lovers and had two or more dogs at any given time. We rescued all of them from various situations, so Jean saw firsthand the difference your kindness and compassion can make in a life. She learned that with tolerance and patience, you could build a bond of love and loyalty with all different canine personalities. Much like she did with her human family, come to think of it.

Mommio: That would be me. Sometimes the village wise man and other times the village idiot, but always with the best intentions and a heart filled with love. I had made some promises to both Jean and I right out of the starting gate, or more accurately in this case, the womb: my daughter would be treated with love and respect by everyone in her home, or they wouldn't live there. She would feel safe and protected because I would always have her back. Always. She would have a hometown and graduate high school with her kindergarten friends. Her dreams would be encouraged, and she would have a college education. I would make sure she always felt loved so she would feel secure. I knew firsthand the damage done to a child's psyche without these things. Jeannie was going to have a stable childhood, a bright future, and heaven help anyone or anything that got in my way.

A tall order considering my age and lot in life at the time she was born, but I meant every word and managed to deliver it. I did it with determination driven by love, sheer stubbornness, and the right attitude. I never approached any obstacle whining, "Oh no, what am I going to do now?" My thought process was always, "I need a plan." I'd come up with one and then roll up my sleeves and do my best to make it work. If it didn't, I'd come up with another plan. It got us through.

Friend-mily: I met a couple at work, Charlie and Judy, and we soon developed a strong bond. We spent many nights around the kitchen table playing cards, or just talking, laughing, and making memories. They were Auntie Judy and Uncle Charlie to Jeannie and always lived up to their titles. When their beautiful daughter Lyndsey was born, they asked me to be her godmother; still one of the highest honors of my life. *I cherish my Lyndsey* *and have always celebrated her moxie and fearlessness when speaking her mind.*

We would camp and canoe on the Saco River in Maine; Judy and Charlie in their pop-up camper, and Jean, Cathy, and I in a tent. Cathy and I would tether an inflatable canvas boat to our canoe for Jeannie, her friend, and their Cabbage Patch dolls while Charlie fastened a makeshift baby seat to the middle bench of their vessel for Lyndsey. Now that I think about it, we must've been quite the sight paddling down the river! We spent evenings sitting around the campfire toasting marshmallows and telling tales. They were great times and created many special memories.

We always spent Christmas Eve together at our house, and most times, my Aunties from New York would be there too. How we all fit into that tiny living room, I have no idea, especially with the number of gifts under the tree for the girls.

I do know this: those Eves, filled with so much love and intimate connection, were magical. That was the real gift we gave one another, and to Jean and Lyndsey as well. We were more of a family than most families—we only happen to have different gene pools.

Ours was not a conventional family, and our household was anything but typical, but it worked for us, and we all thrived during our time together. I genuinely believe the uniqueness of the situation allowed us to form deeper and stronger bonds with one another.

Grandpa, Mom, and Charlie have been called home. Cathy married years ago and has moved on. Judy remarried and has a different life now, and Lyndsey lives in upstate New York with a blended family of her own. Life has taken us in different directions, and we have sadly lost touch, but I know one thing for sure: we all carry the memories and love of those yesteryears in our hearts. Happy visions forever seared in our minds.

THE LONGEST YEAR

B Y THE TIME WE MOVED INTO MOM'S, I'D BEEN AT KMART for five years and was tired of working nights and Saturdays. When they started opening Sundays, it was time for me to go, but I had no idea where. My education ended with a GED, and the only experience I had was in retail, which would mean the same hours. Not one to let reality stop me, I started applying for everything under the sun.

Somehow, I managed to talk my way into a bookkeeper/secretary position at a small rug company, Monday–Friday, 8:30 a.m. - 4:00 p.m. I loved the hours and people but hated the job. I felt like a caged animal sitting at a desk all day. Not to mention, I can add two plus two and get five (even with a calculator), and that's only a slight exaggeration. Then there were my typing skills. I could still type "Now is the time for all good men to come to the aid of their country," at eighty words per minute (it was my final exam in ninth grade typing class), but anything else was painful to watch. I knew things weren't working out, and this time I didn't have a plan. It wouldn't be long before I developed one.

Cathy's young niece Wendy, who took dance lessons, often spent weekends with us. Needing something to do one rainy weekend, we laid plywood down on the basement floor, hung a couple of door mirrors on the wall, and mounted an old handrail for a barre. Before long, Wendy and I were spending hours in our little makeshift studio. While she practiced for her recital, I would work on getting my flexibility and strength back. My muscles were screaming, and my technique was beyond rusty, but my heart would beat happier with every move. Once again, I felt a unique comfort only dance provided me. *How could I have forgotten this feeling?* I loved rediscovering all the different pieces of my dance puzzle and putting it back together.

I was also developing a plan; I was going to open a dance studio. I had been a certified teacher from the time I was fourteen but needed to brush up on things. I took some college dance courses and continued my stringent regiment in the cellar. After a lot of work and a few self pep talks, I felt ready to move forward.

Our village played a significant role in getting my first studio up and running. The space I rented was cheap but needed work. Charlie rented a machine and scraped up the tile floor so I could have it replaced. He made benches for the waiting area and crafted my very first BELLE'S SCHOOL OF DANCE sign for the front of the building. He hung the mirrors and barres on the wall and built steps out to the rear parking lot. Mom and Judy made bench cushions and drapes, and Cathy and I scrubbed and painted until everything shined.

In the fall of 1982, I opened Belle's School of Dance with only forty students and all the heart and confidence I needed to succeed.

Many a night during that first year, Judy and Mom would sew for hours, making costumes for my spring recital. Lyndsey, barely three months old, sat in a tote seat on the kitchen table, and Charlie and I kept her occupied by letting her suck on chocolate-covered Girl Scout cookies until she spit up, and we got caught. That's when Jeannie read and sang to her, and all was right in Lyndsey's world. And mine. Sharing and working on my dream with the people I loved most made it all the more rewarding.

By the studio's third year, I was making enough money to move out of Mom's, but with things working out so well for all of us, I chose not to. Mom appreciated our help with Grandpa, he enjoyed all the company, and finances were better for everyone. My studio hours were after school and evenings, and it was good to know my little girl could come home from school to her great-grandfather instead of going to an afterschool program. If Jeannie needed help with her homework before I got in, Mom and Cathy were there. She'd be bathed and in her PJ's when I got home, so she could sit with me while I had something to eat and tell me about her day.

Gone were the days of Jeannie getting picked up, dropped off, picked up again, and rushed around when we'd finally get home. The help and support Mom, Grandpa, and Cathy gave me with day-to-day living allowed me more time to enjoy my daughter. I will always be grateful to them for giving me that gift. Also, because of their support, Jeannie had stability in her life, a solid foundation, and I was able to fulfill my dream as a dance instructor. She had a home. We all had a home. It made no sense to leave, nor did I want to.

As you can imagine, there were pluses to being an only child living in a house full of adoring adults.

Halloween and Jean's birthday parties were major events. Big bashes were a piece of cake with three of us to run things. Mom, Cathy, and I were quite the team when it came to parties.

There was never a limit on Jeannie's guest list, and every party had a theme. A 50s dance party, a pool party, a magician, a clown, Strawberry Shortcake and friends, Smurfs, you name it. We even had a backyard camping party, complete with a campfire, cooking hot dogs on a stick, s'mores, tents, and ghost stories (boys sent home before lights out).

I made the mistake of asking the boys why they found flinging toasted marshmallows off a stick onto a wooden fence such hilarious fun. "We're pretending they're boogers, Miss Belle!" Oh, that explains it...sort of, I guess. *Boys will be boys.*

Jeannie wanted a rabbit, so meet Mr. Nibbles. When she fretted he was lonely and cold outside, we briefly moved him into her room. Once I discovered how bad even a clean rabbit cage smelled indoors and caught him chewing on an electrical cord, I convinced her Mr. Nibbles would be much happier back on the farm with his bunny friends.

My friend Patty had a horse, Beau, and when Jean expressed an interest in riding, she offered to give her lessons. Patty's one stipulation was she also learn how to take proper care of a horse after riding. Jeannie soon started bonding with Beau, and it wasn't long before my daughter wanted a horse. *Uh oh, time for a reality check.* I made a deal with her. If she helped Patty muck the stalls and water and feed all the horses for a month, we'd talk.

"Why all the horses?" she asked.

"Because it costs a lot of money to board a horse. Patty takes care of the barn to help pay for Beau to live there," I said.

"What's mucking a stall?" was her next question.

"Patty will show you," I managed to say without grinning. My scheme worked. I don't think Jeannie lasted two days. Hey, I might've been indulgent, but I wasn't crazy. A horse? No way.

Patty was also the one who introduced us to camping. We were sitting around the kitchen table one night, and she mentioned she used to love to camp. She hadn't been in years, and neither Cathy nor I had ever been, so we decided to go for it. We bought a six-man tent, sleeping bags, and all the camping essentials. We could have gone on a cruise for what we spent on all the gear. We were ready.

Off we went for a Memorial Day weekend in the woods equipped with everything but a reservation. *You need to book in advance to sleep on the ground in the woods—who knew?* By the time we found a place that had a vacancy, it was late afternoon. It wasn't the best campground around, but we didn't care, at least we'd found one. Cathy and I proceeded to unbox the tent and waited for Patty's instructions. That's when we learned she used to camp in a pop-up camper and had no idea what to do with a tent. *No problem, it has directions, we'll figure it out.*

Next, we needed firewood. It didn't take us long to realize it had rained the day before, and there was no dry wood. *That's okay Patty will grab a bundle at the campground store when she gets the ice.* As if there would be any ice and wood left on the Friday evening of a holiday weekend. She eventually found some about a half hour down the road, and we were back in business.

We cooked hot dogs and beans over the campfire and had s'mores for dessert. After sitting around the fire and talking for a while, we decided to turn in early. We planned to do some light hiking on the Appalachian Trail in the morning. I grabbed a flashlight to take Jean and her friend for a final trip to the bathroom and realized how far from the facilities we were. *It didn't look that far in the daylight.* One coyote howl later, and I decided to teach the girls how to pee behind a tree and figured their teeth wouldn't rot out in one night.

When we woke up the next morning, we discovered why our site was still available the day before. It was right on a creek, convenient for washing dishes and faces, and provided lots of fun for the girls. However, it was also home to a million mosquitoes and mayflies that swarmed our campsite once the fire went out. We were all eaten alive—huge welts all over our bodies (all over, if you catch my drift). Not to worry, the first aid kit had calamine lotion and alcohol. On the way back from hiking, we picked up some more anti-itch cream and lots of bug spray. We drowned that tent in bug spray. No way were we going to be any beast's supper two nights in a row.

I woke up in the middle of the night to thunder and lightning and had to smile. *Perfect; what else could possibly go wrong on this trip?* As if on cue, it started to rain. I mean torrential downpouring rain. Inside our temporary abode. Did you know if you spray insect repellant directly onto a tent's surface, it will affect the waterproofing? It says so right in the booklet, the one nobody read.

We all piled into the car, shivering, soaked, and out of humor. We couldn't change into dry clothes or towel off because everything was floating in the tent. When we drove to the laundromat to dry the clothes we had on, we didn't have any quarters. Being the early 1980s and after midnight in the boondocks, there was no place open to get change. It was a perfect ending to the saga.

Not to be deterred, we continued going on our camping trips until we got it right. We eventually got to be pros, but that first trip was a real comedy act. I'm so glad we didn't give up. Some of my fondest memories are of camping, canoeing, hiking, and enjoying nature in all its beauty. *Thank you, Gaia (Mother Earth).*

WELL, LOOK WHAT

THE CAT DRAGGED IN

O R MORE APROPOS IN THIS CASE, THE LAWYER. WE HADN'T seen Steven in years. He stopped coming around before Jeannie was a year old, and she was now eight. The whopping twenty-five dollars a week in child support had also vanished, but I was somehow managing without it (eyeroll please). He was adhering to the court order to keep Jeannie on his medical plan, which was more critical, so I had decided to leave it alone.

Jeannie suffered from chronic ear infections and periodically had tubes placed in her ears to help them drain. It was an out-patient procedure, but still, it was surgery. The last insertion, when she was eight, finally did the trick, and Jeannie was free from earaches. No more pain or surgery! Yay! Gone were the custom-molded earplugs for hair washes and showers. No more worrying every time she went swimming that the plugs would leak, and she'd get sick again. Both of us were relieved to have the years-long ordeal behind us.

About six weeks later, we went for the final follow up appointment, and the receptionist asked if my payment would be check or cash. Confused, I pointed out post-op visits were covered, and she said my daughter was no longer insured. My first thought was, *Thank goodness; it didn't lapse until after the surgery.* My second thought was, *That S.O.B.!* Those thoughts might've occurred in a different order.

My studio, only open a couple of years, couldn't support health insurance, much less a family plan. It was time to hunt down Jean's so-called father. Last I'd heard he was a member of the pipefitters' union and working out west somewhere. I figured the job must've ended, hence no insurance.

I needed a lawyer but had no idea where to find one. One day, while stopped at a red light, my eyes were drawn to a man carrying a briefcase and entering a small building. When I spotted the attorney at law sign, I intuitively knew he was my lawyer; I just knew. I wrote down his name and called for an appointment the minute I got home.

Mr. Smith, being in family law, was kind and patient while he listened to my story. He then told me we needed to hire an investigator to find Steven. I didn't know where I was going to find the money to pay him, never mind a PI. When I told him as much and got up to leave, he softly asked me to sit back down. He said I didn't need to worry about paying him; the court would order Steven to do it. The investigator, however, was a different story. *I'm down to paying only one—I'll find a way.*

Mr. Smith asked me Steven's last known address, and I told him I had no idea but knew he was a member of the pipe fitters' union. He gave the tiniest of smiles and said to give him a couple of days. I later learned Mr. Smith had a friend in the union who was more than willing to help nail a deadbeat dad. He asked around and found out Steven was temporarily back in town, which was a big break for me. We had found Steven and it hadn't cost me a dime.

We were assigned a court date, and Betty and Edmond posted his bail to keep him temporarily out of jail. Unbeknownst to me, they also made it clear they were not giving him the seven years back child support he owed or paying for either lawyer. Without their money to pay restitution when we went to court, he knew the judge would order him to jail.

Steven started working on me immediately and knew precisely how to play me. Jean. He said he wanted to see her, get to know her. I told him I would broach the subject with her, but it was ultimately Jean's decision. When I sat her down to tell her he was back and wanted to see her, I watched the different emotions my eight year old daughter was feeling dance across her young face. Confusion, curiosity, anger, hurt, hope, fear. *I'm so sorry little girl.*

She had one question, "Will you be there?"

I assured her I most definitely would be, and she asked if she could think about it. I told her to take as long as she needed, and I was with her one hundred percent either way. After a day or so, Jeannie said she'd go as long as I went with her. I called Steven to set it up. There was no privacy at our house, and I knew this would be hard enough for Jeannie; she didn't need an audience, even a supportive one. I suggested a nearby park, and he agreed as long as I drove.

When Steven got dropped off at our house, I could tell immediately he was high. He was also filthy. His hair hung in greasy strings halfway down his back and his stained clothes reeked of stale booze and pot. I could only imagine what was spinning around in my daughter's head. The three of us piled into the car and headed for the park.

The first words Steven spoke to his daughter in seven years were, and I quote, "Never trust anyone in this world. They're all out to screw you, even your parents. Especially your parents. They'll never have your back."

I looked Jeannie square in the eye via the rearview mirror and reminded her she knew that wasn't true. That wasn't her world. She nervously nodded in agreement. *God, I'm so sorry you're going through this sweetie!* Steven never once asked Jeannie anything about her life, her likes or dislikes, her pets, school, nothing. He just slumped in the passenger seat and complained about how tough he had it.

As we pulled into the park and I stopped the car, Steven pulled out a hash pipe and proceeded to fill it.

"What are you doing?! Put that away! Now!" I growled.

He laughed and slid it back into his pocket. "Still the uptight bitch, I see."

I decided it was time for Steven to have a come to Jesus moment, and I was just the lady for the job. I suggested we get some fresh air, and Jeannie couldn't get out of the car and onto the playground fast enough. Steven and I sat on a bench, and I could see Jeannie shooting nervous glances in our direction. *Put her mind at ease, Belle, no hysterics.*

To the naked eye, I was calmly sitting on a park bench, having a pleasant conversation with a homeless guy. In reality, I was clawing my ex-husband down to his core as only a mother protecting her wounded young can do.

"What the fuck is wrong with you?!!" I quietly screamed. "Can't you see how scared she is of this situation? Don't make it harder for her by doing your best doom and gloom routine. Parents don't suck. Your parents suck. You suck as a parent. I do not. Jeannie trusts me, and the people who surround her, and is secure in the knowledge we will always be there for her. I'll be damned if I'm going to let you take that security away with your jabbering nonsense and drug-induced sadistic view of the world." *Smile and wave to her, Belle.* "And if you ever pull out drugs in front of her again, I will sever your manhood—count on it. And for Christ's sake, take a shower, you're disgusting."

He just smirked. "Yup, still the uptight bitch." *Like I care what you think of me, you piece of trash.*

He was straight the next time he called and wanted to see Jeannie alone. No way. I'd promised her she wouldn't have to go alone, and I didn't trust him to take care of her physically, never mind emotionally. I told him he would have to be patient. The situation was new to her, and she was understandably wary of him and confused. He couldn't just pop into her life after all these years and expect her to be comfortable around him. I was Jean's security, and until she told me otherwise, we were a package deal. Steven didn't like it, but he agreed to the status quo.

Meanwhile, the court date was around the corner, and Mr. Smith reviewed the proceedings with me. We would go before a judge, produce the original order, and if Steven didn't pay restitution, they would immediately take him to jail.

By this time, Steven had shared with me his parents had washed their hands of the situation, and he was on his own. He had found work and reinstated Jean's health insurance but couldn't come up with the back child support.

On the day of court, as Mr. Smith and I were waiting in the hallway for our case to be called, I said I'd be willing to let the back support go if Steven proved monthly Jean was insured and paid my legal fees. Mr. Smith pointed out that they could only enforce that if Steven's whereabouts were known and pleaded with me not to drop it. He told me we might never have another opportunity to find him, much less get him to court. He made me promise to think hard about it.

When we stood before the judge and had our case read, Mr. Smith looked at me, and I shook my head no. He asked the court for a minute to speak with me. He begged me to think about my daughter, what that money could mean for her. I assured him I was thinking of Jean. Steven was making an effort to see her, and I didn't want to do anything to jeopardize that. As much of a mess as he was, he was her father.

Mr. Smith shook his head. "Did it occur to you; he's making an effort so you'll give him a break?" Of course, it did. I knew Steven's selfishness and how devious he could be. "Do you honestly think he's going to stick around?" he asked.

No. No, I did not. I knew Steven too well, knew his drug abuse and his inability to stay in the real world for long. But I had to give it a shot. I had experienced firsthand the exclusive feeling of a father's love and then the pain of losing it. My daughter had only felt the pain of loss, and if there was even a minute chance she could experience the love in the future, I had to try. With a heavy heart, Mr. Smith went back into court, and we let Steven go.

The next day, Steven showed up on my doorstep, high as a kite, and insisted on spending the day with Jean alone. He mumbled we'd had enough visits now, and she should be okay with him one on one. He had a canoe on top of his father's truck and said he planned to take her fishing. With the threat of jail gone, Steven had wasted no time swooping in for the kill. He knew I would never let her in a car with him in that condition, much less on the water.

I called his bluff by not immediately saying no, left him on the stoop laying an egg, and went in to talk to Jean. I found her scared and shaking in the living room; she had heard him.

"I don't want to go, Mommy, please don't make me go!" I assured her I would never make her go, and it was still her decision. "I never want to go without you ever!" She was crying hard now.

"No problem, sweetie, you won't have to. But I want to make sure you realize that means he won't be back," I told her. She nodded her head yes, and I went to sweep the chickenshit off my stoop.

After he left, I sat down on the back stairs, and it was my turn to cry hard. Not because of the money, or being used; I figured that was the way it would go down, but I had to try. No, I cried because my daughter had been hurt again by this man.

In trying to do the right thing, I had failed to think it through. Jeannie had no idea her father was that much of a mess. Whenever she asked, I told her he had a drug problem, was terrified of responsibility, and a pessimist. His absence had nothing to do with her; he was just incapable of taking care of himself much less a family. All very true. And I told her he was a free spirit, artistic, creative, and loved music, also true. In other words, I gave her the ugly truth laced with the romantic ideals I had as that young girl in the tree so long ago. Jeannie was unprepared for the reality of him and, understandably, frightened of him. She lived in an environment where people like Steven didn't exist.

In trying to give her a father, something I knew she missed and needed, I set her up for disappointment and confusion. I should have reminded myself of who Steven was before subjecting her to him.

After some time, Mom came out, handed me a glass of iced tea, kissed the top of my head, and sat down next to me without a word. That's when I started to think about what had gone right.

Jean had witnessed firsthand who Steven was, and questions like what-ifs and who is he would no longer haunt her. I would keep a close eye out to help her through the emotional fallout it caused, but surely it would be better than not knowing and always wondering.

I reminded myself of just how far she and I had come and what a bullet we had dodged eight years ago. Against all odds, I had managed to create a safe, stable world where my child lived and thrived. I took some pride and a lot of comfort in that.

Then a thought hit me. If Steven hadn't been her father, if she didn't carry his genes and DNA, Jean wouldn't be who she is, wouldn't be the same Jeannie. Steven was a deplorable excuse for a father, but he was a superb sperm donor; I had to give him credit there. And that's how I thought of him from that day on, a sperm donor.

Also, I now had a good lawyer, Jean had health insurance, and my finances were unscathed. All very bright spots. Sometimes you only need to look at things from a different angle to put them in perspective—that and a glass of iced tea and your mom's quiet love.

LESSONS LEARNED FOR TWO

JEANNIE NEVER REQUIRED MUCH DISCIPLINE. I HAD MY "Meanie Mommy Look," as she called it, and that pretty well took care of most issues. If she were acting up in a restaurant or a store, I'd give her The Look and ask her if we needed to go to the ladies' room and have a talk. Since we never used the ladies' room for anything other than its designated purpose, I'm guessing the look worked—the look and her sensitive heart that is. To hear me say I was disappointed in her behavior worked as well as any punishment I could've meted out. That's not to say Jean didn't have her moments. She was, after all, a normal kid. Honestly, more often than not, we both needed a scolding, and each of us ended up learning a lesson.

When Jeannie was around six years old, we were in the checkout lane at Kmart, and she asked for a candy bar. I said no because it was too close to supper time. After we got home, I saw her take a packet of Skittles out of her jacket pocket, and I flipped out. You would've thought she'd stolen the Crown Jewels the way I carried on.

"You stole these? One of the few times you're denied something, and you decide to take it like some spoiled brat?" I yelled.

I marched her right back to the store to confess her crime and pay for the candy. Her confessor was the assistant manager, my immediate boss, and he knew Jeannie well. Somehow, he managed to get through her confession with a straight face, and he even maintained his composure when she asked if she was going to jail. He told Jean he was sure she learned her lesson that crime didn't pay, and he appreciated her coming clean. He didn't think it was necessary to call the police this time, but if it ever happened again, he would.

She was inconsolable on the way home and sobbed, "I'm sorry, Mommy do you still love me?" *What?!*

"Of course, I do! I will always love you, no matter what," I assured her.

She was afraid she'd lost my love over a packet of Skittles. Jeannie learned the consequences of stealing, and I learned the emotional harm overreacting could cause. I made a note to cut back on the drama.

Jeannie had long, blonde hair. It was beautiful, but very fine and prone to knots, so she hated having it brushed. One morning I was trying to get a particularly stubborn knot out, and things were not going well. Jean and I were still not morning people, and a bad situation was getting worse by the minute.

Amid the escalating tension, my mom asked ever so sweetly, "What do you want in your lunch today, Miss Magee?"

My daughter was so angry at me, her kneejerk response was, "I DON'T CARE ABOUT YOUR STUPID LUNCH!"

My kneejerk reaction to her sass was to smack her on top of the head with the hairbrush. "Don't you ever speak to your grandmother like that again! And think before you speak or act out of anger!"

Really Belle? Because you just smacked her with a hairbrush without thinking.

Sometimes it felt like I was raising both of us, probably because I was doing precisely that. Jean's lesson was to respect her grandmother and control her anger. Mine was to practice what I preached.

There were also times when I was the only one who needed to learn the lesson.

We were planning one of our camping trips, and I asked Jean who she wanted to invite. "No one," she said.

"Don't be silly, of course, you want to take someone," I said and started naming her friends.

I got a resounding, "Why can't I ever just go by myself with you guys?!" Why indeed. Without realizing it, I was going overboard, giving Jeannie what I had missed most growing up, the companionship of friends. Jean's childhood was very different from mine. She had plenty of time with friends. What she didn't have was downtime. My childhood was fraught with too much downtime and not enough friends. I remembered how lonely it was at times, and I had my brother. Because Jean was an only child, I worried about her being alone and was depriving her of much-needed privacy and quiet time. My daughter was not me; she was Jean Elizabeth Pierce with her own needs, wants, and temperament. It was an AHA! moment for me and a valuable lesson learned.

Another way Jean and I differed was the pace in which we moved. I was here there and everywhere all at once, and Jeannie gave meandering a whole new meaning. I would have her hook a finger into my belt loop to keep her moving in a store. Hurry up was a foreign concept for my daughter. Of course, sometimes, it pays to slow down...

Late one afternoon, Jeannie announced she needed supplies for a school project by the next morning. We had just enough time to rush off to Kmart before supper, and I decided to get it done. My mom's car was last in the driveway, so I took it.

On the drive, I lectured Jean about the importance of preparedness, not waiting until the last minute, being focused, blah blah blah.

I looked over at her, and she was happily bobbing her head to the song on the radio. "Are you even hearing me?" I asked.

"Yes, Mom, I'm listening," she said. *Was that an eye roll I just saw?*

With me rushing her as best I could, we picked out and paid for the supplies and headed back to the car. Still yapping in her ear about responsibility and lists, I was having trouble getting the key to open the car door. I was getting more frustrated and crankier by the minute, and Jeannie kept saying, "Mom, Mom, Mom," but I ignored her until the key finally turned.

As we got in the car, I noticed a set of fuzzy dice hanging on the rearview mirror. *Uh oh...*

"I tried to tell you this wasn't Grandma's car, but you didn't hear me, you weren't listening," my daughter scolded with a smirk. We both cracked up laughing and hightailed it out of there. Point taken little girl. *God, I love this kid!* Jeannie learned to be better prepared, and I learned to slow down.

Because I was never able to join anything growing up (due to constant moving), I encouraged Jeannie any time she wanted to join an organization or try something new. I wanted her to explore all the possibilities available to her and learn to enjoy different things. The one rule I had was she stayed until she completed the commitment she'd signed on for.

The only exception I remember making to the rule was dance lessons. When Jean was six (before I opened my studio), she wanted to take dance lessons. I was thrilled! I found a place close by and enrolled her for tap, ballet, and jazz. Jeannie hated it from the first lesson. *How can anyone with my genes hate dance?* She pitched a fit every week when it was time to go and would pout for a day later. And boy, my daughter could pout. I had taught her well.

Whenever I asked Jeannie why she hated it, she said it was boring; they didn't do anything. If I asked her to show me what she learned in class, she would just plop down on the floor. Jean had committed for the year, and she was going to stick it out until recital, even if it killed me (and it was looking like it might do just that). Not to mention, I had paid for the studio uniform, shoes, a semester of classes, and a fifty dollar non-refundable deposit on recital costumes.

Within a half hour of the first parents' night, I understood Jean's problem. The teacher sat by the phonograph (eating) and told the girls to get in a circle for the awakening flower dance. Seven little girls promptly sat down on the floor. Jeannie had been showing me what she learned after all. At ages six and seven, these dancers were not babies and should have been learning basic steps.

When it was time for the girls to change into tap shoes, I took Jeannie out of class and went to the reception desk. I asked the woman for a refund on the remainder of the semester and the costume deposit back because my daughter would not be returning. The answer was no. They had placed the costume order, and they certainly weren't going to refund lesson money because a child changed her mind.

"She isn't changing her mind; I am. I've been involved in dance all my life, and have never seen anything as lame as that ballet class. And I know this year's costume catalogs haven't come out yet, so there's no way you could have placed orders. Now, can I please have my money back, or do I need to share my observations with the other parents?"

She said they'd mail me a check which, of course, they didn't. I had to stop in a couple of times before I got it, but get it I did. It was a matter of principle.

Jeannie saw how to stand up for what was right, and I learned there could be an exception to every rule. Even mine. Because I broke that rule, Jeannie's attitude towards dance was not permanently scarred. When I opened my studio, she joined and couldn't wait for her Saturday lessons. She became a beautiful dancer and enjoyed it right up until she left for college.

I chuckle when I remember the first time Jeannie lied to me. I know it was the first time because she was so bad at it. I don't even recall what the lie was about, but I do remember her mumbling, not being able to look at me, and turning all red. One Meanie Mommy Look, and she cracked like an egg. I immediately launched into the, "I'm disappointed in you," routine followed by my "The importance of trust" lecture and ended with a touch of guilt. It was a mother's masterpiece if I may say so myself. Of course, anyone that bad at lying was already punishing themselves and didn't need a masterpiece. Still, I felt the need to drive home the fact that we were not liars.

Not too long after that, she and her friend Kelly were in the backseat chatting about their day at school. Christmas was coming, and there had been some discussion at lunch about Santa Claus. Being in fifth or sixth grade, they were in the minority as far as believing. I should note that Kelly's dad Mike is still a believer, and I'm not entirely sure it's the spirit of Saint Nicholas he's referring to. Me? I was only trying to keep the magic alive for as long as I could.

Kelly and Jeannie were quite indignant at being made fun of at lunch and felt superior in their knowledge of the truth. Cathy was giving me the "It's time to tell her" look, which I was successfully ignoring until I heard Jeannie say, "I told them he was real for sure because my mom says so, and she would never lie to me. We are not liars!" *Okay it's time.*

Explaining the difference between little white lies to keep the magic of childhood alive or to spare someone's feelings and lies to get out of trouble or get something you want was a tough one. I must've managed it though because Jean's still a lousy liar, and she's incapable of intentionally hurting anyone's feelings. Two noble things that can make adulting more difficult at times but are well worth it.

I BLINKED

HIGH SCHOOL. SO QUICKLY, TOO FAST! *I MUST'VE BLINKED.* Jean had gone steady in junior high school a couple of times, but it consisted of school dances, phone calls, and group activities. I soon found out now that she was in high school, it would be the real deal.

The first boy she brought home was Ron. He was two years older, which I wasn't crazy about, but he didn't have a car, and that eased my mind a bit. He was polite and quiet and older. Did I mention older?

An aside: When Jean was in fifth or sixth grade, we finished the basement and made it her room so she would have a place to hang out with her friends. This was pre-boys.

I came home from the studio one night and went skipping down the stairs to say hi. I found Ron and Jean stretched out on the daybed in a significant lip lock. *Get your paws off of my daughter, you hound!*

"Hi, guys, what's up?" I greeted. Suddenly, I was looking at two startled and very red faces. *Whew, everything's still clipped, zipped, and buttoned.* I babbled on, "Jeannie, is your homework done? No? Well, it's getting late, and you need to get to it. Do you want a ride home, Ron?" I wasn't surprised when he said he'd walk that particular night.

After he left, I sat down on Jeannie's bed to talk. I threw everything I had out there. "A few years ago, we covered the changes your body would go through and what that physically meant for you. But you're dating now, and we need to discuss the feelings and sensations that come with those changes."

I went on to share how I remembered the first time they were awakened in me, how hard it was to control them, and how confused I felt. I went over the STD, pregnancy, and reputation lecture again for good measure and ended with the "Never get coerced into doing something you are uncomfortable with" talk. *I think I've covered everything.* In true Jeannie fashion, she never said a word, but I knew she had listened and taken it all in.

I kissed her goodnight, and on my way upstairs said, "You only get one first time, sweetie. Once you do it, it's done, and you can't take it back. Make sure it's with someone you want to remember."

As I left her to do her homework, I was mentally smacking myself on the forehead. *Hormones! How could I have forgotten about the damn hormones?* From that night forward, Jean's room was for group activities only.

Jeannie told me years later that the "You only get one first time," comment was what had done the trick. I had found that one floating around in thin air at the last minute and grabbed it for my closing. I'm so glad I did.

I always stressed to Jean, if she ever found herself in a situation where she was uncomfortable, call me and I would come and get her, no questions asked. One night she took me up on my offer. Ron was having a party at his house, and yes, there would be supervision and no drinking. *Yeah, right.* I decided to trust her judgment. It wasn't long before the phone rang. She wanted to come home. Immediately. *Don't panic, Belle.*

"Are you safe?" was my only question.

"Yes, I just want to leave," she whispered.

"Okay sweetie, wait out front, I'm on my way."

"NO, don't pick me up here!"

What the... I told Jean to walk to the end of the street and wait for me there. Ron lived more than five minutes away, but

I got there while she was still walking. My Honda Accord had sprouted wings. Jean got into the car, and I asked if she was alright. She nodded yes, and that was the end of my questions.

Mind you, I bit my tongue until it bled, but if the need ever arose again in the future, I wanted her to call. I knew she wouldn't if I didn't hold up my end of the bargain. Besides, she had just proven I had every reason to trust her judgment. To this day, I don't know what happened. My guess is the party, unsupervised, had alcohol and drugs flowing freely. Jeannie just wasn't ready for it.

Ron was gone soon after the party, and she dated Bill through the rest of high school and her first year of college. He adored her and treated her with respect and kindness. Bill was Jean's age and a sweet, quiet innocent. *Perfect! I love sweet, quiet innocents dating my teenage daughter.*

I felt strongly about teaching Jeannie how to take care of herself in situations. That meant her taking some battles on herself, with the help of my coaching and profound advice, of course. Okay, admittedly profound is a real stretch, but I tried to sound at least like I knew what I was talking about.

One such battle was for Jean's position on the field hockey team. She came home one afternoon, upset about the amount of time she spent on the bench. Jeannie never missed practice, worked her tail off, and had improved on the things the coach told her needed work. She knew she was just as good as the girl who played all the time but wasn't getting a chance to prove it. I should mention this coach was very intimidating, tough as nails, and Jeannie hated confrontation. She asked if I would talk to her. *Hmmm, let's try this first.* I told Jean she made an excellent case for herself and had presented it well to me. If she did as well with the coach, she would most likely get her a shot.

Jean went to the coach and got her chance. I knew how hard it was for her to plead her case, but wanted Jeannie to learn how to stand up for herself. I believed, and still do, that children can't develop confidence if they never have to handle situations for themselves; never have to face adversity. Nor can they develop coping skills when others always fix everything for them. I'm sure this wasn't the only time Jeannie might have felt I didn't have her back, but I hope now, as an adult, she realizes and appreciates the lessons. And knows if that coach hadn't been fair and given her a chance, she would've heard from me.

Of course, there are times when a parent has to fight the battle.

The AP math class Jeannie needed in her sophomore year was full. The principal told her to take a different course, and she could double up on math in her junior year. Not optimal but a solution—until that principal left before the end of the year. When Jean went to schedule her junior year, they said she couldn't take both math classes and would have to go to summer school. *Ah, no, I don't think so.* I scheduled a conference with the vice-principal, Mr. Jones, who was the acting interim principal. He was aware Jeannie was an excellent student and apologized for the misunderstanding, but said his hands were tied. I quickly pointed out it was not a misunderstanding, but the former principal's solution to a problem caused by the school's scheduling issues.

Mr. Jones eventually agreed to help and suggested a tutor for the course she missed. That way, Jean could learn the content during the school year and take the final exam when she felt ready. He gave us the name of a tutor and assured me the school would provide the necessary course material. Crisis averted.

I've often wondered if Mr. Jones remembered he was my guidance counselor in my junior year of high school, and that's part of why he stuck his neck out for us. He must've been right out of college when I was a junior and tried hard, but couldn't stop me from quitting school. He never showed any recognition during our meeting about Jean, and I never mentioned it, so I have no way of knowing.

I am sure of this: it was no coincidence the same man, in different roles, was involved in pivotal decisions concerning the education of both Jeannie and me in our junior year. Mr. Jones couldn't save me at sixteen, but nineteen years later, he helped my sixteen-year-old daughter in a big way. I love the crazy twists and turns life takes sometimes.

Jeannie's junior year of high school was hectic, to say the least. She played field hockey, tennis, was class president, president of the Spanish Honor Society, and Homecoming Queen. There were sports dinners, class dinners, dances, meetings, practices, and a job. *She needs a car.* The Christmas she got her driver's permit, I gave her my beloved Honda, and for reasons still unknown to me, bought myself a Cougar. I hated driving that car from day one. It was horrible in the snow, had blind spots to spare, and I couldn't find a seat position that felt comfortable. *Oh well, adjust, it's yours now, and it is sexy looking.* I named her Lola.

Driving home from the studio one evening, Lola and I got into an accident. A vehicle, coming the opposite way, was driving slowly to check out cars on a dealer's lot. He must have seen one he liked and suddenly swerved to turn into the dealership. Lola and I were in the way. While we waited for the police, a car salesman said he saw it happen; that I had nowhere to go and no warning.

When the cop arrived and asked if anyone had seen the accident, the sales guy was mute. *Really, buddy?!* When I ratted him out, the officer was not amused. "You guys, all you care about is selling your cars. How would you feel if this was your wife or daughter?" The guy ended up doing the right thing, and with the paperwork completed, they towed Lola away.

The next evening Jean called the studio and told me she had been in an accident. After assuring me no one was hurt, she told me it was her fault—she'd rear-ended a guy. He'd stopped short in her lane to look at a car on a dealer's lot, and she didn't have time to react. *Our insurance company is going to love us.* Our accidents were parallel: the same dealership, witness, officer, time (around eight thirty), and cause (drivers checking out new cars when they should've been driving).

I now believe it was the universe at work. At the time, my studio had recitals every other year, and Jean's junior year would be her last performance. We planned to dance a lyrical ballet together to Bette Midler's "Every Road Leads Back to You." Whenever we worked on it, I remembered what was to come and would feel such a sense of loss. I think this was their way of reminding me how connected my daughter and I were, and to reassure me that connection would withstand the upcoming changes.

That, and a reminder for both of us to be more aware of our surroundings. A slap upside of the head we both needed at that busy time in our lives.

It was time to start thinking about college. Jeannie's SAT scores were above average, and she was high honors in accelerated classes. She played sports and was an involved, well-rounded student. Jeannie had done her part, and now it was time for me to do mine. I was a single self-employed parent and knew it would open financial opportunities for loans, grants, and scholarships. I had saved enough for a couple of years but knew I would need much more.

I hired an education planner, Mr. Fin, to find the money available, deal with the forms, and point Jean toward the right colleges. He took down the mountains of information he needed (everything but her shoe size and my real hair color it seemed) and started his research. Within a couple of weeks, we got a customized binder of college choices based on Jean's grades and accomplishments. It also included estimated percentages of financial aid and her chances of admittance with her family background. We limited it to five choices, including a safety school, and she applied for early acceptance. Mr. Fin had delivered.

Jean was waitlisted at Boston College, didn't like Boston University's campus, and Tufts was a long shot. It was time for us to book some flights.

Ithaca had offered her full tuition, so they were our first stop. When we found a foot of snow on the ground at the end of

April, I didn't hold out much hope. As we toured the small quiet campus, I lost what little I had. The college and the student body had a very artsy, eclectic feel to it. It was pleasant, but not my daughter.

"Mom, I wouldn't be happy here, it's not for me." *I know, but it's a free ride!*

"Okay, well, you have some time to think about it," was all I said. Jean didn't even want to visit her safety school, Canisius, who also offered her full tuition. I got it. I had spent enough time in the Buffalo area to know it gives snow, wind, and cold a whole new meaning.

Sigh, bye-bye free rides.

The next stop was Clemson, South Carolina. Clemson is the quintessential college campus that sits on a hill overlooking a small town. It's a big school, at that time about eighteen thousand undergraduate students, and steeped in tradition and sports. When we took the tour, the campus buzzed with life. Jeannie liked the feel of it, and I was happy with the safety of a small town. More importantly, it was a high quality education for less money. They didn't offer Jean full tuition, but it was an excellent financial package and scholarships. We had a winner!

Jeannie graduated Seekonk High School in the spring of 1994 with a Clemson Tiger Paw painted on her mortarboard and surrounded by friends, many who she had known since kindergarten.

I have two pictures of her and her friend Steve. The first shows them hugging and smiling in their little kindergarten cap and gown, and the other has them grinning ear to ear in high school caps and gowns, their friendship and history shining through. I cherish those pictures and the childhood continuity and stability they represent. My daughter had the security of a loving family, a hometown, and childhood friends.

I had broken another unhealthy family cycle.

Maybe I did have this, after all.

A FORK IN THE ROAD

A friend whose daughter is younger than Jeannie once said to me, "If I can get her through high school, the hardest part will be done."

I laughed until my sides ached. "Au contraire, my friend, that's when the hardcore parenting gets started." I told her to buckle up; it's a bumpy ride.

CLEMSON OFFERED TWO DATES FOR STUDENT ORIENTATION, one in May and the other two days before the first semester began. Even though Clemson is over nine hundred miles away, I thought the May date would work best. That way, Jean could learn her way around campus and have a chance to meet a couple of people. Maybe it might help ease her into the many changes about to happen in her life. It was a mistake, a big one, and had the opposite effect I had hoped.

At four o'clock, after a full day learning the ins and out of campus life, parents left, and students stayed on campus for the night. I spent the evening thinking about how much fun Jean must be having. I knew she was an introvert, especially in new social settings, but figured there would be more of them in the group, and they would find one another. I was wrong. I hadn't considered the majority of out of state students would combine their orientation with the start of classes, which left Jean surrounded by outgoing, gregarious southerners.

I instantly knew the next morning it hadn't gone well. Jean's face said it all, and my heart broke for her. "I hate it! I don't belong here, and I'm not going to school here," she announced. *You have no choice little girl, that ship has sailed.*

"Jeannie, we've already paid for the semester, and this is the school you chose." There isn't time to apply to another school," I said. She wasn't giving up that easily.

"Boston College waitlisted me, and if they don't call, I'll take the semester off."

"Jean, you can't give up based on one weekend. You have to give it a chance. I'm sorry you're upset right now, but Clemson is your school for a year."

Silence. I looked to the backseat, and she was crying quiet tears, the kind that rips a mother's heart out. Worse yet, they were tears I was causing. *I'm so sorry little girl, but this is something you have to do—a hard lesson you will understand someday.* A time having Jeannie's back wasn't easy for me or readily apparent to her.

It was also the first time I felt hopelessly lost in the wilderness called parenting. Despite being ridiculously young, inexperienced, single, and a product of my upbringing, I had always found a path, a way through the woods. But this time, I couldn't see one and found myself uncertain of the right way to go. And that scared the bejesus out of me.

As the summer wore on, and she had time to digest everything, Jean started to settle into the idea. By August, when we had to leave, she was in a much better place. We packed up the car and set out for the next step in life's journey together, as it had always been.

Her Auntie Cathy, away on business, was going to fly to Clemson a few days later, help set up the dorm room, and drive back home with me. The three of us shopped at Walmart, buying stuff for the dorm room, purchased her books, planned the meal card, and bought a trunk full of Clemson apparel. We located the buildings where her classes would be and strolled around town.

Before we knew it, classes were starting the next day, and it was time for Cathy and me to go. *Go??? Without my little girl??* At that moment, I had to face the inevitable, and it hit me hard. Life had brought us to a fork in the road. For the first time since the day she was born, our very next steps were going to be in different directions. Jeannie was taking the first step on her own journey. Our journeys would always be intertwined and inseparable, but it was no longer just one journey for two. *Keep it together, Belle, don't lose it yet.*

Jean kept trying to stall our departure, as did we, but eventually, it had to happen. Cathy was driving, and I turned around to see my daughter standing on the curb, crying, waving, and all alone. Another image forever seared in my mind.

I cried so hard from Clemson to Richmond, Virginia, that we couldn't even stop to eat. I was that much of a mess. Cathy and I spent the night in Richmond, and by the next day, I had somewhat calmed down. I reminded myself of what a fantastic opportunity this was for Jean; that this was what she and I worked so hard to achieve for her. I needed to pull it together and be strong. It was going to be a tough year of changes and firsts for Jeannie, and she would need me.

It was still the days before cellphones, so the minute I got home, I put a smile in my voice and called her. She was down and overwhelmed but sounded better after a pep talk, and we chatted. I hung up and cried, again. *Is making her stay the right decision? The best thing for her? I think it is but hearing her so upset... I don't know.* I was still lost in the wilderness.

By Parents' Weekend in October, Jeannie had met three girls (still her closest friends today) and didn't seem so overwhelmed. Come Thanksgiving break, Jean was confident and spoke with a slight southern twang. She had also blatantly defied me for the first time, which I secretly loved. *She's coming into her own.*

Jeannie's hair had been long and poker-straight until puberty when it became extremely curly. I loved it; she hated it. Jean always wanted to cut it short but I said no, it would be too hard to control. She also wanted a bellybutton ring that I firmly vetoed. When she came home that November, Jean's hair was cut short, and a ring was in her red and swollen navel. I was wrong about her hair; it looked great. I loved it; she hated it. I was right about the navel piercing. By the end of break it was oozing green pus, and she was at the doctor's office. I tried very hard, unsuccessfully, not to say I told you so.

By the end of Christmas break, she couldn't wait to get back to Clemson, and I no longer cried all the way home from the airport. We had both survived our first steps, and I no longer felt lost in the wilderness. I had instinctively stumbled across the right parenting path after all.

Early in her sophomore year, Jean broke up with high school Bill to date Wes, whom she had met at Clemson. I was happy to see her start dating other guys. I liked Bill but wanted her to enjoy college and date other people while she was there. I had been unable to explore the dating world when I was young, and I was happy to see her taking advantage of the opportunity. I could tell Jeannie was quite taken with Wes and couldn't wait to meet her new guy on Parents' Weekend.

Wes was born and raised about forty-five minutes from Clemson. He was full of southern charm, good looks, charisma, and lots of bullshit. Jean's new beau was outgoing, gregarious, fun, and had a great sense of humor. He was also a sophomore for the third year running, due to the fact his major was Frat Brother 101. Wes loved sports, beer pong, betting, partying, and, apparently, my daughter. *She's just testing different waters, which is what you wanted. It won't be long before she sees through him and moves along.* Once again, I was wrong.

I could see a change in Jean that weekend. She had fully embraced college life, had many friends, talked about parties and football games, and showed me her fake ID. For the first time, I saw a red solo cup in my daughter's hand and noted how comfortable she was with her new appendage. No matter. Her grades were good, and I was glad to see her so happy and gaining confidence. Looking back, I think a little part of me was living vicariously through her. I had been married for two years and was pregnant by her age—such a different life.

Jean's junior year brought about the usual college changes. She rented an apartment off-campus with friends and brought her car to school. I rode down with her, helped get the girls settled into their new digs, and headed for the airport, leaving four excited roomies behind. What fun for her! What a feeling for me to be able to give this to her. Jeannie also switched her major to Biology, which I saw coming. She had gone from a good to an average student, and pre-med was about to get pretty intense. *Well, you wanted her to have the complete college experience.*

One change that didn't come about was Wes. He was still in the picture, and I suspected the reason for Jean's drop to average grades. I had failed to add Jean's inexperience with boys and her giving heart into the Wes equation. Jeannie had made it her mission to save him, much like I had made Steven mine. She was going to get him on track, help him study, and make sure he graduated. I also grossly underestimated his ability as a conman and the strong pull of first love. It sounds as though I didn't like Wes, but actually, I did. I just hated him with my daughter. But I knew from my own experience that the surest way to further enamor her to him was to voice my disapproval. I had to tread lightly or repeat the mistakes my father had made with Steven and me.

The semester progressed uneventfully until Christmas break. As you know, once a student turns eighteen, all correspondence from college is addressed to them, not the best plan if you ask me, but no one ever has. Jean's grades arrived in the mail, and to respect her privacy (something I've been obsessive about ever since Mom and my diary), I handed her the envelope unopened. I gave her time to look them over, then went to see how she had made out. I found her crying in the TV room. Jean was on academic probation. *WHAAAT??!!!* I. Lost. It. There was no letting my crazy out anywhere but directly at her. The situation called for monumental Meanie Mommy action.

"ACADEMIC PROBATION?! YOU?! How did you get from a 3.9 to academic probation?" A rhetorical question since I already knew the answer.

She took time out from crying and repeating I'm sorry over and over again to unwittingly throw gasoline on my fire. "I don't know," she said.

"Don't lie to me, Jean, you're not a stupid girl. You know exactly how it happened. You better get your priorities back in order!" I was livid.

"I'm sorry, Mom! I will, I swear! I can't believe I did this!"

"Neither can I, Jean," I sighed. *Nor can I believe I let it happen.*

I told her to find a college close to home that offered the classes she needed to repeat and enroll for the summer semester. Depending on her grades next semester, and if she passed the summer classes, maybe I'd let her go back to Clemson for her senior year. Maybe. I walked out of the room and gave myself a 4.0 for having never actually said the name Wes. I was terrified to realize he had this kind of pull on her, but I was determined not to blink. I knew from my past it would end badly if I did.

Jean brought her grades up, passed the summer courses, and was off to Clemson for her senior year. The year flew by, and before I knew it, it was time for graduation. I was a hot mess, experiencing so many different emotions all at once. They formed a ball and bounced around inside me like a pinball in a machine. Pride, excitement, anticipation, love, relief, hope, fear, worry, sadness (what if she got a job far away?). Mostly though, it was pride and love.

Mom, Cathy, and I flew down the day before graduation, checked into our motel, and hurried over to Jeannie's apartment. I couldn't wait to see her and hug her to pieces. As we had our reunion and said hi to all the roomies, this adorable puppy came bounding out of the other room. She was all kisses, wiggles, and wags as she leaped onto her mom's lap. Jean's lap. *A dog?! With no idea what her immediate future will bring, she took on the responsibility of a dog?*

About that time, I noticed nothing was packed. I suggested we load up her car and box the rest of the stuff to ship home. That's when Jean informed me the car wouldn't make the trip. It hadn't been running right all year, and a mechanic told her it wasn't worth the money to repair. *I've heard that happens when you never change the oil.*

And then, drumroll, please, someone came in and commented on how Jeannie must be so relieved. That is how I discovered my daughter didn't know until that morning if she had enough credits to graduate due to a potential incomplete. *Who ARE you, and what have you done with Jeannie?* That was it. I suggested (strongly) she and I start packing up her clothes.

Once in her room, I tried to remain as calm as possible, which barely resembled calm. I told her she was more responsible and mature at the end of high school than she was now.

"You've always taken care of your car, have always taken pride in your grades," I said. "Getting a dog without telling me when you're about to move home? Letting us fly down for graduation, knowing it might not happen? It's all unacceptable," I said.

I went on to tell her I found her behavior sneaky and dishonest and not anything like the responsible, considerate girl I knew her to be would act. I was hard on her, maybe too hard, but I was disappointed and hurt. And those two feelings were completely foreign to me where she was concerned. In true Jeannie fashion, she said nothing, but for the first time in her life, I was afraid she hadn't heard me, much less listened.

Jean had been easy to parent in high school, so I was woefully unprepared for college. I hadn't had any college parenting prep courses. I was just as upset with myself for dropping the ball as I was with Jean for her behavior. What kind of a nitwit sends a kid off to college, on their own, and expects them to make all the right decisions and choices? Me. My answer was me. The way I saw it, we had both let each other down.

Despite everything, graduation day was phenomenal. When I saw Jeannie walk across that stage, all disappointment and hurt dissolved into glitter and fairy dust. I was crying, cheering, and hugging everyone around me, even strangers. Jean positively glowed with pride and happiness. I have a picture of her striding toward us in the parking lot after the ceremony, radiant, confident, and full of promise. That picture still sits on my bureau.

Yeah, you've got this little girl.

We rented a van, loaded up Jean's things, including my new grand-dog, and waved goodbye to Clemson. It was time to bring my daughter back to the real world to start the next leg of her journey.

Together, we had fulfilled the last of the promises I made to both of us all those years ago. We did it by following our North Star.

A SEEDLING BLOSSOMS

ONCE JEAN GOT HOME, SHE STARTED TO REGAIN HER FOOT-
ing on solid ground. She reconnected with high school
friends and proceeded to enjoy the summer. Wes? He didn't disappear instantly, but I could see the spark in my daughter's eyes
fading and was happy to see distance was working its magic.
Jeannie took the summer off to regroup and relax before starting
the job process, but come August, it would be time for reality.

Well, come August, Jeannie had another plan. She was going
back to Clemson to take the courses she needed to be a teacher.
Since Jean had never expressed any interest in teaching, a bell went
off in my head (pun intended). Or maybe she'd go back to get her
Master's in biology; instead, she wasn't sure. *Not sure? That sounds
like a non-plan to me.* My question of how she was going to support herself and pay tuition put a quick end to the Clemson plan.

I mean, I got it—she was about to leap into the abyss of
adulthood, and I couldn't blame her for trying to put it off. I
understood her apprehension about such a huge change, but it
was time for it to happen. I went into my best Mary Poppins
impression and told her she was going to do great! She would
land a fantastic job she loved, and adulting wasn't as daunting
as it seemed (I lied). Life was waiting for her!

"So, write that resume, hone your interviewing skills, and
let's get to it!" I refrained from adding spit spot, but it would've
been a fun add-on. Jean was not amused but got on board.

She got a job in medical research in Boston, fifty-five miles from Seekonk. It's a long commute during rush hour, and she soon decided to move to the city. Erin, a girl she knew from high school field hockey, shared a Boston apartment with her brother, Jeff, and Jean made arrangements to move in with them. The only problem was she couldn't take Sahara, her dog. Jeannie asked if the dog could stay with me until she found a pet-friendly place at the end of their current lease. I told her no. For those of you that aren't dog lovers, you might not grasp the angst of this decision. Those of you who are, understand the pain and heartache this caused me, and more so for my daughter.

Sahara had been through a lot, and I could tell it had affected her. In her first year, she moved away from her roomies and Wes into a house with a very bossy beagle (my dog) and strangers. Now her mom would be disappearing. Sahara was a great dog but shy, and I felt depressed. Jeannie leaving her would have broken her heart. Jeannie had taken on the responsibility of a pet in an uncertain time of her life. Now she needed to handle the consequences of that decision on her own. Another time my having her back looked like desertion to her at first, I'm sure.

Jean's solution was to drive Sahara down south to stay with Wes until she could take her to live in Boston. Months later, when the time came to bring Sahara back north, Wes refused to give the dog up. Not to be deterred, Jean jumped in her car and drove seventeen hours to collect her fur baby. When she showed up at Wes's house, late at night and unannounced, his answer was the same; no.

It was a time before cellphones, so Jeannie drove to a payphone and called me. My daughter was beside herself and didn't know what to do. The one thing set in stone? She was not leaving without her dog. I listen to her alternate between crying and yelling, and when she ran out of emotion, she came up with a plan (she is her mother's daughter). In the morning, she would go back to Wes's house and appeal to his family for help. She slept in her car in front of their place for a couple of hours, then rang the doorbell. Things did not turn out the way she hoped. After Sahara's initial greeting, it was apparent to Jeannie she had become Wes's dog. She sat by his feet, went to him to be petted, and brought her ball to him to play. The final blow was when Jean and Wes stood at opposite ends of the yard, called to Sahara, and the dog went running to Wes. Jeannie was devastated but knew the right thing to do and said goodbye to her fur baby.

I'm sure if you asked her today, Jean would tell you it's still one of the biggest heartbreaks of her life. She drove back to the payphone and called me hysterically crying. As my daughter told me the story, I could hear the break in her heart become a chasm. As hard as it was for her, she had made the right choice for Sahara. My heart was breaking and swelling with pride for her all at the same time. Jeannie had put Sahara's wellbeing before herself and, in doing so, showed her true character. It was a hard lesson learned but learn it she did, and I knew it was the last lesson I would have to initiate. With Jean making that selfless decision, my seedling was growing strong. Strong and towards the sun.

BACK IN BOSTON, ALL PARENTAL HANDS WERE CALLED UPON TO help the roommates move yearly. The apartments went from three bedrooms to two, which is when I figured out she was now living with Jeff and his sister, not Erin and her brother. And the final move was to a one-bedroom place with only two roommates. Jean and Jeff have been together ever since, twenty years and counting.

While still in their twenties, Jean and Jeff bought a loft in Roxbury, a section of Boston not known for its safety. They assured me urban renewal was only a year or two away. *God, I hope so.* On my first visit, I had to move the empty whiskey bottles, plural, to park my car. Thankfully I could leave the dirty underwear untouched in the parking space since it wouldn't pop my tires. On another visit, Jean had to out curse a coked-out prostitute to get her away from the building's door so that we could enter. Urban renewal could not happen fast enough for me.

The loft itself was beautiful and had a great view of Boston, a young citified couple's dream. Jean, being Jean, when things weren't happening in the common areas of the building as promised, she joined the association. When she wanted to plant some veggies and saw the community garden was in complete disrepair, she became president, took charge, and turned things around. Jeannie was quick to embrace the concept, "Be the change you want to see happen." As her mom, the change I most wanted to see happen was a change of address—thought but never vocalized. They eventually bought a house in South Boston, but not until years later. Better late than never! *Whew! They're safe now.*

I mentioned earlier how I love the twists and turns life takes at times, but here I will add, not always. There was a twisty turn during this time I most certainly did not appreciate. "The Return of The Sperm Donor." A sequel no one wanted to see, least of all me. *Why now, when she is coming into her own?* I hadn't seen Steven since that fateful day when Jean was eight, but she had seen him on rare occasions at his sister Sharon's house.

A little background: Sharon, Steven's older sister, was the only one in his family who consistently stayed in Jeannie's life. Without her and her husband Mike, Jean wouldn't have had contact with, or knowledge of, that side of her family. Sharon and Mike included Jeannie in holiday celebrations, family events, and made sure she had a relationship with their children, Jean's cousins. Because of them, my daughter at least got to meet her half-brother (from Steven's second marriage), paternal grandparents, and her father's other siblings. Whether that's a good or a bad thing, you'll have to ask Jean. But I have always appreciated Sharon, Mike, and their children for including Jean in their life.

Steven claimed he had found Jesus, seen the error of his ways, and wanted to have a relationship with Jeannie. My thoughts are, Jean, being a smart girl, wasn't buying it, but the little girl in her needed to meet with him. So, she and Jeff met Steven and his... live-in girlfriend? Third wife? (I'm not sure which title was hers) at a restaurant. Jeannie never said much about the meeting, but I got the distinct impression Jesus didn't join them for dinner.

To make matters worse, the woman rambled on about how attentive Steven was to her son and had even helped put him through college. Jean was livid. When the Donor called a few days later and said he wanted to meet with her alone to get to know her better, she refused. She reminded him he'd had her entire life to get to know her and hadn't bothered. Jean decided to walk away, and I hope it gave her some sense of closure.

I later heard, through the grapevine, it wasn't Jesus Steven had found, but a new line of work. He'd stolen money from all members of his family, including his son from his second marriage. If he intended to make Jean his next mark, he had grossly underestimated her. She had his number—that and a calloused heart towards him that was earned and well deserved.

Steven was found dead, a couple of years later, at a house in Florida. I can't remember if it was the home he shared with the woman or her son's house, but the circumstances were shady. There was no autopsy, so the cause of death is unknown. They assumed it was either an overdose or a heart attack. He was fifty years old. Rumor has it, the woman and some members of Steven's family couldn't agree on the arrangements or who was paying for it, so they ended up doing little to nothing. A tragic but fitting ending to a sad and wasted life.

They say when you hold on to anger and resentment, you hurt only yourself. I usually agree, but not in this case. I had let go of the things that happened between Steven and me years ago. We were both so young, children really, and I did know who he was when I married him. No, it's not the anger and resentment for me that I hold against him; it's for my daughter. His abandonment of Jean, such a beautiful gift, is inexcusable and unforgivable.

I hope I managed through the years to make her understand it was nothing she did or didn't do that caused his behavior towards her. He was an addict, and addicts care only about themselves until if and when they get clean, which Steven never wanted to accomplish. They lie, cheat, and steal, and it's never their fault. They blame everyone and everything but themselves for their bad behavior; it is what addicts do.

I pray she has managed to heal as much as one can from such a thing. And I want her to know I will always carry a cold stone in my heart for him; it is, after all, what mothers do.

THE SUNFLOWER

EANNIE WORKED IN MEDICAL RESEARCH, FIRST IN ACADEMIA
and then pharmaceuticals, but after five or so years, she knew
it wasn't what she wanted to do for the rest of her life. It was
time for a career change, and Jean knew just what she wanted to
do: architecture. She enrolled at the Boston Architectural College and began a long, grueling journey.

Around the time Jeannie started school, the drug company
she worked for began renovations on their labs. Jeannie became
the liaison between the architectural firm and her company.
During a conversation with the lead architect, she mentioned she
was going to school for architecture, and he shared the firm was
looking for someone with Jean's knowledge of labs. Impressed
with her work ethic, they offered her a paid internship, and the
rest, as they say, is history.

For almost ten stressed and crazy years, Jeannie learned a
new profession on the job and through a heavy course load at
college. There was a constant stream of information poured into
her brain that immediately needed processing because more was
on the way. For years Jeannie functioned with no weekends and
little sleep. What she did have was Jeff's full support, and determination to spare. Oh, and a very enthusiastic cheerleader: me.

You've got this little girl!

It was during this time I learned my daughter relaxes by doing;
there is no such thing as too much on her plate. When school

159

and work would get overwhelming, she'd design and sew baby clothes and make Moses baskets to sell online. Another time, Jean relaxed by crocheting numerous caps for newborn babies in Boston hospitals and making pillowcases out of fun material for the children's hospital. *Do you know what else is relaxing, Jeannie? Sleeping, you need to sleep!*

I honestly do not know how she managed it, but she made it all work and realized her goal. In 2011, Jeannie graduated with her master's degree in architecture.

I was bursting with pride as I watched Jean present her thesis at the Boston Architectural College. Proud not only for her accomplishment but also for what she had chosen as her project. A project near and dear to my heart as you will later learn.

Jean had designed a cancer center that paired traditional treatments with alternative healing therapies. Everything was geared towards the patient's peace of mind and comfort while receiving treatment. There were walls of floor to ceiling windows overlooking the bay to capitalize on the calming effect of a water view. Plants, couches, and waterfalls were strategically placed throughout the center so patients could rest or meditate comfortably. It was a fully functioning hospital with the tranquil feel of a spa. Patients could get Reiki during chemo treatments, a massage to relieve anxiety, or acupuncture for pain. It had warm and inviting counseling rooms for group therapy or private sessions. A café provided nutritionists' advice and healthy food choices. The center courtyard with trees and flower and vegetable gardens gave patients and their visitors a safe space to enjoy the fresh air and do some gardening. The facility was also a green building, environmentally responsible and resource-efficient including the site, design, construction, as well as operation and maintenance.

Jeannie's thesis not only showcased her talent as an architect but also her progressive thinking, open-mindedness, empathy, and environmental consciousness.

Way to go, little girl—you nailed it!

2011 was also the year she and Jeff decided to get married. They love New York City, so no one thought twice about them taking off for the Big Apple the summer Jean finished school. Little did we know, they eloped to get married the Jean and Jeff way. At midnight, the two of them stood on the Brooklyn Bridge, and with all of NYC swirling around them, privately shared the words they had chosen to seal their bond. They came home, man and wife, both in their eyes and the eyes of those of us who love and understand them. In the eyes of the law, however, not so much. They planned a small intimate ceremony in Jeff's Nana's backyard, to make it legal and to celebrate with their immediate families.

Jean, being Jean, decided to design and make her dress two weeks before the wedding date, even though she was studying for her boards and working crazy hours. My daughter called me the afternoon before the ceremony, sounding cool as a cucumber. Could I come to Boston after work? She needed me to pin the final alterations for the dress on her because she couldn't get the right fit on the dress form. *Oh my God—it's not done yet?!* I told her I would be there ASAP, but thanks to Friday rush hour traffic, it was close to seven thirty before I arrived. "No worries," was her greeting, and she was right. Within a couple of hours, the dress fit perfectly. *Whew, we made it.* Ah, not quite. Jean brought out a few yards of material and shared some of her creative visions for a sash. *Clearly, I'm the only one nervous about the deadline.* After a few different variations and a couple of more hours, we had the sash she wanted. *Success! The wedding ensemble is finis.*

"Oh, Jeannie, it's stunning and perfect for you!" I said with a hug.

"We have more to do, Mommio; we need to design my headpiece." *Surely she jests!*

In a flash, I was looking at a cap and all kinds of embellishments while Jean ran different ideas by me. With a glue gun and some more time, we had a beautiful bird's nest headpiece. This time I didn't dare say anything about being done for fear we'd be designing shoes. Which, by the way, she had already done. Work from the ground up as they say.

I left Boston sometime between 1:00 and 2:00 a.m., exhausted and exhilarated at the same time. I was oh so happy to have spent Jean's wedding eve with her, helping with such momentous projects and basking in our bond. I knew a memory, as warm as fresh baked cookies, had been made that evening, and I smiled all the way home.

That night, I came to understand how Jeannie had gotten through the last ten years. She works, thinks, and creates best under pressure. She remains calm and collected while shoveling twenty pounds of manure into a ten-pound sack with only seconds to spare. Pressure makes diamonds, as the saying goes. She's also relentless when she sets her mind on a goal and isn't afraid of the hard work it takes to achieve it. Jeannie will do whatever it takes to get it done, and heaven helps anyone who gets in her way. She lives as she has learned.

I'm sure both of these traits are part of why she is so successful in her career. Jean is now part-owner of a young Boston firm that has far surpassed their expectations and business projections. She has an excellent reputation in her field of expertise and had an article written about her in the *Boston Business Journal*.

As proud as I am of her professional accomplishments, it is the person she is, her core's essence, that I celebrate most. Jeannie is all things kind, and her aura is one of love. Her creative vision is a wonder to me and evident in all that she does. Be it baking, sewing, knitting, crocheting, quilting, or planting flower pots her unique touch shines through. She designs everything in her head, her way, and then brings it to life, just as I did through my choreography and dance, and now my writing. Patterns, instructions, and recipes are made to be altered if followed at all. Much like I've lived my life.

I want to think the need and nerve to color outside the lines come from me, but she gets the rest from previous generations.

The love for knitting and crocheting comes from my grandma, the love of baking and sewing from my mom. It is all lost on me, although all three ladies tried their best through the years to get me on board. I have all the patience in the world for children, the elderly, and animals, but dropped stitches, crooked seams, and burnt cookies send me over the edge. Did you know you can scrape the bottoms off burnt cookies with a lemon zester and serve them? Sadly, I do.

I smile when people tell me I don't take enough credit for the great job I did raising Jean. "Look at her," they'll say, "she is who she is because of you." I disagree; she is who she is because of her. She was born to uneducated teenage parents, one who was an addict and both with less than stellar gene pools. Somehow, she managed to capitalize on the genes worthwhile and learned to hold the rest at bay.

I'll take credit for getting us out of the cesspool she was born into and surrounding her with loving people. Credit for giving her the most stable life I could and loving her with every fiber of my being, even when I was screwing up. But I did not make her who she is; she did.

I provided her with the tools to build her character, but she picked up the hammer and nails. I taught her life lessons, but she chose to learn them. I pointed her down the right path, but she took the steps and followed it. I showed her to believe in herself and to fight for what she wants, but she picked up the boxing gloves and entered the ring: her choices, her decisions, her pat on the back.

I continue to give Jeannie unconditional love and she returns it. My daughter stands tall and strong; she is beautiful and resilient, like a sunflower. She is, always, My Saving Grace.

PART IV

LOVE'S ILLUSIONS

What follows is the start of my years with Bobby. A narrative told in my voice, both as a healthy ego and as a broken shell. A relationship seen with my eyes blinded by love and my eyes wide open. A love felt by my heart both when it was whole and when broken. It's our life together as it happened for me, as I remember it.

As Dickens so eloquently wrote, "It was the best of times, it was the worst of times."

A RINGING IN MY EARS

ONE DAY, IN THE SPRING OF 1987, I WAS AT MY FRIEND HOL-ly's house having a cup of tea and some laughs when her husband Michael came home from playing softball. On his way upstairs to shower, he lamented how it was a shame Holly hadn't been to one of his games in years. Taking the not so subtle hint, Holly said she should go to one but didn't want to alone. She asked me to go with her. *Ummm...no.*

"Why would I want to watch a bunch of middle-aged men in polyester shorts run around a field and sweat?" I asked her.

"Oh, come on, it'll be fun, and we can get a bite to eat after the game," she bribed. Sold—I love to eat.

Off we went to Mike's next game while visions of burgers danced in my head. The game was underway when we got there, and Mike's team had taken the field. As I surveyed the sights, feigning interest, my eyes landed on the pitcher, and it was an instant attraction. *Belle—look again. He's not your usual type.* The second look confirmed it. Even sweating and wearing those ugly shorts, his Y chromosome was speaking to my XX.

When the team came off the field, Mike jokingly asked if anyone had caught my eye. I surprised him with, "Yep. The pitcher, Number Five." *Please don't tell me he's married.*

"DeCosta?" Mike asked with raised eyebrows (he knew my type).

"Yes, I want that one," I quipped. Bobby told me months later that he was standing on the mound, hoping I wasn't Mike's wife because, and I quote, "I was gonna be his next one." Bobby's idea of sweet talk, and it made me laugh.

My new favorite pastime quickly became going to Mike's softball games, and Holly and I had a perfect attendance record for the rest of the season. Despite my best efforts at flirting, it was still over a month before Bobby called and asked me out to dinner.

When he picked me up that night, it took all I had to maintain my veneer of cool calm and collected. I was excited about our date, and seeing him in something other than softball attire was a bonus. His ensemble was nothing fancy; a buttoned-down shirt, navy blazer, a pair of Nantucket looking pants, and Topsiders with no socks. He wore the look well—very well. We went to an elegant restaurant, had a great meal and an even better time. On the way home, I had my bare feet up on the dash, with my heart singing the song, "Love Is In The Air," when he said he had something he needed to tell me. *Uh oh.*

He was living with someone. *Of. Course. You. Are.* And he wasn't quite ready to end it. *Of. Course. You're. Not.*

"Well, you're about to miss out on the best thing that's ever happened to you," I told him. *Wow—did I just say that?!* I thanked him for a lovely evening and his honesty, kissed him on the cheek, and went into the house, screamed into my pillow, and I cried myself to sleep. *Well, so much for that.*

I was surprised when Bobby called the next day and asked if I was going to the game. I told him no, I had heard him loud and clear the night before. If and when he was ever ready to leave his situation, he could give me a call. My statement met with silence… then more silence. "I told you last night; it is over. She and I have been talking about it for a while but haven't pulled the trigger yet. She'll be out by the end of the summer," he said. That's not what he said the night before, but I liked what I was hearing now better, so I went with it.

By the end of summer, Bobby was living alone, and we were an item. Utterly besotted with the man, I thought he was the funniest, classiest, sexiest guy around—and so did he for that matter. That was okay with me; I was comfortable in my skin and found his swagger somewhat attractive at the time.

When I met his large family and two children from his first marriage, we all hit it off right away, so no glitches there. There were, however, some glitches elsewhere. Warning bells sounded in those early years, announcing certain behaviors, but being a confident lady, I mostly turned a deaf ear. I had everything under control.

One evening, entering a restaurant, Bobby caught two guys looking my way and commented, "When the old queen walked into a room, heads turned." *Wow, what a strange thing to say.*

"You mean like theirs just did?" I replied with a wink. DING: counterattack a compliment.

Once he showed up three hours late for a date with a couple of beers under his belt and no phone call. "Give me a hard time, and I'll leave," was his greeting. "Bye-bye" was my send-off. DING: never apologize.

Bobby sometimes crossed a line with things he said to me, or about me, for a laugh, but I usually had a comeback. DING: a lack of boundaries.

During that first summer, he asked me to go to Martha's Vineyard for the day, and the date he chose was Jeannie's actual birthday. When I asked him to pick another day, he said no, that's the date he had planned. DING: no compromising.

I owe my daughter a huge apology. I went. I knew it was wrong, and I still went. I tried to justify it to myself by saying Jean's party wasn't until the weekend, but it didn't work. I have never forgiven myself and never will. It was unacceptable, selfish, and unforgivable, and I have no one to blame but myself. Jeannie never said a word, but I know it must have hurt her. It was not one of my shiniest moments as a parent. *I'm so sorry little girl.*

Bobby also had a softer side. He made me breakfast in bed and romantic dinners when I could spend the night. We'd watch football games and movies in front of a fire with wine and popcorn. *It's all good; we're just getting used to each other. It will settle in just fine.*

The last time I remember feeling completely secure in myself with Bobby was the summer after we met. We rented a house on Cape Cod with another couple and one of Bobby's single friends. For the first few days it was just the couples, and I was having a great time. Then his buddy arrived, and I became the fifth wheel. I'd get up in the morning, and the two of them would be out to breakfast. After getting our stuff together for the beach, I'd go downstairs to learn they had already left. I'd get out of the shower after the beach to discover they had gone for a beer. Bobby wouldn't tell me he was going, but would just leave. DING: here's your place.

When I said something about it to Bobby privately, he got right up in my space and followed me around the bedroom. It went something like this: "Am I spending enough time with you now? Is this close enough, or do I need to put my nose up your butt? Do I need to tell you when I go to the bathroom?" Ding: bullying tactics.

I was so hurt and angry over his recent behavior the underlying aggression played out in that little scene didn't register right away. The obvious belittling of me did, however, and I'd had enough. The other couple was leaving for home that afternoon and said yes to my request for a ride. Bobby came into the room, found me packing, and walked out. We never said a word to one another. DING: zero communication.

On the way home, the three of us stopped to have a final vacation cocktail, and the bartender, Karl, and I hit it off. He was a school principal in a town north of Boston and had tended bar at the Cape for summers since college. When he asked for my number as we were leaving, I didn't hesitate to give it to him.

I admit I was surprised when he called. Karl was a good looking bartender in a resort town and probably had stacks of phone numbered cocktail napkins. We talked for an hour or so then picked a restaurant halfway between us to meet for dinner later that week.

He was easy to be with, intelligent, soft-spoken, respectful, interesting to talk to, and interested in what I had to say. It was a nice time with a nice guy, and ended with a nice kiss. It was all so nice. A few more weeks of long phone conversations and dinners, and it was still just nice. *Belle, give it a chance; he's an excellent kisser and you love to kiss. I know, I know, it's a nice kiss.*

I knew Karl played tennis and was a fan, so I suggested an afternoon at the Tennis Hall of Fame in Newport for our next date. Jeannie was a ball girl for the ongoing tournament, and I knew I could get tickets. We made plans for that weekend.

After we hung up, I went to the studio to start preparing for my September classes. The Cape couple stopped in when they saw my car, and we talked for a bit. They asked if the bartender ever called and were surprised when I said we were dating.

They were gone less than an hour when the studio phone rang, and it was Bobby; they must've given him a heads up. He missed me. I missed him too, plain and simple. That was the end of Karl, and the day I sealed my fate with Bobby.

Whenever I tried to clear the air about what happened at the Cape, Bobby would ignore me or change the subject. Finally, he told me to leave him alone, it was over and done, and I needed to let it go. Then he didn't call me for a week. DING: withholding attention when challenged.

One night, Bobby and I were at dinner, and I started filling him in on my past. How and why I had gotten married at sixteen and quit school. About having Jeannie at nineteen and leaving Steven because of drugs, blah, blah, blah, when he stopped me.

"I wouldn't tell too many people that, Honey—it doesn't put you in a very good light." DING: I also heard an unspoken message, "Don't embarrass me. Be ashamed of who you are." *Maybe I should be less proud of everything I've overcome and more concerned about how it looks.* That's how and when Belle started morphing into Bobby-Belle. A version of me I felt would fit his idea of acceptable. A learned behavior from all my years of new schools.

When I flew to Virginia to meet him for a corporate party, I landed in a small remote airport. At 7:00 p.m., my plane was the last one in, and they started to close the airport. I was getting nervous and contemplated getting a cab but couldn't because a) there wasn't one, and b) I was in the boondocks and had no idea where I was going. Bobby showed up well over an hour late. He had been at happy hour and lost track of time. DING: where I placed on his list of priorities.

There were also plenty of positives during this time, including a whirlwind of trips, bonding with his family, and enjoying my newfound friends. I've always said some of Bobby's best assets are his family and friends.

Holidays with his family were noisy, delightful events! Thanksgiving at his brother's house was right out of a Norman Rockwell painting, albeit one that included a lot of football and beer. Christmas at his mom and dad's house was a sea of wrapping paper, kids of all ages, and a buffet of his mom's signature dishes. There would three different childhood memories being told all at once and laughter to spare.

The yearly Fourth of July Cape vacation became a couples/family tradition. A few of us would rent a big house for the week, and other friends would come and go. Some had a place of their own and would come to the Cape the same week. Those vacations were intimate times of friendship and bonding. At any given time, there would be twelve to fourteen of us taking over the beach or sitting around the dinner table. When we went into Chatham shopping, it was like a school bus of rambunctious kids were dropped off on a field trip. We could be a loud, boisterous group when enjoying our friendship, and we made no apologies for it. It was a good time had by all.

No relationship is perfect, Belle; you've got to take the good with the bad. There's a lot of good here, and you have a handle on the bad. Just relax. Silly me.

SEASONS CHANGE

———

IN THE WINTER OF 1993, I ASKED BOBBY IF WE COULD TALK. Jeannie was a junior in high school and would be leaving for college in less than two years. We had been dating for almost five years, and I needed to know where the relationship was going. *God, I hate that line.* There are many changes in the first year of college, and I didn't want to add coming home to a house where she'd never lived into the mix. To my complete and utter surprise, Bobby said, "Let's do it." He agreed with the points I'd made about Jean and also felt he was ready. *Wow, that was, well, it was...easy? Scary?* Both.

We started looking for a house but couldn't find anything we both liked. The realtor suggested one particular house, insisting it had everything we both wanted, and she was right. I instantly loved all the light, openness, and different levels. Bobby took one look at the built-in pool and hot tub out back and gave it a thumbs up.

I was beyond happy when our offer was accepted! Until the realtor looked at Bobby and said something to the effect of, "I was glad to hear you were house hunting with someone this time. I knew the two incomes would qualify you for the type of house you wanted to purchase last summer." *What?!* When we got in the car, I quietly asked why he never mentioned he was house hunting last summer. With a cocky shrug, Bobby said it was no big deal. He was sick of living in a small apartment and wanted to see if he could find something.

"Looking for a house is no big deal, Bobby, but keeping it from someone you've been dating for five years is," I said.

"It didn't concern you, Belle," was his response.

No? Because here we are a few months later buying a place together. A house more suited to your taste than those you qualified for on your own. I can't say if my fear was on target, but it certainly looked that way to me; it definitely hurt that way.

In July 1993, despite that nagging thought in my head, we moved into 75 Ferncliffe Road, Seekonk, Massachusetts. *I'm probably just being too sensitive.*

I was over the moon with Jean, Bobby, and I being in our own home! We had pool parties, friends over for dinner, and quiet nights in front of the fire. When it would snow, Charlie, Judy, and Lyndsey would come over for a cookout—burgers on the grill and a soak in the outdoor jacuzzi. Jeannie and her friends were always in and out, watching movies in the family room or enjoying the backyard. I reveled in living the typical suburban life as well as being a couple.

Bobby and I started our tradition of an open house on the Sunday before Christmas. Mom and I cooked for a week preparing for the army of friends and family that would come; people from all walks of our lives, past and present. It was one of my favorite days of the year. Our home was full of the people who mattered most to us, enjoying themselves and each other. Santa always stopped by and sat each child down on his lap for a final check on their lists.

Christmas Eve moved from Mom's house to ours. Sadly, we had lost my grandfather by then, and my aunts, due to age, stopped making the winter drive from upstate New York. But the rest of the crew was still intact. I did my best, but it was never the same as it was at Mom's. We needed that house, wallpapered in our memories, and carpeted in love, and dog hair, to truly feel the magic of our special Eves. We were still family and loved our time together, but I never managed to recreate the Eves of yesteryears.

Before we knew it, it was Jeannie's last year of high school. Her senior year was bittersweet, as well as hectic. One day she would be eagerly awaiting the change college would bring, and the next day she'd be clinging tight to the familiarity of home and her friends. Added to the emotional rollercoaster she was on (and therefore me), there was the process of visiting, choosing, and applying to colleges. Bobby's being there made it easier for me to maneuver things both physically and mentally. It was such a comfort to have him there when after prom was at our house. I was worried about the probability of alcohol and the kids in the pool and hot tub all night. And it was nice to have an extra set of ears at the education planner appointments in case I missed something. *We're a team, a couple.*

Bobby also arranged his business trips so he could meet Jean and me at Ithaca and Clemson to tour the campuses with us. He was supportive, respectful of Jean's and my decisions and relationship, and gave his opinion only when asked (the latter being unheard of for him, which made me appreciate it all the more).

As you know, Cathy and I moved Jean to Clemson for her freshman year, as it should have been. But come sophomore year, Bobby was at Clemson building loft beds, lugging carpets, and moving furniture. He was just as excited as I was about parents' weekends and always made sure Jeannie could fly home for Thanksgiving and Christmas. *I love sharing all of this with him!*

All good and wonderful things, but...

One afternoon that first winter, Bobby and I spent a cold, rainy day watching movies and (Wink). We had just finished Winking when a buddy called, wanting to grab a couple of beers. I was disappointed when I heard Bobby say sure, but decided to be a sport. I asked where we were going and was told, "He asked me, he didn't say anything about you going." *Ouch— there had to be a kinder way to say that.* When Bobby saw my eyes start to well up, he added, "I spent all afternoon with you, what more do you want?" *To not feel like a pastime until something else comes along. To not feel like you should be leaving money on the bureau.*

When the lease was up on Bobby's company car, a Sable, he negotiated a company stipend instead of a new car to upgrade his ride. I came home from the studio one night, and he told me he was trading my Cougar in the next day and buying out the lease on the Sable for me. I waited for a laugh that never came. *Dear Lord, he's not kidding.* I think my head spun completely around. Not only was this the first he told me of his cockamamie plan, but he had already made the decision. I said I didn't like the Sable and pointed out the Cougar was in my name and not his to trade. I got the silent treatment for the next few days for not cooperating. *Am I being ungrateful and selfish?*

I remember when a friend of his told me I had nice legs, and Bobby countered with, "Please, I can barely get her head through the door now." *Oh no, do I come off as arrogant and conceited?*

And when we were at a business function, and someone commented on my sense of humor. I was happy to be making a good impression on Bobby's business associates until Bobby whispered to me, "That's because he doesn't know the real you." *Do I present two faces?*

One time, in an airport, Bobby was walking ahead of me, yet again. Fed up, I stopped following him, and he turned to asked what was wrong. I told him, not for the first time, it was demeaning and embarrassing. So he started walking in exaggerated slow motion, loudly saying, "Is this better, Honey? I wouldn't want to embarrass you." As people turned to stare, I felt my face get red hot, and a woman commented I should run like hell the other way. Mortified, I never brought it up again.

On another trip, Bobby only had enough points to upgrade one ticket to first class. Instead of keeping both tickets coach, he upgraded himself, and I sat in coach. I got off the plane and found him at the end of the jetway, a big grin on his face. "How was it back there with the cattle, Honey?"

I overheard a passenger say to his wife, "That guy's an asshole." I felt like a fool I was but said nothing. *If I say something, it will ruin the trip.*

As you've previously read, these behaviors were not new. They were escalating, sure, but nothing novel. What was different was my response to them—the way they affected me. My confidence whittled down, I was no longer standing up for myself. It was less confrontational and hurtful to be quiet, to let it go. The bully tactics and belittling were taking their toll. Not only was I accepting unacceptable behavior, but I was also starting to question my role in the whole thing. Is it my fault? Am I to blame? Am I overreacting? Am I unappreciative? The answer was no. No, I was not. But I was moving into an emotional house of cards.

Unfortunately, it would be years before I could see clearly, and get the help I needed to break the cycle.

THE WAVE

———

O N THE OTHER SIDE OF THE RELATIONSHIP...
I enjoyed our Sunday morning ritual of Bobby in his chair and me stretched out on the couch, sharing the Sunday paper. A little background music, some coffee and cinnamon buns, and we'd stay tucked in until noon.

One Sunday, in early November of 1995, I saw the wedding announcement for a student's wedding we had attended. As I showed Bobby her picture, I wondered out loud if we would ever take the leap. "I don't know, what are your thoughts on it?" was his question. We agreed there was no way we wanted a formal wedding; been there, done that. A few minutes passed, and he asked, "What would we do then Vegas?" I suggested one of our pool parties or Christmas Open Houses, so the people we cared most about would be there. We could avoid gifts by making it a surprise. A few minutes later, I heard, "Okay, let's do it."

"Sounds good, when?" I asked, thinking next summer or beyond.

"Our open house next month works." And that's how we decided to get married.

Bobby felt strongly about having our vows blessed for his parents' sake, and I agreed. He was raised Catholic, I was raised a stay at home Methodist, and we were both divorced, so that ruled out a priest. At that time in my life, I didn't have a religion, much less a church. Also it was a home wedding on the Sunday before Christmas, a busy time for clergy. Since I didn't know where to start, I did what any red-blooded American would do at that time and opened the Yellow Pages.

Out of dozens of calls, only one clergyman said he was available. When Bobby and I met with him, we could see he was an odd, somewhat creepy fanatic. Back in the car, we agreed there was no way that nutcase was officiating our wedding, but now what? It was Thanksgiving weekend, and we were running out of time.

When we got back to the house, Jeannie, home for the holiday, was laughing with friends about the times they played basketball for Seekonk Congregational Church. *That's it! Why didn't I think of that church?* I called, left a message, and the pastor returned my call the next day. He wasn't available, but his new assistant pastor was and would be happy to meet with us. Success! We were ready to roll.

It snowed the morning of our wedding, so Bobby was out shoveling when his business phone rang. I ran to answer it, assuming it was the pastor confirming the time. Au contraire, it was his mother calling to say they weren't coming. His dad had been in the emergency room all night with kidney stones, and they were home now but exhausted. I went out to the garage to tell Bobby, and he said things could go on as planned. A gallant gesture, but no, there was no way we were getting married without his mom and dad. He went up to his office to call his mom, and I went to the kitchen where I had left Jeannie, Mom, and Cathy cooking. Clueless as to what was going on, they were trying to figure out why I was so upset just because his parents were going to miss a party. I mumbled something about having PMS and went upstairs to take a shower.

Bobby met me in the hallway and told me his parents were coming. Once he told his mother we were getting married, she said they'd be there if she had to carry his father in on a stretcher. His parents were the only ones who ever knew. I wish you could have seen Bobby's sister, Doreen's face when they came through the door! She had been at the hospital all night with them and now here was her dad at a party. They kept our secret, and Doreen only had to stew, good-naturedly, for a short time before the ceremony.

Our house was a tri-level with a finished basement, so we had party-goers on the main level (kitchen, dining, and living room), seven steps down in the family room, and seven steps down from there to the man cave. About an hour before the ceremony, we announced our wedding to the guests on each floor. People's reactions as we told them the news was like a wave at the ballpark. Gasps and words of surprise waving down through the levels, followed by a wave of cheers traveling back up—it was so awesome!

While I went upstairs to change into my wedding suit, our guests made some changes of their own. They created an aisle leading from the stairs, across the living room and ending at a makeshift altar. The ladies had collected candles and poinsettias from around the house and created a gorgeous arrangement. On my way back upstairs to make my grand entrance, I saw two of Bobby's sisters-in-law pinning a boutonniere on his jacket, the three of them laughing and sharing the moment. I remember thinking the happiness on their faces mirrored the joy in my heart. All the kids piled at the bottom of the stairs, and as I started down... They sang "Da Da Ta DA." It was the most beautiful rendition of the wedding march I had ever heard.

On December 17, 1995, in our home, with our daughters Jeannie and Robin as our witnesses and surrounded by family and friends, we took our vows. Kenny G's Christmas CD played softly in the background, and the Christmas lights cast a soft romantic glow. It was perfect in every sense of the word except Todd, his son, wasn't physically there. Not knowing there was to be a wedding, Todd had decided not to come home from Seattle, Washington that year. When we got the wedding film developed, I chose a picture of Robin, Jean, and Bobby and I to enlarge. Then I cut Todd's head from another photo and glued it floating above ours to show he was there in our hearts and minds.

I awoke the next morning smiling, with my right hand wrapped around my new wedding band and the doorbell ringing. It was Steven's mother, Betty, asking for Jean. No, I'm not kidding. I hadn't seen her in almost twenty years, and she showed up on our doorstep my first day as a new bride. *How did she know where we lived? Oh yeah, Sharon.*

I'd heard she had lung cancer and could tell by looking at her she wasn't winning the battle. I wish I could say that softened me towards her, but I'd be lying. I told her Jean had spent the night at her grandmother's because it had been our wedding night. As I stared her down with twenty years of anger and hard feelings, she handed me a card to give Jean. *How dare she try to make amends now so she could go in peace. What about Jean's peace?*

As I watched her leave, I attempted to understand what the universe was trying to tell me. It certainly was no coincidence she showed up when she did. Was it to let me know the past is always present, even in new beginnings? Was it to remind me these people's blood and DNA ran in my daughter's veins, and therefore we would forever be connected, like it or not? Or was it merely to make me appreciate how much I had upgraded in the mother-in-law department?

I smiled at that last thought and closed the door. *Let it go, Belle, it's Jean's decision whether or not to see her.*

She's got this.

Or at least I hoped so. I rolled up my sleeves and started to clean up the party mess; that was a mess I still had control over.

THE RINGMASTER

AND HIS MISTRESS

BOBBY AND I HAD THE SHORTEST HONEYMOON PERIOD OF any couple I know. Less than a month after we were married, Bobby had a five-day business trip to Puerto Rico, and he took a single buddy instead of me. In addition to the hurt of being passed over as a new bride, I had to endure all the comments from his brothers and friend when he returned. I realized they were giving him, not me, a hard time, but it was still embarrassing.

The early years of marriage were more of the same relationship we had always had. It got off to a rocky start, but there were also special times. Bobby would make birthday dinners for me and give me thoughtful Valentine and anniversary cards. We also got our first dog, BJ. I had dogs my entire adult life, but Bobby never had, even growing up. To me, dogs are four-legged children with fur and have the run of the house, including furniture and beds. Realizing what an adjustment this would be, I waited until Bobby was ready. The day after he gave me the thumbs up, I was at the shelter, and BJ picked me out. He was a beagle/lab mix, all black and a little bigger than a beagle. With the other dogs barking and carrying on, BJ just walked up to the front of the pen and sat, waiting for me to put his leash on and take him home. So, I did. Bobby ended up loving that dog as much as I did, and it's a good thing too. That little dude ruled the roost.

We spent my fortieth birthday on the island of St. John. Bobby and I always traveled in style, but this condo was exceptional.

It was private and sat on a small cliff right over a secluded inlet. The floor to ceiling folding glass doors allowed a panoramic view of the water, and if we left them open, little banana birds would fly in and serenade us during breakfast. The balcony was literally over the water, and we would sit and watch the cruise ships sail by. The bed was in an open loft, and I loved feeling like a bird in a nest, looking out over the water and at the stars. Bobby was attentive and loving, which made an idyllic vacation even more romantic.

On occasion, Bobby would help me solve studio problems. My studio recitals were in an auditorium that seated twelve hundred people, which we always sold out. One year, the fire department almost shut us down because people were standing in the aisles. Bobby came up with a plan. I had the aisle and seat numbers printed on the tickets, and Bobby got his buddies to be ushers. No one got in without a seat number, and the guys were there to help everyone find their correct seat. Problem solved, and it was an added touch of class to the evening. It was a great relief having Bobby take care of the chaos out front so I could focus on the organized chaos backstage. It was so nice not to have to wear all of the hats anymore.

Bobby was there to share in Jean's college graduation, help with her yearly moves in Boston, and lend advice when asked. In other words, he was a good stepfather, and that meant the world to me. Bobby being Bobby, he never told her, but he was proud of Jean. Proud of her accomplishments and proud of her character.

All good and wonderful things, but...

I came home one afternoon to find a guy from Sears going over a contract with Bobby to vinyl side the house. Bobby had already decided on the style, color, and who was going to do the job. What he hadn't done, however, was discuss any of it with me. The same scenario played out for the new deck a few years later. Two examples of the many times I felt like nothing more than a tenant living in his house.

After a knee injury, Bobby decided to quit softball and focus on golf. The Christmas after his decision, he gave me a golf bag and clubs as a gift. He intended to start playing golf when we traveled and wanted me to learn so I could play too. I found out later that day Bobby had gifted me his old clubs and bought himself a new set. Not wanting to ruin Christmas, I said nothing, which by now was the norm.

A year or so later, we took a Palm Springs golf trip with his brother and sister-in-law. As we sat around the fire pit enjoying the evening, his sister-in-law mentioned she couldn't wait until we joined Wanno, and we could golf together regularly.

Wanno, short for Wanumetonomy, is a country club in Middletown, Rhode Island, where Bobby's family and childhood friends belong. I loved going there, but Bobby said financially, it made no sense to join a club when he traveled so much on business.

So, imagine my surprise when his next comment was, "I just signed us up at Segregansett Country Club." *WHAT?!* I was unaware he was even thinking about such a thing. He had never said a word to me about it. What's more, I had never heard of the place much less played golf there.

I stared in stunned silence as he continued his little song and dance. "Yeah, well, the price is right, and it's close to home. We have an interview Monday night, but I know the guys on the membership committee, so it's just a formality."

Finally finding my voice I said, "I can't go on Monday, I'm at the studio."

"It's just a formality, Belle, and you don't need to be there."

"But I would at least like to see the place and introduce myself," I said.

"You can do that after we join."

When we got back to the room, I got one question out before he shut me down.

"What the hell were you thinking?!" I not so quietly asked. He glared at me.

"I have no problem making it a single membership instead of a family; it'll save me some money," was his nasty response. *I have to let this be, or it will ruin the rest of the vacation for everyone.* Controlling behavior, left unchecked, only escalates.

Segregansett, aka Seggie. Bobby's mistress; the other woman. One trip to the club and I knew why we were there. A lot of the members were his 1980's crew, his party partners, and softball mates. I was afraid it spelled trouble, and I was right. Don't get me wrong; I liked these guys. It was Bobby's mindset and attitude around them that I couldn't stand. That's on him, not them.

He would say something like, "The last thing I want to do right now is to go back out there and play nine holes." Some guy would yell across the bar, "Come on, Bob, be a sport."

"You don't know how long those holes are, Mack." Ha-ha's all around—except for me.

The few times we teed off with other couples, it was plain for all to see Bobby was not having fun. It had what I believe to be his desired effect. To save face, I stopped asking him to play and was on my own.

The women's group had a block of tee times on Tuesday, Thursday, and Saturday mornings. You showed up and were assigned a foursome. I was terrified the first morning I went to play, and it turns out I should've been, I was in way over my head. This was not the casual golf I played. There were no mulligans or give me putts and more rules than I knew existed. And if you missed a shot or a putt that cost the team, you heard about it. After eighteen holes, I would leave the course and go directly to the studio, mentally and physically spent (it never took more than a few minutes in the studio with my dancers, however, to turn my day around). I was so nervous I'd be nauseous on the way to the course, but I kept going. How else was I going to meet people? *Just think of it as being the new kid in school all those years, you handled that. Yeah, except this is supposed to be fun.* I hung in there until one day I hit a breaking point—my point of no return.

We were playing a game with no stroke limit. Players had to hit the ball as many times as needed to put it in the hole. *Dear Lord, this is guy golf!* The seventeenth hole is a par three over water and uphill. I had cleared that water countless times before, but once one ball got wet that day, I knew I was sunk. Nerves. I stood there and put what felt like a million balls in the water before I got one over. At the end of that round, I picked up my one remaining ball and went home. I was all done. Every time the women's group teed it up, it was like tournament play, and I just wanted to play golf, not join the LPGA.

Not long after that day, I met my friend Kris, and we found other like-minded ladies to play with us. I ended up meeting some of my dearest friends at Seggie and love them to pieces. So, eventually, things leveled off for me, but that first year or so was brutal. It's been almost fifteen years since I was a member there, and my friends tell me the women's group there now is lovely. I am so delighted to hear that!

Bobby played with a large group of men who played nine holes every Thursday night and eighteen on Friday afternoons. They would play, eat, drink, then drink some more. They had datebooks printed up, and at the beginning of April, they would sit at the bar and make matches to play every Saturday and Sunday for the year. Not a regular golf season, the year. Unless there was snow on the ground, they played. If a guy didn't commit, he risked getting shut out on weekends. Add the nineteenth hole taking as much time for Bobby as the round of golf, and it spelled disaster for my marriage.

Naturally, things come up on weekends throughout the year, and other guys would get substitutes to fill in for their match. Not Bobby. "I can't, I have a match that day," became his mantra. Sunday mornings reading the paper were gone, as were pool parties and afternoons in Newport. No more friends over for dinner. He spent weekend evenings in his home office catching up on work he had neglected Thursday and Friday. We never went out to dinner or over to friends' houses anymore. "I'm too tired," or "I don't want to go," was his usual response. If I pressed him to go, he would be miserable at home, ruin my mood, then be Sammy Sunshine once we got there.

One summer, I had a full hysterectomy due to fibroid tumors, and my surgery was on a Wednesday. That meant Bobby was at the golf course Thursday through Sunday, and I was on my own; he did not miss a round. My surgeon nicknamed him the Phantom Husband because she never saw him at the hospital.

If I said anything about how much time he spent at Seggie, he would go to the extreme, always. "Fine—I'll quit," he'd pout.

"You don't have to quit, just come home on Fridays after your round so we can do something together. Or, play a round with me once or twice a month," I'd say.

"No. I'm going to quit and be miserable—then you'll be happy."

"Bobby, between golf and business travel, you're never home," I tried to reason.

"What do you suggest I do, quit my job?"

I tried again, "Of course not, just adjust some of your time to include me."

"Now I have to quit my job to make you happy," he'd counter.

I can't tell you how many times variations of that so-called conversation went on, but it was a lot. Until I finally gave up. You can't reason with a self-centered bully incapable of compromise, and that's what Bobby was when it came to Seggie. I was tired of my head spinning, and besides, my pain was getting worse.

In the fall of 2001, I noticed my knee would throb after I ran, or my back hurt after teaching dance. No problem, Advil became my best friend. *Keep moving, lady.* By April of 2002, I was eating Advil like candy, and still had to give up jogging. I could no longer walk eighteen holes and took a cart for the back nine. At my studio, I counted down my dancers, bent over, with my hands on my knees. "Five, six, seven, eight..."

It was time to see a doctor. The first orthopod I saw in Rhode Island told me it was arthritis in both hips, and I would have to live with it. They didn't do replacements on people under fifty years old. *But that's five more years!* My second opinion resulted in the same story, but at least he offered some relief. He put me on NSAIDs for inflammation and sent me for physical therapy and cortisone shots. Eventually, I needed nerve blocks for my back because my gait was messing up my spine. All of this went on for quite some time, and through it all, I kept moving. Until one day, I couldn't. *Now I know how the Tin Man felt.* In a year and a half, I had gone from jogging, golfing, and dancing to barely being able to walk. No way I was going to make four more years. It was time to go to Boston.

Boston has some of the best orthopedic and spine surgeons in the world. The problem is getting an appointment with them sometime in this century. Through her career, my friend Debbie knew the best of the best and got me in to see him.

Dr. Max examined me, took some X-rays, walked behind me down a hallway, and said, "Both hips have to go."

"I know, but when? I've had two doctors tell me four years," I whined.

He just shook his head no and said, "I can do them in August."

Woo-Hoo! He sent me across the hall to the spine surgeon, to make sure he concurred the hips were causing the back pain, which he did. In March of 2003, I scheduled a bilateral hip replacement and started counting down the days like a child going to Disney World. *YES!! I'm getting my life back!*

A month later, in April 2003, I was diagnosed with Stage 2 invasive breast cancer.

PART V

CHARACTER BUILDING 101

BLINDSIDED X'S TWO

———

SPRING AT MY STUDIO WAS ALWAYS A BUSY TIME, PREPARING for the June recital. Even so, I ran out one day to have my yearly mammogram, figuring I'd be back within the hour. As usual, I had to wait while the technician made sure the film was readable. *Is this taking a long time, or is it me?* The tech came back and said she was sorry, but we needed a do-over. After the second set of films, she was back in no time.

"The radiologist wants an ultrasound." *It must be those pesky calcium deposits again.*

"Ok, I'll schedule an appointment."

"No, he wants one now." *Uh oh, this can't be good.*

As I laid there shivering from the cold gel and fear, I tried to calm down by reminding myself there was no family history of breast cancer, and I was only forty-six. It almost worked until the radiologist called me in and showed me the worst picture of me ever taken.

"You need to get to an oncologist immediately; this is serious. How did you not feel something this size?" he asked. *I was too busy trying to keep my hips functioning; that's how.*

When I got to my car, I started shaking so badly I couldn't drive. *Cancer?! Cancer?!* I called Bobby, who was on his way home from a business trip, and broke down. He told me not to panic, he would be back that night and we'd handle it—it would be okay. From that call on, Bobby was my rock and by my side through the entire ordeal. He was a different man towards me; he was a husband.

I asked my gynecologist who she recommended I see, and without hesitation, she said Dr. Flan. I called his office, and they gave me an appointment right away. I instantly liked and trusted him, and so did Bobby. He was soft-spoken, had kind eyes and a gentle, calm manner. Dr. Flan looked at my film, examined me, and told me to be prepared to have the biopsy come back as some form of breast cancer. He didn't like what he saw or felt. I had to wait a week to have my biopsy, so the NSAIDs I was taking for hip pain would be out of my system and not cause excessive bleeding. Soon after the biopsy came the lumpectomy and a full diagnosis.

Those couple of weeks felt like an eternity to me, and even longer for Bobby, I'm sure. I wish I could say I was one of those brave warriors who hear the word cancer and instantly declare they will beat it; they will survive. I was not. My father died of cancer at my age, and I was scared senseless, literally. I couldn't be reasoned with nor consoled. I was dying. Period. I tried to let this defeatist attitude only show up at home, or with the people closest to me, and still function normally at the studio and in the real world. I had over two hundred dancers counting on me to showcase their hard work in a couple of weeks, and the show must go on as they say.

As predicted, the results came back positive, but thankfully the lymph nodes were clear. I heard Stage 2, invasive, 2mm tumor with iffy borders, and I flipped my brain's switch to the off position. I had to; this was something I couldn't wrap my head around. I was petrified. *I'm dying. I'm forty-six years old, and I'm going to die, just like Daddy did.* Somewhere in another dimension, I heard Bobby asking questions and getting information for the battery of diagnostic tests I needed to see if my cancer had metastasized. Then I heard something about a nuclear test to make sure my heart was healthy enough for chemotherapy treatments. *CHEMO?!* That brought me out of my self-induced coma.

"Am I going to lose my hair?" Dr. Flan nodded yes and kept nodding when I asked about my eyebrows and eyelashes. *Not only am I ill, but now I'm going to look sick, and people will pity me!* I know it sounds so vain and shallow on the surface, but I zeroed in on that one fact because it was something my mind could comprehend without shutting down. It wasn't about my entire body being scanned and tested to see how much of my innards this cell eating monster was devouring.

The tests revealed my cancer hadn't metastasized, and Dr. Flan presented my case to the tumor board. *I have a tumor board. Me. How can this be happening?!* They agreed on eight treatments of chemo—four of Adriamycin and four of Taxol—followed by six weeks of daily radiation. If all went well, at the end of my extensive "Spa Treatment," my five-year survival rate would be eighty-five percent.

Bobby took one look at my "Are you kidding me?!" face, stared me straight in the eyes, slapped me a high five and said, "We'll take those odds and win." It worked the intended charm. Once he had me talked down off the ceiling, we decided to start treatment after my recital, which was a month or so away.

As the NSAIDs left my system, and my pain and immobility returned, another thought slammed into my consciousness. *My hips! I can't replace them now—what if I never can? Are cancer patients able to have that kind of surgery, ever?* A lifetime of immobility and pain terrified me more than not surviving cancer. Bobby and I met with Dr. Max to explain the situation, and he assured me I could have surgery after the cancer treatments ended, as long as my white blood cell count was normal.

I gave him my treatment timeline and asked how soon after he would be able to do the surgery. The doctor told me January 13, 2004, was his first open date, which was less than two weeks after my radiation was scheduled to end. He added he had other patients go through similar breast cancer treatments, and they rarely stayed on schedule due to infections and/or weakness. Dr. Max suggested I call once I completed my regimen, and he would fit me in ASAP. I told him to schedule me for January thirteenth; I would be there. And that's when I became an unstoppable warrior. I had a goal set, a plan in place, and a mission to accomplish. The cancer was a dragon to slay, but slay it I would. I was still scared but no longer defeated. *Cancer, you're going down.*

On top of losing the meds that managed my hip pain and mobility, they whipped me off the hormone therapy I was taking since my hysterectomy. It sent me into instant, full-blown menopause, which any woman who has ever had the honors will tell you is a fun time all on its own. I was a hobbling crazed zombie living my worst nightmare and still kept the studio and me up and running, with a whole lot of help from my tribe, of course. There were countless acts of kindness and love shown to me that year, and I remember every one. They still bring a smile to my heart all these years later. I would like to share some with you.

From that first visit with Dr. Flan, Bobby made sure I never went to an appointment or treatment alone, even the daily radiation trips. On the rare occasion he had to miss one for business, he lined up a friend to take me. If Bobby was going to be gone overnight, he arranged for someone to stay with me. He never let me give up hope or doubt I would make a full recovery.

Bobby's strength and support also gave me another significant gift, the gift of ignorance. For me to remain positive, I had to stay off the internet and ask no questions of the chemo nurse or Dr. Flan. I was focused on one thing only; January 13, 2004. I was able to accomplish this because Bobby took on all the knowledge and worry, asked the questions, and did the research. He handled it all. There was no Phantom Husband this time. Bobby shielded me from my reality and stayed informed, protecting me in my ignorance. He took care of me and dealt with me, which wasn't always a day at the beach to be perfectly honest.

The 2003 recital went off without a hitch, despite all the chaos with my health. However, after a few summer chemo treatments, when it was time to schedule and plan for September, I knew I couldn't pull it off. I had always selected music and choreographed for each group to best showcase their talent, and I knew I lacked the energy for the hours of work that entailed, never mind teaching classes. To make matters worse, my assistant, the only other instructor who had ever choreographed and taught on her own, had quit, pregnant with her second baby. Bobby came up with an idea. "It's the studio's twentieth anniversary this year, and you have twenty years worth of routines, why not use them? A trip down memory lane," he suggested. *Yes! Brilliant.*

Now, to find teachers. I had this problem solved if I could get them to agree. I had four adult student teachers who had been with me for most, if not all of, the studio's twenty years. They were more than capable of teaching a class on their own but had never done so. They all had full-time jobs, and one had a young family. I was asking a lot. They agreed instantly, stepped up to the plate, and hit home runs! Without my dancing earth angels, the studio would have closed, and twenty years of my heart and soul would have vanished. Those special ladies made many sacrifices that year to keep us up and running, and they did it beautifully.

My Jeannie came up with the most creative and loving idea to make what I call my Group Hug. She sent a packet out to all the people in my life, which included a beautiful letter and a blank cloth square. Jean asked them to draw, sew, or embroider a time or feeling that best represented their relationship with me. She then took the squares and made them into a magnificent quilt, a king-sized hug that provided me more comfort in my darkest, most private moments than you can imagine. How Jeannie found the time to put it together with school and work, I have no idea, but it is the greatest gift I have ever received. Both Jean's and each of the square's creators' love radiates through every stitch. Because of the markers used on some of the squares, the quilt isn't washable, and dry cleaners are afraid to touch it. That's fine by me; the stains add to its comfort and charm. They are a reminder of what that hug and I have been through together and survived.

When Debbie called me the morning of my first chemo appointment, I mentioned I was upset because I hadn't found time to plant my annuals. As Bobby and I pulled into our driveway after the treatment, I saw Debbie and her husband Paul, busy planting my flower pots with colorful blossoms. The vision of those two hearts, planting life that would thrive, not die, that summer, was precisely what I needed to see at that moment. That act of kindness was the first of many times Debbie, Paul, and their daughter Emily would stop me from falling into the dark hole that year.

We had a set foursome that played in a charity golf tournament in Newport every year. Three good golfers and me (let's just say no one has ever called me Captain on a golf course). By the time the tournament rolled around in late August, I had gone through a few treatments and was in less than stellar form. Add in my non-functioning hips without pain meds, and I wasn't going to help them do anything but slow down play. Still, they insisted I be their fourth; we were a team. That meant more to me than they'll ever know. One of their husbands had team golf shirts with the pink ribbon logo made for us, and we wore them with pride. It was a day of laughter, friendship, and some terrible golf on my part. They couldn't have cared less about the golf; they cared about me and gave me a beautiful day to remember at a not so great time in my life. That kind of understanding and support is priceless.

The third day after chemo was always my toughest due to dizziness and nausea. I would feel like I was on a small boat being tossed about in rough seas. The men at Segregansett played a two-day tournament in early fall, and after the Saturday round, there was a dinner for the players and their wives/dates. The dinner was on my third day, but it was important to Bobby, and I wanted to go. I stayed in bed all day and slept so I could make it. When I awoke, my dinghy was still in choppy waters, but I was determined to go. In a total chemo fog, with no sense of time, I did the physical therapy stretches needed to get my hips almost functioning, then showered and dressed. By the time my mom dropped me off at Seggie, I was late, really late. *God Belle, you're nothing but a broken down rusted out old wreck. You belong in a junkyard.* I ran in at my snail's pace to find the president of the club, and our dear friend, Jimmy, had the staff wait to serve dinner until I got there. "We weren't going to eat without you," was all he said, but it meant the world to me. It made me feel like a brand-new shiny red Porsche.

IN THE MIDST OF THIS, MY BROTHER JOHN, LIVING IN FLORIDA, was in the process of divorcing his second wife. She was from overseas, and he was determined to pull her green card and send her back home. Still being in the Air Force, he could do this, I guess. I had been trying to talk him out of it because they had a son together, but he was too angry to listen. I was afraid if John sent them out of the country, he would never see his son again. On one of my infamous third days (naturally), John called and had had a few too many beers. I was fresh out of patience and let him have it.

"What is the matter with you? You can't send her away! Being a good father has to trump getting even with her," I said, not so kindly. *Easy Belle, he's hurting.*

All of a sudden, he started talking about our father and how we were molested as children, how awful it was for us... *Where the hell did this come from?! What is he saying?!*

"John, what are you talking about?"

"Belle, our father molested both of us, don't you remember?" *No, no, I don't.*

"John, Daddy never touched me. He touched you?" *I can't believe this!*

"He did more than touch me." *Dear God, I can't be hearing this, right!* I started to cry.

"When John, when did he do this?"

"Over many years, Sis," he said with a cynical chuckle.

"Why didn't you come to me? Why didn't you ever tell me?" I asked. *I would have protected you, little brother, I would have found a way.*

"Because it was happening to you too," he said.

"No, no, John, it wasn't." *Was it? I'm so tired and foggy I can't think straight right now.*

"When you got married, I figured good for you. You found a way out." I was crying hard by now.

"I begged you to come too, but you wouldn't leave! I would have never left you there had I known! I would have done SOMETHING!"

"It's all in the past now, Sis." And with that, he hung up, and I threw up.

This story is ludicrous! He's been drinking; I have chemo brain, it's, it's...OH MY GOD, IT'S TRUE! Just like that, the telltale signs in Erdenheim, Seekonk, and Alexandria flooded my mind and drowned my soul. How could I have missed it? What kind of sister was I? Where the hell was Mom?! *Oh yeah, on Sunnybrook Farm with Rebecca.* I was distraught, beside myself, broken for him.

Then came the tossed salad of thoughts about myself. Had I been molested and repressed it? Were there signs I had missed in myself over the years? *Go back through the years, Belle, remember, think!* I chopped, diced, and sliced my memory until I was sure that horror had not occurred. But oh, what an awful time to have had to relive the darkest parts of my childhood! It took a strength I didn't know I had to explore that unthinkable possibility in my weakened state.

First the breast cancer and now this; I've been blindsided twice in six months. They were equally devastating.

John refused to discuss it with me ever again. Whenever I tried to get him to talk about it, my brother would close up like a clam and said it was in the past and to let it go. *How can I let this go knowing he surely cannot?!* Did he feel betrayed by me because I hadn't suffered the same atrocities? Had he found a morsel of comfort in assuming he was not the only one and now even that was gone? Did he not believe me? Or couldn't believe me for the painful loneliness it would cause him all these years later? Had too many beers allowed him to unintentionally blurt it out so I would stop chastising him about his wife and son, and he now regretted it? These questions haunt me to this day, but I could hear the anxiety and fear in his voice whenever I brought it up. I realized I was doing more harm than good, and I let it go.

My baby brother, the lone wolf.

———

BY MY SEVENTH CHEMO TREATMENT, I WAS IN TROUBLE. ON THE ride in, I announced to Bobby, "I'm not going," and asked him to turn around.

"You have to go. We've made it this far on schedule, and you can't quit now." *We, he said we. Okay, I'll do it for him, but I don't know if I can make it this time.* My can-do attitude was gone, and I was teetering on the edge of the black hole.

The third day after my seventh treatment, I was all done. I had no fight left in me. *This isn't living; this is dying.* I gave up and did a swan dive into the black hole. I was so bad I didn't even let Bobby see it. *He's worked so hard to keep me going; I can't let him know I've quit.*

After Bobby left to play golf, I went to curl up into the fetal position when the doorbell rang. It was one of his cousins dropping off tickets to a function. When he asked if I was okay, I shook my head no, and started to cry.

"This has got to be over; this has to end," I sobbed. A big strapping guy, he embraced me in a bear hug and rocked me while I cried.

"I know, hang in there, Honey, soon."

The whole scene took less than five minutes, but it turned me completely around. I shut the door, grabbed the catalogs, and went to work picking out and pricing costumes for June's recital. I decided the show must go on—all shows. The healing power a human touch possesses never ceases to amaze me.

Other than those three days of the seventh treatment, I never completely stopped, never entirely caved. *The hips hurt too bad to function today? Do extra therapy exercises this morning and get moving, Cupcake.*

You need fresh air! Grab Kris and play nine holes, she could care less how slow you are or how badly you play.

If the wig doesn't stay on, put double stick tape around what used to be your hairline, and it won't come off in a hurricane. When you get home, rip that tape off your scalp with one fast yank and slather antibiotic cream on the raw spots. You'll be fine.

Nauseous? Throw up, grab your antacids, and go out to dinner. Can't stand looking at the sick woman in the mirror? Then don't look right now; tomorrow's another day.

Can't teach? Well, someone has to schedule classes and decide which group is dancing what. Support your Dance Angels!! And rewrite those years-old routines in a script and language they can follow instead of your crazy shorthand.

Too tired? Too bad! Get out of bed and do your part woman; your team is most certainly doing theirs. Don't let them down. If you stop, this thing will definitely swallow you whole.

Did this Belle always show up at the party? No, of course not. I remember a night Debbie called and could tell I was down. "Come over for dinner; we want to see you. Emily misses her Miss Belle."

"Oh, Debbie, I just can't. I can't stand the thought of putting on that freaking wig and makeup. Not to mention a smile and a brave face. I don't want Em to see me like this. I need to be positive and set a good example for her," I said.

"You are always a positive example for her, and she could care less what you look like, she misses you," my friend said.

I went as I was, and Debbie was right. Emily showed no reaction to my depleted state. *She truly does see me from the inside out.* Listening to Emily's stories of school and other adventures, told with her usual humor and enthusiasm, worked wonders for my spirits. Some people are lucky enough to inherit the right kind of heart and be taught the best way to use it. Emily is one of those fortunate people.

Another time I was feeling hollowed out, Jeff's mom and stepdad, invited Jean, Jeff, Bobby, and me down to the Cape. They have a great place on a marsh in Sandwich, Massachusetts. They are also fellow dog lovers, so our four-legged family members got to come along too.

Fall is a beautiful time on Cape Cod, and the combination of sea air and great company was just what I needed. We sat on the deck and watched BJ and my grand-dog Hannah romp in the marsh with boundless energy and joy. Well, Hannah, a border collie, had boundless energy. BJ had little beagle legs and a big belly, so he was more about the joy, but just as entertaining to watch. I remember being curled up on the floor with the dogs while we all watched TV, and experiencing this incredible floating sensation of peace and contentment. That weekend, life-affirming and full of love, got me right back on track.

My eighth treatment went off as planned, completing the most intense portion of my spa regime on schedule. Thanks to Dr. Flan, his staff, and the shot I got the day after every treatment to boost my white blood cell count. And thanks to my dream team of family and friends.

On Tuesday, January 13, 2004, I kept my date with Dr. Max.

THE TWINS

I WAS DR. MAX'S FIRST SURGERY OF THE DAY, SO BOBBY AND I were up and at 'em at o'dark thirty to be at the hospital for 5:00 a.m. By the time I saw Dr. Max and his entourage of residents, I was prepped and pretty drugged up. The last thing I remember saying was, "You install them, and I'll rehab them." The last thing I remember seeing was a table in the operating room that looked more like a tool bench in a garage. It had saws, mallets, plates and screws, rods, and face shields. *Holy shit!* was my last thought before the anesthesiologist put me out.

The first time I remember coming to after surgery (I'm sure there were times before), I was in a semi-private room with Jeannie, Bobby, and Debbie around my bed. They had placed my angel figurines on the nightstand and covered me with my Group Hug. As promised, Debbie had red nail polish with her, and she set about transforming my naked toenails into a thing of beauty. Jeannie gifted me a stuffed giraffe with the perfect neck for hugging, and I had brought the stuffed elephant she made me in elementary school. I was watched over, wrapped in love, had comfort to hug in both arms, and some kick-ass toenails. The three of them had covered all the bases. I also had this magnificent button in my hand that took my pain away every time I pushed it. Poof, just like magic. Satisfied I was set for the night, Jean, Debbie, and Bobby left, and I gave my new best friend a poke and drifted off to la-la land.

Am I awake? Am I dreaming? Everything appears to be swirling in a fog. Did I die? Who is standing at the foot of my bed? Is it Saint Peter? Am I in Heaven? As my vision cleared, I realized I was seeing Dr. Max, looking gorgeous in an Armani suit and red tie, obviously on his way out. *If I had died and this was heaven, I'd honestly be okay with it.* After reviewing my chart, a look of bewilderment crossed his face as he took in my décor.

"Do you like what I've done with the place?" I quipped, earning myself a dazzling smile.

When he pulled back the Group Hug to examine me and saw my red toenails, he just shook his head and laughed. He said the surgery went well, everything looked excellent, and he would see me tomorrow. I thanked him for my new set of twins, pushed the button, and nodded off.

Here's the thing about the button; it only worked magic until the anesthesia from my eight-hour surgery wore off. Starting sometime in the middle of the night, I would hold that button down to no avail. Every time I came to, I'd call the nurse over to check for a puddle under the machine because I was sure it was malfunctioning. *It was working so much better earlier in the day.* She'd patiently check it each time, make sure my cuddle buddies were tucked in my arms, and told me it would be working again in a few minutes.

"Okay, thank you," I'd slur and pass out. Nurses are saints.

Early the next afternoon, they tried to get me up to prevent blood clots. A physical therapist parked my new set of wheels, a sleek silver walker, by my bed, and swung my legs over the side. I could've sworn I got up that day, but Bobby informed me I did not. He said I shook my head no, so they put my legs back on the bed, and I went back to la-la land. My memory is of the following day when I did get up, meaning I had lost a whole day to drugs. With that realization, coupled with the visions embedded in my brain of Daddy and Steven, I bid farewell to my magic button and went to a pill every four hours. I had a big job ahead of me, and I couldn't afford to miss another day of work.

I will never forget the first time I walked after surgery. When I stood up, I felt disjointed, like a marionette, which come to think of it, I was. *Just put one foot in front of the other Belle.* After a few steps, I started to feel a little more confident and walked the distance to the doorway. The physical therapist congratulated me, then told me on the walk back I had to pick my feet up instead of shuffling. *Surely, she jests! Only one foot on the ground at once? It's too soon—I'll fall!*

She took one look at my face and said, "If you're too weak, we can try it tomorrow." *Too weak?! Step aside, woman, and watch me cut a path back to that bed.*

Mission accomplished, and I was so proud of myself. Thoroughly exhausted, I got back into bed and laughed out loud when I saw how few steps I had taken; no more than a dozen round trip. *Oh boy, the twins and I have a lot of work to do. I'll take a little snooze and then another stroll later.* I did, and I only shuffled on my first steps—progress. *Nicely done today, twins, day one is behind us.*

The nurse packed ice around my hips for swelling, and I fell asleep, shivering but smiling. I was on the road to recovery. *Tomorrow I'll walk three times and maybe even out the door.* I did make it out the door and a couple of steps down the hall, but only twice. *That's okay. It was more than yesterday. Tomorrow I'll walk it three times with no shuffles.* And I did. I had secretly given myself a one-year deadline from my cancer diagnosis to get back up and running, and I only had a few months left. I needed to keep moving.

I was discharged from the hospital that afternoon and sent to a rehab center. I was hoping to stay at the hospital's rehab, but there were no beds available, so off I went to my second choice. As the ambulance attendants wheeled my stretcher to the door of my new hotel, I asked them to stop a minute so I could breathe in the fresh air and see the sun. After what felt like a nanosecond, they informed me it was bitter cold, and they needed to get me inside. I thought they were total wusses until I remembered they weren't on that little numbing pill every four hours and decided to cut them some slack.

Had I realized my second choice for rehab was a nursing home, I would have hopped off that stretcher and jogged home. Because I had seen the hospital's rehab center, I assumed I would be in a similar facility. I was wrong. *There's been a terrible mistake; this is a nursing home! Once they put you in a home, you never get out. Oh my God, is Bobby putting me in a home? What aren't they telling me?* I don't do well on drugs as far as logic and reasoning go, but then again, does anyone?

When I got to the room I was convinced I was being left to rot in, I needed to pee. The certified nursing assistant put me on a bedpan and left. The number one concern after joint replacement surgery is an infection and here I was, with my fresh incisions sitting in a bowl of urine, growing more hysterical and irrational by the minute. It is in this agitated state my sister-in-law Chris and friend Nancy found me. *Yes, they'll save me!*

"Why am I here? This place is where people come to die, not to heal! I don't belong here, and I'm not staying!" I said (or maybe slurred).

When another CNA appeared to take the bedpan, I demanded to see someone in charge. The floor nurse came in, listened to my tale of woe, then assured me I was in the right place. She told me they had an amazing physical therapy department, and I was in the best of hands, then gave me a pill and told me to rest. I'm sure Chris and Nancy thoroughly enjoyed their visit with me that first day—not! Fortunately, they still loved me anyway. Bobby came in after taking care of the paperwork, and I told him I was not staying—period! I was asleep before I heard his answer.

When the night nurse woke me to take my vitals, I felt rested and, therefore, a little better about things. I was unprepared for how much the move would take out of me physically and mentioned how I hated feeling so weak and sleepy all the time.

She said, "It's only been four days, give your body time to rest."

To which I replied, "My thinking is it's already been four days, time to stop napping and get moving."

She chuckled and shook her head. "You won't be here for long." *No, I won't.*

Maggie was my night nurse for the duration of my stay. She was my caretaker, confidant, cheerleader, and comfort. Nurses are saints.

The next morning, Sunday, I asked for a bedside commode, and to take a shower. I was denied both requests.

"Physical therapy has to sign off on it," the nurse said. When a young therapist came in to give me my Monday PT schedule, I asked if she could help.

"Sure, if you think you're up to it," she said.

She left and came back with a wheelchair because we were going to the end of the hall and it was too far to walk. *Well, I'll use it for today, but that's it.* Once in the shower room, she helped me onto the shower chair, handed me the showerhead, and closed the curtain. My first shower in five days, and it was heavenly. After I washed up, I let the water rain down on my head and turned my face up to a make-believe sky. I must've been that way for a while because she asked if I was alright.

"I'm fine, I was just baptizing the twins," I said.

She helped me dry off and wheeled me back to the room where the most beautiful toilet sat by my bed.

"Are you ready to learn to safely get out of bed and on and off the commode?" she asked.

"I'll ace this in no time," I told her.

HA! Not so much. I had to scooch to the side of the bed like an inchworm on my back. Then grab the railing and swing both legs, at the same time, over the side and into slippers. Hold onto my walker, sidestep until I was in front of the commode, turn around and back up until I felt the toilet's edge. Then drop my panties, with one hand remaining on the walker, and sit. Reverse and repeat for the return trip. *By the time I get back to bed, I'll have to go again.* You would think one run through would've been enough, but let's remember the drugs, exhaustion, and ensuing fog. Every time I had a misstep, I had to start all over again. "You could fall," was all she kept saying. Fall out of bed, fall without slippers, fall pulling my pants down, fall sitting down, fall getting up, fall, fall, fall.

I finally got it right, and she asked if I needed anything else. "Yes, ice, lots of ice." I had done too much, and my hips had blown up like balloons. I was asleep before she got back.

When I awoke from my ice packed morning nap, I discovered I had a new roommate. She was screaming at a CNA, and the smell of raw sewage filled the room. *Oh my, isn't she lovely?* This scenario would be my life, morning, noon, and night until I left a week later. She was cranky, mean, and had more bowel movements in a day than I thought humanly possible—all in her bed. Thank goodness I had the bed by the windows, which I kept open to help with the smell. It was so bad that when people visited me, we had to leave the room and sit elsewhere. To keep her oral toxicity away from me, I kept the curtain between us closed and listened to music through my headphones. *You can handle anything for a short while, Belle, stay focused on why you're here.*

I woke up bright and early Monday, excited to start PT. *I feel stronger every time I wake up!* I performed the dance of the commode, washed up, choked down some toast, and waited. When PT came in, they helped me change, and wheeled me down to the therapy room. *Today is the last day I will sit in this chair or need help to dress*—a promise I made to myself and kept.

The floor nurse that first day was right; I was in good hands. The physical therapy department was top-notch in both personnel and equipment. The room was humongous and had rehab sessions for everything imaginable, all happening at once. It was such a positive environment you couldn't help but roll up your sleeves and get to work. Every therapist in that room was dedicated and focused on one thing; achieving the best quality of life possible for each patient, a sometimes painful process. I, for one, couldn't wait for their enthusiastic and loving torture. All those years of dance had prepared me well. I knew if I worked through it, it would pay off in the end.

The first lesson of group PT was how to safely get out of bed, use a bedside toilet, and take a shower. *But I already know this!* My young Sunday therapist spotted me, pulled me out of class, and did a one on one session with me. She gave me strengthening exercises I could do in bed and lectured me on the evils of chasing pain instead of controlling it.

"Take your meds, even if you're feeling better. The pain will catch up with you during therapy; trust me," she counseled. Naturally, I had to find out for myself—the hard way. She let me drive my shiny new wheels down the hall and back again, then asked if I had any questions.

"Yes. How do I put my pants on?"

My young therapist laughed and said, "Patience." *Clearly, this child does not know me.*

My afternoon session was with a different group. They gave us two gadgets: one to put on our socks, and one to grab things off the floor or out of reach. We then learned how to use them to get dressed by ourselves. Thanks to my young therapist moving me to a new group, I only had to be patient for a few hours. *Hmmm, maybe she does know me after all.*

The next morning, Tuesday, I awoke at 3:30 a.m. It was the exact time I had gotten up one week ago to the day, to shower before surgery. I took it as a sign and decided to shower in celebration of just how far I'd come in seven days.

Giddy with excitement of the forbidden, I performed my dance of the commode, stuffed the hospital toiletries in my robe pocket, and silently wheeled my walker out of the room. I peeled out, raced down the deserted corridor at my breakneck crawl, and pulled into the shower room undetected. *Success!* I took off my robe, knocked the shower chair out of the way, and started to dance with my walker. Well, I don't know if you could call it dancing, exactly, but it felt that way to me.

"I'm singing in the rain, just singing in the rain..." A knock on the door and in walked Maggie with a towel.

"You're probably gonna need this." *Uh oh, busted.*

"Maggie, I just had to—"

She cut me off, "Let's get you dried off and back into bed before we both get in trouble."

I hadn't thought about her being held responsible. Once tucked in, I started to apologize, "I'm so sorry, Maggie, I wasn't thinking—" She cut me off again with her signature chuckle and head shake.

"In all my years, this is the first time I ever had a patient go missing in the middle of the night. Make sure it's the last," she scolded with a wink. I was forgiven.

Wednesday morning, I got out of bed, washed up and dressed, all by myself. I didn't even care that it took me forever. I was just excited to have accomplished it. On my way to PT, I remembered Jeannie's mantra when she was two years old: "Me do it, me-self!" It made me smile to think of it as mine now.

At lunch break, I decided to get the ice I needed on my own and bring it back to my room. I placed my ice bags in plastic bags and tied them to my walker. The ice machine was at the opposite end of the unit and past the nurses' station. I smiled and gave a theatrical nod when the nurses clapped for me on my return trip, ice on board. *Once a performer, always a performer.* That little excursion took almost half of my two hour lunch break, and I was drained and sore, but I didn't care; it was worth it. It marked another milestone towards my independence. I iced down the twins, ate half a sandwich, and caught forty winks before heading to afternoon PT.

I never missed a PT session the entire time I was there, morning or afternoon. I took every class they offered: exercise, strengthening, stretching, plus my group's PT. If there was a class going on in that room that could help me, I was there. Then I would do the exercises I'd learned in bed before going to sleep. Strength equaled mobility, equaled independence, equaled HOME.

On Thursday morning, PT awarded me with a set of crutches for all my hard labor. They were my gold star, my A+, not to mention they provided me with better mobility. I could now stand up straight and move more freely. More importantly, they meant I could start studying for my final exam, stairs. Stairs were the last thing I had to master before PT would let me go home. I walked up and down the hallways for most of the morning session, proving to them I was steady enough to try the stairs. Finally, during the afternoon session, a therapist took me to the stairwell, where we walked up to the first landing (seven steps), and back down.

I have to lift my foot so high, and I'm nervous, I'll fall!! It's okay, Belle, Just one step at a time. Come on, girl. You've got this. When we got back down, he asked how I felt.

"My armpits are killing me," I responded.

He laughed and said, "I meant your balance and strength. Your armpits will be fine if you put your weight on your hands."

"Oh, got it—then let's go again."

And we did a couple of times until he said, "Enough for today."

"Just one more time, please?" I begged. *I want to go home!*

"No, your arms are too tired, they're shaking."

I was so determined to keep going I hadn't noticed. And I had also forgotten to be nervous.

Friday was the first day I didn't take a nap. I showered, walked the halls, went to PT, climbed the stairs, walked the halls, went to PT, climbed the stairs, and made the decision I was ready to go home.

Saturday morning, I announced I was ready to be discharged. There were no PT classes on the weekends, and I would just be hanging around. My case supervisor came in and told me it wasn't possible because my PT team leader wouldn't be back until Monday, and she had to sign off. *Great, yet more time with my lovely roomie and her Eau de Crap.* For the first time in a week, I felt sorry for myself.

I cried, got angry, then I reflected. *Last Saturday, you were sitting on a bedpan, completely helpless and weak as a lamb. You couldn't shower, dress, walk, or even use a commode on your own. Look how far you've come in seven days! Are you going to celebrate or mope around feeling sorry for yourself?* Celebrate, of course. I got up, showered, and spent the day visiting other patients from my PT group to say goodbye. *I will NOT be here on Monday.* I got back to my room, opened the window, put my headphones on to drown out the cranky, and counted down the hours. *Two more nights but only one more day.*

Sunday, I packed up my angels and put my few clothes in a bag. My cuddle buddies and I watched our beloved Pats win the Super Bowl, then I snuggled under the Group Hug and tried to sleep. I couldn't. Between the Pats victory and going home the next day, I was flying high. When Maggie came in, she took a look around and asked if I was going somewhere.

"Yep, I'm going home tomorrow!" I cheered.

"They tell you that?" she asked.

"Nope, I told them."

She let out a laugh and said, "I bet you did. Told ya you wouldn't be here long," she said with a wink.

"Thank you for everything, Maggie."

"You were a breath of fresh air, child," she said as she tucked me in for the last time. Nurses are saints.

Monday afternoon, after mounds of paperwork, I climbed into Bobby's car (well, it was more like stopped, dropped, and swung in), and we headed home.

Home! BJ, my bed, iced tea, fresh air, sunshine—I could not stop smiling! BJ curled up next to me and didn't leave my side. That little dog made it his mission to keep me company and feeling loved. I had in-home PT, a visiting nurse, and a phlebotomist come for a week or so, but after that, I was left blissfully on my own. I started outpatient PT three times a week and got stronger every day. I got off of all my meds and had a clear mind for the first time since my initial chemo treatment nine months earlier. Dr. Max still hadn't cleared me to drive, so Bobby carted me around everywhere and anywhere I wanted to go and never complained.

I started going to the studio for visits and, by the middle of March, was staying to observe some classes and offering my two cents worth. Bobby and I started going out to dinner with friends, and I went to see my dear friend and hairstylist so that he could dye my crew cut. I was pain-free, a feeling I hadn't had in years. I was slowly but surely getting my life back.

There is a quiet spot in Saint Thomas that Bobby and I loved, and in April, we decided to go for a short trip to detox from the past year. I had graduated to a cane, which meant traveling would be less of a hassle. On the afternoon we arrived, we went down to the pool so I could do my water therapy.

As I worked out, I saw a look come over Bobby's face, and it instantly made me feel self-conscious. Not only was it the first time we were being seen in public together without me being "done up," I was in a bathing suit. My radiation burns were fading, but I still had red patches on my chest, matching eight-inch angry scars on my thighs, and I was sporting a crew cut. I was also way too thin and too pale without clothing and makeup. *I'm reading too much into it—I'm being overly sensitive.* Or was I?

That was the only time Bobby was seen with me in a bathing suit on that trip. I went to the pool and beach alone. "Honey, I have calls to make and work to do. You go ahead, and I'll come down for lunch." *Lunch, when I'm wearing a beach coverup and hat.*

The night before we left, after a nice dinner and cocktails, one thing led to another, and we tried "Winking" for the first time since the effects of chemo had started. It's understandable, after the ordeal we had been through, to have, shall we say, equipment failure. But a woman knows when her man isn't turned on by her, is not attracted to her, and in my heart, I felt that was the case. *He sees me differently now and doesn't like what he sees.* Bobby never said, nor did anything to make me believe that wasn't true.

The celebration I was so looking forward to turned into a lonely two days, and a fear that the Phantom Husband was making a comeback.

When we got home, I started driving, lost the cane, and was back at the studio full time, albeit not yet dancing. I was also doing my part for the economy by shopping the malls and outlets with Debbie on weekends. By May, I was back on the golf course and realized the twins did little to improve my golf game. I was disappointed but understood. Some things even miracles can't fix. June found me dancing with some classes, and by July I was walking endlessly on the beach at the Cape.

I hadn't made my deadline of a year, but I didn't begrudge myself the extra two months it took. I'd had quite a lot to deal with between April 2003 and June 2004.

Little did I know a new challenge was right around the corner.

MOM?

A S I LOOK BACK, THERE WERE WARNING SIGNS MOM'S MIND was fading during my ordeal, but I chalked them up to worry over me. *Think what a mess you'd be if, God forbid, Jeannie was sick.* When she asked me how to make a grilled cheese sandwich and how I liked my tea, both things she had been preparing for me my entire life. Or the day Bobby brought her to see me at rehab, Mom just sat in the corner, smiling, never saying a word. *She's alright. She's always handled things that overwhelm her this way. She'll be fine once I've healed.* That was not the case.

Once I got back to the studio full time, I had to face the changes in her were more than just worry. I looked at my payment book and found the majority of clients marked past due; however, when I checked the cash box, it was overflowing. Mom no longer interacted with the mothers and had no patience for the younger students, whom she had always enjoyed. BJ got out the door one day, and she didn't notice he was gone. Thankfully, a student found him in the parking lot. Mom, an avid reader, always had a book close at hand. After a parent teased she hadn't seen her reading in a while, I saw Mom holding a book. *Oh good, she's reading again.* After class, I went to say hi and saw the book was upside down. *Oh, Mummy—No!* It was time to see a doctor.

We went to see her primary care doctor, who gave her a basic oral test, which she failed miserably. Mom didn't know a single

214

answer and kept looking to me for help. *Don't cry—she's confused enough, don't cry.* He gave me the name of a neurologist, and I called to schedule an appointment. I also got on the phone with my brother John. He was out of the Air Force by this time and working in DC. He had divorced his second wife, shipped her and his son back overseas, and, as I predicted, hadn't spoken to them since. *Sometimes I hate it when I'm right.*

I explained the situation and told him I felt both of us needed to be at the appointment. I knew Mom, and there was no way she was going to face this horrible reality when she had so expertly avoided all others. I couldn't let her pretend this one away, however, and knew I would need reinforcements. John agreed to come up and made plans to stay for two weeks.

The three of us went to the appointment and found the CAT scan had confirmed our worst fears. It was some form of dementia, most likely Alzheimer's. Mom just sat there and smiled while John and I asked the doctor questions. *She's already in denial.*

When we got back to my house, John and I tried to get her to talk to us. All she kept saying was, "I'm fine, there's nothing wrong with me. I don't know what you two are talking about."

"Mom, the tests, the doctor—"

She cut me off, "Oh Belle Ann, he's not even MY doctor." John and I kept trying for a day or two, but she was having none of it, and I could see my brother getting more frustrated by the minute. On the third day, John announced he remembered an important meeting, and he needed to get back to DC. He would be leaving in the morning. *So much for reinforcements.* I knew John was lying, but part of me was relieved. I had only been back on my feet for less than two months and had a lot on my plate. I knew him losing patience with Mom would make matters worse.

I have since learned volumes about Alzheimer's, but at the time Mom was diagnosed, I knew absolutely nothing. I didn't realize how far the disease had progressed, nor how long she had managed to hide her symptoms. Having always hidden ugly truths, even from herself, my mother had become a master of illusions. In the summer of 2004, I soon learned how quickly her mind was betraying her.

She would be at my house first thing in the morning, or if I wasn't there, she'd pull in the driveway right behind me. I'd get home and find BJ gone because Mom had picked him up to go for a ride. She once told me they had been to the mall, and I went nuts about leaving the dog in a hot car. Mom giggled and said, "I don't get out silly. We just drive there and back."

One day while in the bathroom, I looked out the window and saw her rocking back and forth on her heels at the edge of the pool. She can't swim. Another day I went to get the laundry out of the dryer and came back to find her playing with the glass top stove, ready to put her hand down on the pretty red spot. Once, while in Bobby's office, I saw her and BJ walking down the middle of the street. Like a toddler, she could be in harm's way in a blink of an eye. Unlike a young child, her mind was wilting, not blossoming. I could only redirect her, and only if she was willing.

Mom kept scratching her arm one day, so I pulled up her sleeve to see why. A raw oozing rash covered her arms, legs, and torso; it must have been incredibly uncomfortable. *Oh my God, she's having an allergic reaction to her new meds!*

"Mom, why didn't you tell me about this?"

She smiled, "It's fine; it'll go away."

A trip to the emergency room revealed an allergic reaction to something topical. My mother shook her head no when asked if she was using a new soap, detergent, shampoo, etc. They gave us a cream to clear it up, and we went to her house so I could find the cause.

I hadn't been to Mom's in over a year. Before I got sick, we had lunch at her house most days and rode to the studio together. After my treatments started, we ate at my place so I could rest before work. After I was well, we continued to eat at my house and I'd drive us to the studio from there.

When I walked through the door, I was stunned. Mom's house was filthy and smelled horrible. Even though it was August, all the windows were closed and locked. Dirty dishes were everywhere, and pots caked with moldy food sat on the stove. I quickly learned what was causing the rash. She had been showering with shampoo thinking it was body wash, and also using it as a lotion to help her rash. There were bottles of it all over the house. Undies were soaking in the kitchen sink, and when I asked her why she said she didn't want to go downstairs to do laundry anymore.

"So, you only wash your undies now?" I asked.

Her answer was a smile and a shrug. I couldn't believe my mother was living like this and I didn't know. My guilt was overwhelming. *I should have known from her behavior. I should have come over sooner; she's my responsibility.* Had I been so selfishly busy with myself I refused to see more than I had to? I added a shot of shame to the guilt cocktail.

I knew one thing for sure: this arrangement wasn't working, and something needed to be done. As I cleaned her house, I mulled over the different options.

She's not bad enough for a home, is she? No! I can't do that to her.

She can't move in with us, what if my cancer relapses? Bobby would have two of us on his hands. It wouldn't be fair to him.

Could he handle it? Could I?

She obviously can't be alone. Think, you need to think, Belle.

I decided I would keep her with me during the day and at the studio, then hire someone to stay with her at night. I had a plan; now I needed to find the money.

I called my brother, filled him in, and asked him to share the expense. John flatly refused. He said our mother had never been there for him, and he wasn't giving her a dime. I understood his response now that I knew what horrible things she had chosen not to see, but I needed his help. And to be honest, I was confused.

Up until her diagnosis, John always treated our mother like a queen, never showing any anger towards her, only love. Had I stopped to think, I would have recalled how successfully I'd hidden my ill feelings towards her long ago, and shown her only love. Maybe John, thinking I had endured the same fate as he, had only been following my lead. Now that he knew the truth, he dropped all pretenses. I can't fathom how deep his emotions towards our mother must've run. I don't know because I wasn't thinking. At the time, my sole focus was on her safety.

"Please, John, for me. I'll deal with everything and leave you out of it, but I need help financially to keep her home."

"No," he said, and hung up.

That was the last time I had any contact with my brother.

As it turned out, the meds her doctor, "who wasn't her doctor," had put her on, seemed to start helping. That, and spending most of her time with me, appeared to level things off for a while. I unplugged her stove, locked her basement door, and checked her house daily. Not ideal, but it worked for a short time.

I needed to get Mom's affairs in order so I could make decisions about her care now and in the future. We went to see a lawyer and Mom signed over power of attorney and health proxy to me, but insisted we include John. I couldn't tell her John had left for good; it would've broken her heart. But neither could I set things up to require his signature that would never come. The lawyer handled it by making John a substitute should I be incapacitated, and Mom was none the wiser. Now I just had to stay healthy—not exactly a given at that time.

In the fall, a friend spotted Mom, at five thirty in the morning, twenty minutes from her house. She was trying to execute a left-hand turn and barely getting it done. I ran into her neighbor a few days later, and she told me she thought my mom was sleeping at my house because her car wasn't in the driveway at night.

When I asked my mother about these things, she told me they were mistaken. "Oh no, it was the afternoon, Honey." She was losing track of days and nights. I checked her car's odometer on a Sunday and again on the following Saturday to find she had driven over five hundred miles. My house was two miles each way from hers, and she rode with me everywhere else she went. That kind of mileage meant she had to be driving most of the night, every night. It was time to take her keys.

I asked Bobby to sit in on the intervention, thinking she would be less likely to give him a hard time. We tried to reason with her, even though I already knew it was impossible. "You aren't safe. What if you get lost or hurt? What if you hurt someone else? What if you run over a dog or a child?" (Harsh I know, but I was desperate).

Nothing swayed her. All she did was look down at her folded hands and say, "But I need my car. What will I do without my car? Why do you want my car? You have your car." She quite simply did not understand.

Bobby finally said, tenderly for him, I might add, "Lois, you cannot drive anymore."

Seeing men as figures of authority, she finally said, "Alright."

I took her home, checked out her house, and tucked her in. The last thing she said was, "Honey, do you still have my keys?"

"Yes, Mummy, you're safe. Please go to sleep."

"Okay," she said, and drifted off.

This isn't working, Belle. It's time, you know it's time. You need to start thinking about placing her. NOOOOOO!!!

The next morning, Sunday, Bobby and I were still in bed when I heard a whisper, "Honey, I don't want to bother you, but I need my keys."

What the...?!

"Mom, how did you get here?" *Christ, it's only 6:00 a.m.* "Did someone drop you off?" A rhetorical question since I already knew the answer.

She had walked two miles of country roads (with no sidewalks) to get to my house. A phone call from her neighbor later that week, in the middle of the night, telling me Mom was walking down the road, forced me to make the inevitable decision.

I did the research and found the place where I thought Mom would feel most comfortable. It was a small, homey, assisted living center in a Victorian house. It was close to me, and she would even have a private room and bathroom. *She'll be safe here. She'll be safe here. She'll be safe here.*

For two weeks, I dropped Mom off for activities and lunch, as if it was a day center, trying to acclimate her to the environment and people. She hated it and knew something was off. "Everyone thinks I'm going to live here like them, but no way," she said.

Mom refused to get out of the car one morning. "I don't want to go in there, you know."

"I know, but it'll be fun," I told her. She rolled her eyes and made me promise I'd pick her up, which I did—on that day.

Bobby and I set up her room the weekend after Christmas. I hung pictures of her sisters and parents on the wall and placed photos of John, Jeannie, BJ, and me on her bureau. I brought all her favorite movies to play on her new TV and DVR combo, her favorite knickknacks, clothes, and lots of chocolate.

That Monday, instead of going home, I brought her to her room. *Thank goodness Jeannie's here with me.* Mom hated it. She hated me. I didn't blame her; I hated me. She laid on the bed and refused to look at me or speak. *I'm sorry, Mom, I'm sorry, I'm sorry.*

The facility suggested I stay away for the first couple of weeks so Mom could adjust to her new way of life, but there was no way I was abandoning my mother. I went to see her every day, and every day she would have the pictures off the wall, and her belongings packed. She'd lay on the bed and refuse to look at me. I would keep talking to her while I put the room back together, kissed her goodbye, and showed up the next day to do it all over again. After some time passed, I took her suitcases home, hoping to solve the problem. The next day she had everything neatly stacked in piles on the floor. *Well, after so many moves over the years, she is a pro at packing.* At my wit's end, I finally took the facility's advice and stayed away for two weeks. It worked. *Imagine that, they know better than you do.* Mom still wasn't happy with me, but the room stayed intact, and she would talk a little.

Mom was starting to settle in nicely, so I was surprised to find her completely unnerved one day. She was pacing back and forth, head down with her hands shoved in her pockets. She wouldn't look at me or answer when I asked what was wrong. I wrapped her in a hug to calm her down and felt her shaking.

"Mom, if you tell me why you're so upset, I can fix it for you."

"I had no idea your father was treating you and John that way," she whispered. *What in the world brought this on...John!*

I made her look at me and reassured her Dad had not treated me that way, which seemed to soothe her somewhat. I got her to lie down, sat with her until she fell asleep, then immediately went to see the receptionist. Sure enough, my brother had called. I went to the administrator with a list of people Mom could talk to without notifying me first, and John was not on the list. *I have to protect her now.*

My mother's mind suffered an even more significant loss after John's phone call. If revenge and hurt was his intent, he got it. If closure was what he was looking for, he had waited too long. By the time he confronted her, our mother was incapable of processing that kind of trauma, never mind addressing it, although I doubt if she ever had been.

I found out John had also sent emails to Bobby and Jeannie, explaining his disappearance and the reason for it. He added I had been abused too and was in denial, something he needed to believe, I guess. Sharing his misguided assumptions with my husband was one thing, but sharing them with my daughter crossed a line. I was, and part of me still is, angry.

John stayed in touch with my mother's sisters for quite a while but stopped all contact with them years ago. No one knows how he is or where he lives. The aunts told me John had married for the third time and that they had twin girls. The last time my aunt spoke to him, the girls were ten, and he was thinking about going back into the Air Force. After that call, all of my aunt's cards and letters went unanswered.

My brother was (still is?) a troubled man, and I often wonder how he's doing; if he was finally able to find happiness, peace. I don't know why he never contacted me after that phone call, especially since he reached out to Bobby and Jean. Nor do I have an explanation as to why I never sought him out. Was it because it was all too much? My illness, his divorce, Mom's illness, my discovery he was molested, his learning I was not, both of us discovering we'd been living misconstrued truths about each other. Yet more trash for both of us to stuff into the already full garage bin of our youths. Perhaps one day our paths will cross, and we will find our answers, but for now, I have laid it to rest.

Mom needed to be safe, and I needed to live. I had earned my right to live; had fought damn hard for it, and won. But words cannot describe how conflicted I felt at that time, putting her in a home. In the end, I knew I had made the right choice for both of us, but boy, was it hard for me to get there, and harder still for her. I wouldn't wish that decision on the devil himself.

2004 was the epitome of bittersweet. I was granted a new life and regained my independence, a rebirth of a kind. My mom's life, as she knew it, was taken away from her, as well as her freedom. Not only did she lose something so precious to her, her home, but mentally, she was becoming a prisoner in her own mind. I cannot even fathom the latter.

Mom's life and mine did share one tragic commonality that year; we both lost John. My baby brother, all alone.

2004 was quite the year.

A NEWLY PAVED ROAD

NORMALCY, FINALLY. GRANTED, IT WAS A NEW NORMAL, BUT welcomed just the same. I never realized how comforting routine and the mundane could be until I had to live without it.

The first adjustment I had to make was at work. With Grandma Lois retired, I had to take over the business end of things, which meant less time for teaching. Fortunately, my Dance Angels stayed on as instructors and also did a lot of the choreography (beautifully I might add). My old normal was choreographing six or seven days a week, September through November, as well as teaching thirty hours a week. There was also costuming, scheduling, and mentoring; all great fun, but time consuming. There weren't enough hours in a day to add Mom's studio tasks, much less visiting her every day. My character building times had forced me to delegate my workload and trust the talented teachers that had grown up in my studio family. It was a valuable lesson learned. I continued to do so, and it allowed me the stress-free time to enjoy all aspects of my studio. It also enabled me to tend to and enjoy Mom.

Once Mom got acclimated to her new home and I could take her out, we started our new routine. We would go out to lunch, or for ice cream, or take a ride. Mom wouldn't sit still for five seconds, but put her in a car, and she'd ride for hours; it was her favorite thing to do. She had a habit of reading every sign we passed by out loud; street signs, building signs, election signs, stop signs, yield signs, you name it. To be honest, it drove me crazy most of the time. Until the day she stopped talking.

Mom just woke up one day and never said another word. She would laugh, say I love you, show happiness, sadness, or anger, all without a sound. On our rides, I would beg her to read the signs for me, to no avail. She just sat there looking out the window, smiling and holding her empty purse. So, I made a little adjustment; I started reading them to her, and she seemed to get a kick out of it.

There was only one time my mother spoke in the last ten years of her life. Years after she went silent, the facility had a sing-a-long, and Mom sang every word to "You're A Grand Old Flag." I like to think of it as her encore.

I was dancing again, albeit minus the leaps, splits, and high kickin'. *I can live with that. It's more than I've had the last three years.* I hadn't danced in recent recitals (for obvious reasons), and I decided I was going to perform one last time, to prove to myself I could. Knowing the June 2005 recital was to be my finale, I wanted to share the stage with my studio's foundation, its heartbeat. My assistant director at the time and her sister, who were the first students to enroll for classes twenty-one years earlier. My original associate director, who had left in 2003 and my instructors, who were between six and eight years old when they joined the studio.

We performed a tap dance to "Together , Wherever We Go," from the musical *Gypsy,* based on the memoir of Gypsy Rose Lee. Talk about going out with a bang! I stepped onto a stage for the last time surrounded by my Dream Team. My first thought as we took our bow was, *Yes—I did it!* Immediately followed by, *I just got outdanced on my own stage!*

That last thought left me grinning ear to ear. I couldn't have been prouder of them. I had trained these dancers, mentored them, watched them grow into beautiful dancers and young women. To see them so confident in themselves and their talent, knowing I played a part in it, was as reaffirming to me as the standing ovation our little tap trio got all those years ago. The difference being, the standing O was confirmation of my ability to dance; this performance was confirmation of my ability to teach. I found myself just as proud, if not more so, of this one.

I'd be lying if I said I didn't shed a tear as I hung up my last costume, but it was only a little one as the slideshow of memories ran through my mind. Remembering all the countless costumes and performances, the opportunities I was given, the pride I took in seeing my hard work come to fruition, and hearing the audience's appreciation.

Then I thought about the pride I felt as my instructors and students basked in the glow of their spotlight, listening to their applause. What a gift it was to share that with them, to be a part of their moment. *As long as you teach, you'll be performing Miss Belle; the best part of you will be on that stage.* Not only could I live with that, I considered it a trade up.

There was one new normal in my life that I wasn't adjusting to quite so efficiently. Mammograms, once just a routine thing, became the biggest challenge for me in my new normal. Only a fellow breast cancer survivor can understand the emotions that surround that test once the results of one threatened to kill you. I had to go every six months, and a week before the test, I would crawl, terrified, into my black hole and stay there until I heard the results. Fortunately, they read them while I waited. Sitting there in my Johnnie, shaking uncontrollably, I would try to fight off the horror my mind was creating.

I couldn't seem to adjust my attitude, no matter how hard I tried. *Come on now; you're here going through this because you lived. You survived! Focus on that.* It didn't work. I fell into that damn hole every time. After five years I only went once a year, but had to wait a few days for the results. As with most things in life, there was a trade-off.

Very few people knew how deeply I feared that test. Publicly, for the most part, I managed to maintain my game face. But an unlucky few got to witness me melt into a puddle of goo every time, which was not a pretty sight.

Something else happened in my early healthy years, something I couldn't adjust to; couldn't quite wrap my head around.

One Sunday morning, there was a knock on the door, a stranger asked for Bobby, and promptly served my husband with a paternity suit. I could tell by the look on Bobby's face that it was true.

"Give me a date," I said.

He shook his head. "This wasn't in the long-term plan."
Well, at least YOU knew about it.

"GIVE ME A BIRTH DATE—NOW!" I said with a little more force (make that a lot more).

I had been well aware of Bobby's reputation as a player. The year before we met, his team had the name Snake, embroidered on the left breast of his softball jacket, and he not only got a kick out it, he wore it with pride.

"It was way before you, Honey," he said and, shellshocked, handed me the papers. "She isn't mine. I didn't believe it then, and I don't believe it now." I looked at the complaint.

"That's not what the DNA test said when she was born."

"Well, it's wrong," he snapped. *Of course it is OJ.*

"And the mother told me she didn't want me in their lives, wanted nothing to do with me." *Was that before or after you kept insisting you weren't the father? Because she did have the DNA test done—that doesn't sound like someone who wanted you to be MIA.*

A closer look at the papers gave me the child's birthdate. One month before he started seeing me. Which, by my calculations, meant he knew one woman was carrying his child while purchasing a home with another woman, whom he cheated on with me, all in less than a year. *Well, if the jacket fits...*

I soon learned my third stepchild was the worst kept secret in Rhode Island, which is why I'm comfortable writing about her now. The child's mother was part of a close-knit group at the tavern that Bob had played softball for and where the team used to hang out. A lot of the friends he made there in the 1980s joined us for our Christmas parties, and some had become very close friends of mine. Others had girls that danced at my studio. The child and her mother had no reason or want to keep the identity of the father a secret and therefore didn't. I found out, a lot of my dancers went to school with the girl and knew Bobby was her father. Even my godchild knew about her. The girl's cousin lived across the street from Lyndsey, and they played together growing up. It felt like everyone knew but me. No one had ever said a word to me through the years, probably because they either assumed I knew or they didn't want to be the one to tell me.

While the above wasn't easy for me to digest, none of it is why the situation affected me so profoundly. It was Bobby's dismissal of her, his ability to convince himself she didn't exist. He's not a stupid man. He knew the DNA test proved he was her father. Still, he chose to believe otherwise because it was more convenient, a better fit for his lifestyle.

Even fourteen years later he was refusing to acknowledge her, refused to answer her calls. She left countless messages on his answering machine and eventually called me on my line and asked to speak with her father. While Bobby stood in front of me, shaking his head no, I had to tell her he wouldn't take the phone. I told her I was so very sorry and hung up. Rarely, if ever, have I meant those words more.

Publicly, I stood by my man. I regurgitated the lame excuses he had fed me to other people. I followed his lead and portrayed him as the victim. I went against my morals and principles to support him. I had sold myself out and knew it; hated it (that's mine to own, not his). Even worse, I felt I had somehow sold Jeannie out. There were differences in my daughter's situation with Steven and this one with Bob to be sure, but there were also similarities, and they hit home with me. Hard.

And at the heart of both scenarios was an innocent girl callously hurt by an unfeeling father. Both of whom I had married.

Sigh...

PART VI

RAINBOWS, BUTTERFLIES, AND UNICORNS

FINAL CURTAIN (S)

---

*A*GE HAS NEVER BOTHERED ME. *I DIDN'T WISH TO BE OLDER AS A child, and I don't want younger as an adult. My turning fifty stands out for me only because of the significant changes that took place in my life, and me, during that decade.*

For my fiftieth birthday, Bobby rented a room at my favorite restaurant and threw me a surprise dinner party. I could tell he put a lot of thought into the guest list, which included people from different areas of my life, and he even had someone bring Mom. I felt touched by his thoughtfulness and the effort he made to give me a special celebration.

That lovely party was a surprise for me in more ways than one. Unfortunately, my fears in Saint Thomas had come to pass. Bobby hadn't had an epiphany that fateful year that made him a more attentive, loving husband. Had he played a role? Did what he had to do for appearances, so important to him? Genuinely cared, but a whole year of showing it exhausted him? I had no idea, but I did know I was back to feeling like an afterthought for him. His lifestyle and the dynamics of our marriage had reverted to their original state.

Some people believe a person's real character shines through in times of trouble, a crisis. I disagree. Anyone can wear a mask, or put on a show for a limited amount of time. I believe it's the person they are, day in and day out that defines their character and shows their true colors, as well as their genuine heart for you.

⸻

AROUND MY FIFTIETH BIRTHDAY, I DECIDED TO CLOSE THE studio. I knew I was no longer able to give it my all, and the students deserved nothing less. I had changed in the three years since my illness, as had my life. I still cherished my time at the studio, but personal time had become just as important to me. I wanted more time to play golf, travel, float in our pool, sit on the beach, walk, shop, read, go to lunch—more time to live. At one time, I was able to do it all, but I no longer could. I was healthy again but lacked the wherewithal and, more importantly, the motivation to go full throttle twenty-four seven. Living had taken on a new meaning for me, and I knew better than to take it for granted.

I'm ashamed to say I took the coward's way out to announce the studio's closing. I did a mailing to my clientele and immediately left on a trip to Florida so that no one could reach me. The studio was closed for spring break, so the students would have a week to process the news.

The letter also announced my new venture, Verve Dance Company. I'd always wanted a small dance company and felt it was now or never. The letter explained Verve was for dancers twelve and older who were serious about developing their skills. Sessions would focus mostly on technique and strengthening. Uniforms and specific shoes were required, and auditions would be held for performances. Verve would be a much more disciplined environment than they had experienced at Belle's School of Dance.

Belle's had a casual, fun atmosphere. I encouraged and supported individualism, so there were no uniforms—quite the opposite. I have a picture of students lacing up their pointe shoes in softball uniforms because their game went into extra innings, and they didn't have time to change before class. We didn't have dance competitions or auditions. It didn't matter if you had two left feet or were naturally talented; there was a place for you, and everyone was encouraged and treated with respect. I was determined if someone wanted to dance, she would dance to the best of her ability and be proud of it. Some beautiful dancers came out of my studio, and others knew it wasn't their forte but stayed anyway because they loved to dance. The only prerequisites I had were you had to be a team player, and you had to leave the words "I can't do it" at the door.

I did my best to keep the last June recital upbeat and positive but I didn't succeed very well. A mother came up to me after the final curtain, and, very upset, informed me I was the only one in the building not crying. *You have no idea the tears my heart is shedding, but it's time.* A coward once again, I didn't go back to the dressing rooms to say goodbye. I couldn't face my students' tears.

I don't usually regret how I handled a situation in life. I go with the belief I dealt with it the best way I knew how at the time, and leave it at that. I do, however, regret the way I handled closing the studio. My students deserved better from me, and I owe them an apology. So...

"I'm sorry, ladies, truly sorry I didn't say goodbye. I loved you all, and the years we had together meant the world to me. Thank you for sharing a part of your lives and allowing me the privilege of being your Miss Belle. It is an honor I will always cherish."

Years too late, I know, but it is from my heart.

Debbie and Emily were recently enjoying time with another friend of mine and her daughter when the girls, who had both danced with me for years, started reminiscing about how much fun they'd had at the studio. All the dances, costumes, and recitals, etc....Debbie was sweet enough to text me to let me know the special memories I had given so many girls and to say I should be proud. I did feel pride when I read her text, but grateful was the first word that came to my mind. Grateful to have shared twenty-five years of memories with so many outstanding young ladies.

DURING THE SUMMER BETWEEN THE STUDIO'S CLOSING AND Verve's debut, Bobby took a picture of me with his cellphone. When he showed it to me and asked if it was a keeper, I told him to delete it immediately and joined Weight Watchers the following day. *Where did those twenty pounds come from? Oh yeah, the donuts and fries.* It was time for me to get physically back on track, and I did. After a year of eating right, walking three miles a day, and training at Verve, I lost the weight and was toned and healthy. I looked and felt better than I had in ten years.

Still, my husband showed no interest in me; if anything, he showed less. I can see so plainly, on the other side of therapy; this was his issue, not mine. But I couldn't see it then. Then his behavior made me feel unworthy of his time, plain and simple. Whether it was intentional or not didn't matter; it was devastating. It was exhausting trying to get his attention, trying to measure up. Many a time, I attempted to talk to him.

To explain that words matter: "*You can't only criticize and never compliment.*"

Actions speak louder than words: "*You can't leer at attractive women and never even look at me.*"

Inaction speaks loudest of all: "*You can't keep ignoring me. I'm here dammit, acknowledge me, I matter.*"

He showed no interest in listening to me, much less hearing me.

It also didn't help the marriage that I was now able to come and go as freely as he, because Verve's format was less structured than the studio's. I would often fly to Florida with a friend, who was remodeling her condo there, to check on the progress. In between picking out bath tile, flooring, and paint, we would sit on the beach and read, nourish our friendship over long lunches, and solve the world's problems on her patio. All very innocent, but Bobby didn't like the role reversal.

"I don't get why two married women have to go to Florida all the time," he'd say.

"I told you, she's remodeling the condo," I would reply.

"And she needs you there?"

"No, I need me there." *For someone who never bothers with me when I'm around, you sure take notice when I'm gone.*

———

VERVE WAS UNSUSTAINABLE FINANCIALLY AND ONLY LASTED A year or two, so I now needed a plan for my next adventure. I had an idea but needed to work out some kinks.

My mom loved tap, so sometimes when I visited, I'd bring our tap shoes and her favorite songs, and we'd dance. Because I was worried about her falling, we would sit and do some simple steps, but it still had the desired effect; it always made her smile.

One day I looked around and noticed the other residents were trying to follow along. *Wow, this is so awesome! But they need tap shoes.* The activities director convinced the administrator to split the cost of tap shoes with me, and that problem was solved. *Now I need to figure out how those who can't move their legs can participate. Rhythm sticks! They can follow the same beat with their hands.* And just like that, I had a new kind of tap class. We had so much fun during those classes, and it was as healthy and rewarding for me as it was for them.

So, when I needed a new career, that was my first thought. *I can do this at other facilities and charge a fee.* Tap shoes were my biggest dilemma to solve. I needed something easy to transport that would fit a variety of different sizes, and I could disinfect after each use. Debbie came to the rescue. She called while shopping one day and told me she'd found ballet style bedroom slippers at half price. Maybe they would work? *Yes!* I ran to the store and bought every S, M, L, and XL they had in stock. I had saved the exchange bin of children's dance shoes from the studio, and Bobby helped me pry the taps off. I found a glue that would withstand the washer and dryer and glued the taps to the bottom of the slippers. I cut wooden dowels into fourteen-inch sticks, painted them gold, and I was ready to go. I dressed professionally, called on a couple of local nursing homes, and I was in business.

I laugh like crazy when I remember my equipment those first few years. Child taps on adult slippers, gold paint flecks from the sticks all over the floor and residents, and an old iPod, and a cheap portable speaker for music. But I was also equipped with enthusiasm, a unique program, and a love for what I was doing.

I limited my new endeavor to part-time but recognized its potential, both as a therapy program and as a business. That realization was a much-needed boost of confidence for me.

With my newfound confidence, I started standing up for myself in the marriage. I stamped my little foot down about where I was going to play golf. I was joining Wanumetonomy. His family was there, I loved the course, it was on the water, and I enjoyed the atmosphere of the club.

He stamped his big foot down and said, "We aren't joining there. It's too far, and we already belong to a course."

"You belong to a course. WE do nothing there together. I'm joining Wanno. We can join as a couple, or I'll go as a single, but I'm leaving Seggie," I said. I was adamant and not budging.

Bobby joined too, of course—his brothers would've razzed him unmercifully had he not. He also kept his single membership at Seggie, which meant more golf and even less time in the marriage for him, but by that point, it was a trade-off I didn't mind. *Miss Belle is getting her moxie back!*

When my Honda got rear-ended, I needed a new car. I test drove a pre-owned Accord and an Acura. I liked the Acura better, but it was two thousand dollars more. Bobby said it was too much to pay for a second car.

"We don't have a second car. There's the car you drive and the car I drive," I reminded him.

I ended up with the Accord. Three weeks later, Bobby pulled into the driveway with his Cadillac CTS. He had never mentioned he was looking at cars, much less buying one. The one time I asked him to park our so-called second car at the airport so I could drive the Caddie while he was gone, I got a resounding NO. I started calling the Caddie his Fat Cat car after that. I didn't mean it as a compliment, and he didn't take it as one. Things were not going well.

I saw the car episode (start to finish) as my payback for Wanno. A way to prove to himself, and me, he was still in control. I don't know if that was the case or not, but it looked that way to me.

There was a price to pay for my newfound moxie—a big one. The more control Bobby felt he was losing over me, the colder he got. He was never big on affection, but now "Winking" had become the only intimacy and touching in the relationship. Bobby's interest in Winking (with me) had waned considerably since THE YEAR, but now, there was even less. It felt as though he was withholding his only show of affection towards me as a punishment of sorts; to remind me of my place. His behavior and the things he would say did nothing to dispel that belief and typically reinforced it. It was humiliating, and after a while, it worked. I lost all confidence in myself as a woman. *So much for moxie.*

With that ultimate putdown, the emotional house of cards I had been residing in for years was complete, the penthouse suite added. I was living in a place that was barely able to withstand a breeze, never mind the perfect storm that was brewing.

Many people didn't know this side of the marriage, nor will they believe this version of Bobby. To the outside world, he was Sammy Sunshine, always jovial and pleasant, a nice guy.

Many people will be surprised the Belle they know allowed herself to be put down and controlled for years. I appeared put together and was always smiling, happy.

The havoc emotional manipulation and degradation reeks

on a woman isn't something others can readily see from the outside. Not even those closest to the situation. It's not a scar visible to the naked eye. The damage it causes is something that happens gradually over time. It can take years for even the victim to know the impact it has had on her life, health, and self-worth. Years before, she realizes she was manipulated to believe she is less than another, which could not be further from the truth.

In February 2011, Bobby and I took a trip to the Cayman Islands. By this time, I was chastised back to my place in the marital pecking order. The only time my moxie would show up was after a couple of glasses of wine, and since we were on vacation, the cork was off the bottle of liquid courage more often than usual. Not good and not well-received.

I bucked him on everything during that trip. Where we were having dinner, the pool or the beach, take a cab or walk—everything. I saw it as a battle of wills, and I was determined to hold my ground; to have a say. How sad I had come to think of my marriage that way.

I am not a jealous person, and Bobby had always checked out other women, but having been rejected by him for so long, my ego was very tender. And very pissed off.

So, when I came back from the restroom on the last evening of vacation and found him chatting up the attractive bartender, I reacted—unpleasantly. I leaned over and whispered something about him taking care of things at home first and instantly knew by his body language he'd had enough. It was time to shut me up, and boy did he ever.

As soon as we were seated at our table, he let me have it. "You can't keep up with me drinking. When you do, there's a personality change, and it's ugly. This trip is case in point. You need to knock off the wine. It's become a real problem for you."

If you want to drop someone who has survived my past to their knees, call them a drunk. With that one statement, he not only shut me up; he owned me. The emotional house of cards collapsed and buried me beneath the rubble. I could barely breathe. In winning the last battle of wills, he had won the war. Bobby had complete control. The marriage was no longer the only thing in trouble; so was I.

On my sweet grandma's soul, up to that point, my drinking was not a problem for me, but it became one then. For well over a year, after work and on weekends, I had a bottomless glass of wine in my hand. I had discovered I needed a lot more wine to stay mute in the marriage than I did to find the courage to speak up. And I had to remain silent at all costs, remembering all too well what happened the last time I stood up to him. I couldn't fathom what his next verbal attack would be, but I knew I was at capacity and wouldn't be able to take it. So, I became a quiet, obedient little wine drinker. Chardonnay was no longer my courage; it was my pacifier and new best friend. Children live as they learn. Not thinking clearly, it didn't occur to me that my new way of coping was confirmation for Bobby that he was right.

And around and around we go.

FORE!

———

I HAD MASTERED THE PUBLIC GOOD MARRIAGE ACT YEARS before, but after the Cayman Islands trip, my performance became Oscar-winning material. "Aren't those DeCostas fun? Always smiling and laughing. They sure know how to enjoy life." We were proof positive all that glitters is not gold. Publicly people saw the same couple, but privately the marriage was deteriorating quickly.

At the Cape that summer, two of my close friends and I were discussing how unfair it is that generally speaking, men are considered more attractive as they age while women are considered old and less attractive.

Bobby overheard us and commented, "Well, if you want me to get it up, give me a thirty-year-old."

Shocked. Silence. One friend told him he had just sunk as low as he could go, and I thought the other one's eyes were going to pop out of her head. When I called him on it privately, Bobby said he was kidding. *Like hell you were.*

"Nobody laughed," I said.

"I did," he said. "You used to have a sense of humor, Belle, what happened?"

You happened. You can't habitually dismiss your fifty-five-year-old wife then make that comment. I finished the bottle of wine to stay silent and numb my hurt then went to bed early.

When my old desktop computer froze one afternoon, I mentioned to Bobby if it couldn't be fixed, I wanted a laptop. "You don't need a laptop, Belle, and you wouldn't like it. The keyboard is tight, and the screen is too small," *said King Tut to the peon.* "I'd still like to look at them if I have to replace that one," I said. Bobby took it to be checked out and returned home later that day with my brand-new desktop, all set up with my data. I poured a glass of wine to swallow my words and scurried back into my place.

At the same time, my business was growing by word of mouth, and I was also maintaining my weight. I loved to walk, and it helped to manage my stress and kept me toned. I enjoyed dressing up for work and loved wearing high heels. For the first time since my twenties, I was out in the working world and not cocooned in my studio dressed in leotards and yoga pants. I started noticing getting noticed, and it was nice. I became a clothes horse and owned more shoes than sense. I was proud of the work I was doing and felt good about my appearance. When out and about, I was happy and secure in myself and my abilities. Then I'd go home, be ignored, and pour a glass of wine to cope. There is nothing lonelier than being married all by yourself.

One spring, Bobby and I went to the Azores with a small group of family and friends. San Miguel is a beautiful island, but unfortunately, we caught a bad stretch of weather. Except for the two travel days, it was cold, windy, and raining. A couple in our group and their friend from San Miguel had arranged a golf tournament so we Americans could get to know the Islanders. It was a great idea but would have been much more fun had the weather cooperated.

The couple's friend also took us to out of the way restaurants where we would dine on fresh seafood, and the best local cuisine San Miguel has to offer. It was all delicious but very rich and spicy.

Now seems like a good time to mention I travel about as well as a linen suit. After days of constant group activities, too much golf, lousy weather, and spicy ethnic cuisine, my system and I were both done. I just wanted to go home.

The second to last night of the trip, some of us were having a nightcap at the hotel, one that I admittedly did not need when I overheard a conversation between Bobby and another guy comparing different male prescriptions. *How odd.*

The following morning, my sister-in-law and I were supposed to golf with a friend she had met during the tournament. I dragged myself out of bed to shower, emptied my stomach into the toilet, and decided I was not going to take one for the team this time. I couldn't rally. While Bobby got dressed, I asked him about his conversation I'd overheard the night before.

His response was something like, "Yeah, well, that has no bearing on you and me."

Cue the theme from *Rocky*, please, and get ready for some theatrical prose. Like a phoenix rising out of the ashes, I rose up out of my black hole in a blinding blaze of glory. ENOUGH-HHH!!! No more. I suddenly saw through him like he was a piece of cellophane. I felt all the anger that had been swimming in Chardonnay break through the surface and become a full-blown rage. I saw the truth. His truth. My truth. The marriage's truth. The truth.

He, of course, had no clue of any change in me and skipped off to play golf with his brothers, proud of his little HUGE zing.

After he left, I curled up on the bed, hugged a pillow, and cried. I cried over the death of the husband I had during THE YEAR, and for what the marriage could have been. I wept for being broken and having let myself down. I sobbed in fear and shame at having started down my father's path. My God, how close I had come! I cried myself dry, then fell into a deep healing sleep. When I awoke, I felt more peaceful than I had since I'd met him, all those years ago.

I knew by the light coming through the window it was getting late, and I needed to get ready for our last dinner on San Miguel. *Thank God we're going home tomorrow.* I grinned when I saw the mess staring back at me in the mirror. My eyes were bloodshot and almost swollen shut. A puffy face, red nose, and snot caked in my hair rounded out the vision. But to me, I had never looked more beautiful. I was back. I could take care of the mess in the mirror with a cold shower and some makeup, but I had no idea what I was going to do about the disarray of my so-called marriage.

When our plane landed in Boston, I checked my voicemail, which included a couple of messages from Don Juan. Don worked at one of the facilities where I ran my program, and we had been flirting back and forth for some time. It was a harmless, fun banter that brightened my day. There was no denying the attraction between us, but we were both married, so we always kept it light and ignored the heavy.

Well, apparently, absence not only makes a man's heart grow fonder but also makes him more brazen. Don acknowledged his attraction to me and told me how much he missed my smile. In another message, he shared all the things he loved about me and why I was so special. In his last voicemail, he described what he thought we would be like together Winking and I was sold. Like I said, he was a Don Juan and his timing was impeccable. Before I could chicken out, I immediately texted him the three little words every man longs to read: Reserve a room. *Oh, look, a plan.*

Fuck you and the horse you rode in on Bob.

Okay, so maybe having an affair wasn't one of my better plans, but I'd do it again in a heartbeat. It gave me my womanhood back and, as crazy as it sounds, my self-respect. I no longer felt less than, not good enough. I saw the affair as standing up for and taking care of myself. I loved feeling in control of my actions and decisions again, even if they were less than stellar. It might not have been the most moral way to accomplish these things, but it worked. And the sex was great. Although now that I think about it, anything would have been better than nothing, so the bar was set pretty low. Still, I remember it as quite the time.

Some will say it was wrong, and others might think it was selfish. In my world, it was long overdue. It brought me back to life. And it was infinitely better for my all-around health than drowning in Chardonnay.

For five months, I felt desirable, pampered, and cherished instead of ignored. Whenever Don Juan called, his first words were always, "Tell me about your day," and then he'd intently listen while I told him. For the last few years, Bob's calls had become, "I can't talk, we're next on the tee. I'm just checking to see if we got water in the basement. No? Great, got to go." Or, "I forgot to clean up the dog mess before I left, and the lawn guy is due, so you'll have to clean it up. Sorry, can't talk, I'll be home Thursday." I'm fine, Bobby, honestly. Let me tell you what I did today, I would say, sarcastically, to a dial tone.

For those months, I had someone who had eyes on me for a change. Don Juan complimented me, talked to me, listened to me. He liked being with me, doing things with me, laughing with me. Don didn't cringe at my touch but welcomed it. He held my hand and was proud to be seen with me. He. Enjoyed. Me. After years of having my needs, feelings, and opinions disregarded, it was candy to my ego to be validated.

I had no grand illusions of who and what Don Juan was—I mean, he was cheating on his third wife with me. Only a fool would believe this was his first rodeo. I didn't care. I had no intention of riding off into the sunset with this man. I didn't have any long-term plans or expectations, nor did I want any. It's a good thing, too, because when Mrs. Juan caught on, she expertly traced and documented our time together. Once she had her proof, she roped and hogtied him and expertly lassoed me to the ground—rightfully so I might add. *I have always regretted my part in the hurt it caused her.*

We were busted.

KARMA

ONE DAY IN EARLY FALL, MY LANDLINE RANG IN THE KITCHEN as Bob was making dinner. When I answered it, a panicked Don Juan told me his wife was simultaneously calling Bob's office line. As Bob went out to grill the steaks, his phone began to ring. Seconds after it stopped, mine started again. This time it was a furious Mrs. Juan calling me every name in the book and demanding to speak to Bob. I hung up, but with the windows open, Bob caught the gist of the conversation. He brought in the steaks, placed them on our plates, and calmly sat down to dinner.

As he began to eat, he casually asked the loaded question. "So, Honey, you got yourself in trouble with this, Don Juan guy?" *Honey?! Wow. And how can he possibly eat right now?* I went with one of his tried and true tactics: the best defense is a good offense.

"Yes, I did. You haven't had any use for me, and I don't believe for a minute you haven't been elsewhere in all this time." *How the hell is he eating? And God, I wish his phone would stop ringing.*

He finally looked up from his plate and with his cocky shrug said, "You know what they say about payback? It turns out it's true." He then waved a dismissive hand at the ceiling and the ringing phone, saying, "And take care of that—I'm not dealing with her."

Having had his say, Bob not only washed his hands of the entire situation, but he also cleared any lingering doubt I had about his infidelity or the fact he didn't care. He finished his meal in silence and went up to his office.

Bob never said another word to me about the affair.

I needed time to think, to process what was happening, and that meant keeping Mrs. Juan away from Bob as he requested. To accomplish that, I had to take her phone calls—and there were many. She would call me at least once a day (usually more) and alternate between screaming what a whore I was and confiding in me like a friend, the latter being much worse. It didn't take long before the constant guilt and incessant name-calling wore me down. Bob had gone silent, but someone else had picked up the mic, and she was relentless.

I was stronger now but also had enough self-awareness to know I needed professional help to maneuver through this kind of chaos; I couldn't do it alone.

My friend gave me the name of a therapist, Dr. Leon, and I made an appointment. As I sat down for our first session, he asked me to tell him a little bit about myself and why I was there. After I gave him the cliff notes on the current situation, he asked me about my childhood. *My life is in turmoil, I need immediate advice on how to stop it from spinning out of control, and this guy wants to talk about my childhood?!*

"Dr. Leon, I came to terms with my childhood and all the issues it caused years ago. What I need is help with my present situation." What I didn't yet realize was the two went hand in hand, and we needed to work on them together.

After a few months of work, Dr. Leon and I shared a belly laugh over my ridiculous statement. "Telling a therapist you're over childhood issues is a giant red flag," he said. I had unwittingly told him more than I knew with that one crazy comment. And I was learning how much my childhood affected the way I navigated through my marriage.

Our father is the first man in our lives, and from the time I was eleven, mine was emotionally unavailable, verbally abrasive, and self-centered. Even though intellectually I knew that behavior was wrong, it was the type of man I had grown up with and therefore was emotionally drawn to—hence, Bob. Also, like my father, Bob's public persona was a fun guy who loved his family. Like my mother, I presented a public façade to support that belief. I was repeating learned cycles from my childhood in my marriage. That knowledge, coupled with being reassured I was not overreacting, hearing things wrong, or expecting too much from Bob, began pointing me in the right direction. I still had miles to go, but in those first few months, Dr. Leon and I had made some progress, and I was about to put it to good use.

On Christmas Eve, Bob came downstairs and showed me a phone number he said kept freezing on his cellphone screen. I knew it was Mrs. Juan's number and assumed Bob wanted me to know she was trying to contact him. *Has she been leaving him messages, and that's how he knows it's her number?* What did she hope to accomplish? Through our countless phone-calls she knew he knew, and that my life was hardly cheery. Why would she bother him on Christmas Eve, of all days? I thought I had managed to keep her away from him as he requested, but now I wasn't so sure. *Now, what am I going to do?*

The day after Christmas, Bob and I went to Marco Island, Florida, as we did every year. Why? How? Because the marriage had been a charade for years. Since we had never addressed the affair beyond that first evening, we just fell back into that same old pattern.

That vacation was awkward, of course, but also different in another way. Bob was more attentive than he had been in years. We functioned as a couple, talking over dinner and walking on the beach together. *Can I trust this husband to stick around this time? Maybe things can be different. Do I even want them to be, or is it too late?* It turned out I didn't need to worry my little head about it.

The minute we got home, I went to my computer to delete an email account Don Juan set up during the affair. I hadn't used it but wasn't sure if he had, and if I was entertaining thoughts of trying to repair my marriage, it needed to be gone. When I opened the account, I saw a scathing email from Mrs. Juan. The way it was written, I knew it was meant for Bob's eyes to see.

I instantly changed my password and simultaneously heard Bob say from his office, "Nice job, Honey." He knew about the account and was logging in at the same time, proving he had been in contact with Mrs. Juan all along. I had suffered name-calling and endless guilt to shield him, and his tent was pitched in her camp from the start. Bob was in cahoots with her, had aided and abetted in her degradation of me. For three months, I had endured phone calls to protect him from the very person he'd chosen as his teammate. His complete silence and refusal to address the affair with me became even more demeaning and crueler with this discovery. Yes, I had betrayed him, but this was a betrayal of a different sort; this was a mind fuck, and it was going to end immediately. *Time to roll up your sleeves, girl, you have a lot of work to do.*

Bob and I never said a word about the computer incident.

Thanks to my ongoing work with Dr. Leon, I was getting the guidance and tools I needed to heal. I was slowly getting my emotional ducks in a row, and because of that, I could start getting my life in order. I had an exit strategy to plan, because I was definitely out of the marriage; that much I knew for sure. But first, I needed to put an end to all the craziness.

When Mrs. Juan called to kick off the new year, I told her I would no longer tolerate her verbal beatings—I was not a whore. Anger had replaced my feelings of guilt and remorse. She had taken one too many bites out of me. "Do not call me again," I said, and hung up. I wish I could say that was the last of it, but it wasn't.

The affair was long over, but Don Juan continued to call and text. I assumed his life had pretty much become a living hell. I had played a part in getting it there and felt guilty. I had no desire to be with him, but he had rescued me when I needed it most, and I didn't feel right deserting him now. I owed him as much. So, we continued some communication, then Bob and Mrs. Juan would see the phone records and on and on it went.

Mrs. Juan would call, I'd let it ring, she'd hang up before it would go to voicemail and immediately call back. The cycle would go on until I answered the call to stop the constant ringing. (It was my business number so I couldn't change it). I finally snapped one day after a ride on this merry-go-round and called Bob on the golf course. I told him it had to stop, I couldn't live like this anymore. Bob told me he'd take care of it, and he did. She never called me again. I was sure they were still in touch regularly, but I bit my tongue—I needed time.

How in the world has this become my life? Oh yeah, now I remember.

A DOG AND PONY SHOW

M Y EXIT PLAN WAS SIMPLE BUT WOULD TAKE TIME TO ACCOM-
plish. That meant holding my tongue with Bob, even
though I was healing. I had to pretend I wasn't different, wasn't
stronger. I also needed to continue wearing the public marriage
mask, which I now found suffocating. *I must be getting better.*

The first thing on my to-do list was to build up my business
so that I could support myself. I upgraded my equipment to a
more durable slipper and better sounding taps. I ordered real
rhythm sticks with better tone, and a Bose speaker that sounded
like you were at a concert.

I picked the brains of geriatric healthcare workers and physical therapists to develop a program that could be adjusted to ben-
efit different disabilities and functioning levels. Patients in skilled
nursing homes, those inflicted with dementia and Alzheimer's,
and learning disabled adults, as well as higher function seniors
in assisted living centers. Jeannie came up with a great name, Tap
N Time, and created an awesome logo. I hired a lawyer to patent
the shoes, copyright the program, and trademark my logo. I had
brochures and business cards designed and printed. I videoed
classes, had them professionally edited, and my son-in-law created a website for me. Then, I got to work marketing and selling.
I made cold calls and mailed pamphlets with personalized notes.
I dressed professionally and armed with brochures, a smile, and a

strong belief in what I was selling, visited the facilities that hadn't returned my call. I offered sample classes and reduced rates to get Tap N Time in the door, knowing once they saw the program, it would sell itself. *Well, look at you all confident again, Miss Belle.*

I'm a force to be reckoned with when I believe in something, and I believed in Tap N Time. I'd seen the program work its magic, had witnessed the elderly and disabled transformed through the music and rhythm. It was an easy sell. In no time at all, I was working full time and had to hire another instructor.

Now it was time to take a look at our joint finances. For years, Bob and our accountant made all financial decisions during a round of golf. I had no idea what we had or where we stood long-term. *How is it you don't know any of this, you silly girl? It doesn't matter; I'm educating myself now.* Fortunately, Massachusetts is a 50/50 state, which made figuring out what I'd have post-divorce much simpler.

When Bob left for one of his business trips, I got busy. I'm surprised his office copier didn't run out of ink or start smoking after my first visit to the files. As I studied the stacks of papers, I discovered our finances reflected Bob's "Live for Today" attitude. *Well, you enjoyed the lifestyle too, missy, and now it's time to pay the piper. Living high comes at an expense.* I figured out I could and would make it work.

Yeah, I've got this. It was good to have my mantra back.

The more progress Dr. Leon and I made, the more secure I felt within myself. "You don't need GPS and Bluetooth in your car," Bob stated. Yes, I did. I was going to get killed trying to read a MapQuest printout or answer a business call while driving. I had them installed, and I bought a laptop. Bob's silent treatments became welcome, and his never being home a relief. His sarcasm and putdowns fell on deaf ears. *I'm getting better.*

February 2013 also marked a monumental milestone for me; I was ten years cancer-free! I can't describe the utopia I felt when the radiologist rounded the corner with her thumbs up. No more living in terror for a week before my mammogram and no more

MRI's. Gone were the days of me poking at imaginary lumps in the shower until my breasts were black and blue. I was just a normal woman, with a yearly test and exam. *I've made it!*

I was on cloud nine and mentioned to Jeannie I should celebrate somehow.

"You absolutely should, Mommio! What would be your number one choice?" she asked.

Without hesitation, I said, "Definitely a party. A party with dancing and good food and friends." *I love this idea!*

"Who would you invite?" she asked.

I rattled off everyone I could think of that had touched my life that fateful year with kindness and love. Bobby's family, Jean's in-laws, the Dance Angels, my hairstylist confidant, the tournament golf foursome, Seggie friends, Wanno friends, Cape friends. Friends, friends, and more friends. *I am one lucky lady!*

Early that summer, Debbie called to see if Bob and I wanted to go to dinner with her and Paul at one of my favorite restaurants. I readily agreed and was surprised when Bob did too. I started to walk up the stairs to the second level of the restaurant, and saw pink and white balloons. As I climbed higher, I began to see the beautiful faces of my inner circle, all yelling SURPRISE! It was a Pink Party, complete with a pink-and-white candy bar, my favorite foods, and a DJ. The cake had two humungous breasts on it, iced in a sexy lace bra, and was quite the masterpiece. Jeannie made a beautiful speech about THE YEAR and how she admired my strength. *There is nothing that compares to the knowledge your child is proud of* you! I was pretty emotional, so I hope I thanked everyone for their support through my ordeal and for celebrating the special milestone with me. I do remember asking them to please mingle and introduce themselves to each other because they were all very special people. Being from different walks of my life, they didn't all know one another.

We laughed and ate and danced and laughed and ate and danced, then did it all again. It was a perfect celebration of life, shared with family and friends. A dream come true for me and a magnificent gift from Jean and Debbie's heart to mine. As I understand it, Bob also had a hand in it, paying for the open bar, so a thank you to him as well. I was glad to see our deteriorating marriage had not seriously damaged his and Jean's relationship, and they could work together.

In the early fall of 2013, Bob overheard me scheduling classes for February 2014. It was the month he wanted to spend in Florida, which I had no intention of doing.

"You go. I don't want to leave my mom, and what about the dog?" He wasn't going for it.

"You're just throwing this relationship away," he said. *Relationship?! He can't be serious.*

"I'm not leaving my life here to spend a month sitting around waiting for you to come back from wherever and whatever," I shot back.

"I told you it wouldn't be that way, but you don't believe me," he said. *No, I don't, because it has always been that way.*

"Well, it's months away, and I hope to have a second employee by then." We both knew I was lying. It was time.

I started interviewing lawyers. The first attorney was like a rabid dog. "Clear everything out of the house while he's away. Take it all and let me deal with him." *Ah, no.* The second lawyer was so young and sweet I couldn't imagine her tough enough to negotiate a playground scuffle, never mind a divorce settlement. For me, just like Goldilocks, the third time was the charm.

Mr. Lawson had an air of capability and quiet confidence. He was a logical, no-nonsense kind of guy and could intimidate with just a look and a soft-spoken word. I hired him.

One thing all three lawyers agreed on was that legally, the affair did not matter. Massachusetts is a no-fault state. I told Mr. Lawson that Mrs. Juan had most likely shared her documentation of events with Bob, which meant he probably had proof. He just gave a cocky shrug that put Bob's to shame and said, "Doesn't matter." I stopped him as he started to make a list of the paperwork he would need by plopping volumes one and two of my copies down on his desk. He gave a little half-smile and said, "Well, that should cover it."

In October 2013, I retained Mr. Lawson and filed for divorce. Bob called from out of town that week, and I told him the marriage wasn't doing either one of us any good.

"Ya think?" he said.

I told him it could go down easy or hard, but it was going to end. There was a lot of background noise wherever Bob was, so I don't know if he didn't hear me or just ignored me. "I'll be home Wednesday," was his send-off, and I hung up.

When he got home, I let him get settled into his office, and then told him I had filed. "Okay, Honey, whatever."

I don't think he believed me.

SHAKE RATTLE AND ROLL

ONCE BOB WAS SERVED PAPERS, HE HAD TO BELIEVE. WITH documents in hand, he said, and I quote, "Well, I guess this is going down. Now what?"

"You need to get a lawyer," I said. He shook his head no.

"If you want out fine, go, but you're not getting anything." *And the fun begins.*

It was my turn to wag my head to and fro. "Massachusetts is a 50/50 state. I get half."

"Except you had an affair," he countered.

"Doesn't matter. It's also a no-fault state." He got a lawyer.

Our respective lawyers set up an appointment for the four of us, and the meeting went as I expected it would. In Bob's world, I wasn't entitled to anything, much less half of everything. It was his retirement, his bank account, his house. Once Bob heard the word alimony, the meeting was over.

Mr. Lawson advised me to continue living in the house until we reached an agreement; otherwise, Bob would have no incentive to sign off. I knew he was right, but could I do it? *Yes, I have to; with Dr. Leon's help, I've got this.* Bob knew the minute I moved out temporary alimony would begin, so he was determined to wait me out. It was a standoff of epic proportions.

The lawyers started sending letters back and forth. Mr. Lawson would ask for more financial disclosure and threaten larger alimony payments. Bob's lawyer would counter with a letter demanding I give Bob money to live there and threatening to have me removed from the house, impossible to do with my name on it. Anything to make it unbearable enough that Bob would sign or I'd move out. It was a tense, stressful situation with no end in sight. Thankfully, Bob often traveled on business.

We started each day with a variation of, "You can't stay here, Belle." Answered with, "Sign the papers, and I'll move out tomorrow." I had to start eating Tums with my morning coffee instead of toast and was relieved when Bob went to Florida for February. The months between October 2013 and January 2014 had felt like an eternity—for both of us, I'm sure. The holidays were especially awkward, going our separate ways and then both returning to a cold house that was once our home.

A couple of days after Bob left, Mr. Lawson called and wanted me to come to the office. He had received a legal document filed in court by Bob's lawyer and didn't want to discuss it over the phone. *Great. So much for some relief.* When I sat down, he handed me the document, and I grew more incredulous with every word I read. It stated I'd had multiple lovers and affairs throughout the relationship, marriage, and separation. I had never been faithful. I repeatedly visited motels with various lovers while he was away on business, earning a living. In short, I was the Whore of Babylon.

I got hysterical, laughing. "Is he serious? This nonsense is a total fabrication! I had one five-month affair because he had no use for me. If it weren't so ridiculous, I'd be insulted." I found it even more entertaining due to the track record of who was sitting in the glass house throwing stones. Then a thought hit me. "Wait, you don't believe this garbage, do you?"

Mr. Lawson sat back in his chair and grinned. "Of course not. It's a tactic some men use to intimidate their wives into giving up alimony."

Unbelievable. This whole thing is getting uglier by the minute. "Will the judge believe it?" I asked.

"It doesn't matter if he does, the law is the law; it has no bearing on the outcome," he said.

"Okay, good. And Mr. Lawson? Now that I think about it, I am HIGHLY insulted."

"I thought you might be," he said with a smile.

I shot Bob off an email telling him how foolish and cowardly his little stunt was, and if he intended to intimidate me, it back-fired. He couldn't bully me out of what was rightfully mine, and if he wanted to get nasty, so be it. Sooner or later, he was going to have to accept the truth and the law. *Sooner—please make it sooner.* I sounded a lot tougher than I felt.

February was also the time for my yearly mammogram. *No worries there now, I'm past the ten-year mark.* I had the test done in between classes on a Thursday and went upon my merry way. Friday afternoon, I got a call from the technician saying they needed more film.

"Why?" I managed to choke out.

"We need a better look at your left breast. *NOOOOOO! God, please no.* My left breast was THE breast eleven years ago. She suggested we schedule a time for Monday.

"Monday? There's no way I'm waiting over the weekend. I'll be there within the hour," I told her.

This cannot be happening!

I called Debbie on my way to try and calm down. She said she'd meet me there and told me to think positive. I can't remember if it was Debbie or me that called Jeannie, but by some mira-cle, she was in Providence for meetings and could be there. They were both sitting in the waiting room when I came out from having the mammogram and promptly set about keeping me from going completely insane. Being a mammography veteran, I knew something was wrong, and I was inconsolable.

I can honestly say it's the only time I remember making a spectacle of myself in public. I didn't care. I was sobbing, wail-ing even. "How can this be? It's too much right now—I can't do this on top of everything else! Why now? What am I going to do? I'm in the middle of a divorce. Oh my God, the divorce! I have to go through with the divorce. I can't stay there. Not now. This cannot be happening!"

Jeannie and Debbie went into the radiologist's office with me to look at the film, the picture I couldn't seem to pull into focus. The doctor told me to schedule a needle biopsy, and I floated out to make the appointment. Jean and Debbie stayed to get the information I couldn't bring myself to hear. The radiologist told them it wasn't anything like I had before, but it was something; she didn't like it.

It was really happening.

After that initial meltdown, I began to pull myself together. I knew two things for sure: a) No matter the outcome of the biopsy, I was getting a double mastectomy. I was no longer going to be terrorized by my breasts. b) I was staying on track with the divorce. I was convinced the stress of the marriage had played a big part in my health, and I needed to move forward.

As expected, the biopsy was positive. Dr. Flan said that other than a negative result, it was the best-case scenario. It was not a return of my original cancer, was non-invasive, and involved no chemo. *Thank you, Jesus.* Radiation was the usual treatment, but because that breast had undergone—I cut him short. "I've already decided I want a double mastectomy." I waved my hand across my chest and said, "The girls have got to go."

Because I wanted implants, Dr. Flan's office made an appointment for me with a plastic surgeon, and the two doctors coordinated their schedules. My surgery date was on Good Friday. Dr. Flan would remove the breasts, and the plastic surgeon would insert the implants. A *one-stop operation, I like it.*

I called my lawyer to tell him what was going on and that I still wanted to proceed as planned. He said he would inform Bob's lawyer and wished me well.

When Bob got back, his first words were, "I was hoping you'd be gone by now," which I met with, "Me too, but you still haven't signed."

He went upstairs, saw the email from his lawyer on his home computer, and came flying back downstairs. "This is how I find out?!" he yelled. *Did he honestly expect any consideration from me after the* Whore of Babylon *document?*

I didn't have it in me to engage with him at that moment, so I stayed silent. Once he calmed down, he said he thought the mastectomy was the right thing to do, blah, blah, blah. And then I saw a look come over his face. "We have to put the divorce on hold until this is over."

Uh oh, time for me to speak. "No, we don't. One thing has nothing to do with the other," I said.

I don't know if Bob was concerned about me or his case, but my feeling is it was the latter. Especially since I knew he had met someone special in Florida (word travels fast). Knowing about her made it hard to believe Bob's concern was for me, and he had the problem of declaring me a whore of epic proportion in open court when I just had a double mastectomy due to a second bout with cancer. A tough sell even for a seasoned sales guy like Bob. And the alimony would most likely be increased because of my health. No, in my eyes, all of the above pointed to his concern being for his case.

I still had to tell my friends I was at war with cancer again, but I wasn't yet up to saying it over and over. *I'll know when I'm ready.* And I did. I was driving home from work one day, when all of a sudden, I felt incredibly resilient, upbeat even. *Funny. I'm alone, but I don't feel alone right now.* I knew the time was right, and I would be able to tell my friends in a way that would ease their worry. I pulled into a parking lot and made all the calls. I rallied my troops and was now ready to do battle. *Cancer, you're going down!*

The day after surgery, Jeannie and I waited for the plastic surgeon to come in to examine and discharge me. By late afternoon, I was afraid of being stuck in the hospital for Easter and asked the nurse to find him. She assured me she'd been paging him all day to no avail. I called Dr. Flan's service, and he immediately returned my call. He said the last surgeon to operate was usually the one to discharge, but after I explained the situation, he reluctantly agreed to let me go. The nurse, knowing no one had examined me since surgery, wasn't about to let me leave without taking a look. When she unwrapped my bandages, she found two black flaps where my new girls should have been. My tissue was dying. Rapidly. Have I mentioned nurses are saints?

Within minutes, two of the plastic surgeon's residents arrived and took pictures with a cellphone. A quick text to the man himself and Voila! He instantly appeared at the foot of my bed.

"Just a bump in the road," he said. I would need to start hyperbaric treatments immediately. *Fine—whatever that is.* Instead of going home, Jean and I took a ride to a treatment center. *Thank goodness she's here. Thank goodness she is who she is.*

Here are the cliff notes on hyperbaric therapy: You lay on a stretcher in a sterilized glass tube, which is sealed shut. The technician slowly lowers the air pressure in the chamber, which increases the oxygen flow to your cells and helps your body heal. After a couple of hours, they slowly raise the air pressure back to normal to prevent the bends before they unseal the chamber (think scuba diving). After a few treatments, you have healthy, beautiful skin and hair but scrambled eggs for brains. Those hyperactive brain cells start bouncing here there and everywhere, and you can't land on a single thought. It's also exhausting. Your entire body's cells are in perpetual motion, a hyped-up state for weeks. But it does get the job done.

I must've been in real trouble because that first night a tech stayed until ten, and one came in on Easter morning for hours, and again on Easter evening. I did this twice a day for two weeks, which saved most of my new girls. I then had outpatient surgery to remove the unresponsive tissue and continued treatments once a day for weeks on end.

After my second surgery, I wanted to get back to work and do something useful. The problem was I couldn't drive because of my two half-moons of stitches, and the post-surgical drains were still inserted (not to mention my scrambled egg brains). My friend Nancy came to my rescue. She would bring me to my daily treatment and read for the two hours I was there. I'd come out of the chamber, stuff my corset's bra, tuck the drains into their pockets, do my makeup, get dressed, and off we'd go. Nan drove, lugged all the equipment, and changed the residents' shoes. My only job was to sit there like a queen and run class, which I desperately needed to do.

Finally, the drains came out, the treatments were over, and I was once again feeling like myself. But I wasn't done yet; the implants had moved. One more outpatient procedure and all that was left were weekly trips to the plastic surgeon until the girls were my desired size. The injections weren't exactly pleasant, but I kept reminding myself when finished, I would never have to wear a bra again. Nothing could have cheered me up more. I've hated them from my very first training bra, and after fifty years of being imprisoned, I was looking forward to freedom.

THE SURGEON'S BUMP IN THE ROAD ENDED UP BEING MORE LIKE a detour over a mountain range, but fortunately, I had enough gas to make the trip and the best co-pilots ever, my friends.

A friend of mine said she didn't believe me when I told her the decision to have my breasts removed was a no brainer—spoken like a woman who has never faced breast cancer. I once saw a picture of a woman on Facebook doing a breast cancer walk, and her pink T-shirt read, "Hell yeah, they're fake. The real ones tried to kill me." That sums up my attitude perfectly. Besides, it's two fewer body parts that will sag. And no more bras. Have I mentioned no bras?

Forget diamonds. Camisoles are this girl's best friend.

CLOSING CIRCLES

AND OPENING DOORS

WHEN THE EARLY JUNE COURT DATE ROLLED AROUND, BOB and I were no closer to an agreement than we were in October. The judge gave us a continuance until July 31st, but said if there was no agreement by then, we were going to trial.

Things got even uglier at 75 Ferncliffe Road. We were purposely doing things to push each other's buttons, petty, childish things. Bob's "You can't keep living here," became, "When I get back Tuesday, you'd better be gone." Of course, publicly, he was thanking the people who helped me and answered inquiries about my health like he was concerned and in the know—something that infuriated me beyond belief. *If this doesn't end soon one or both of us is going to snap.*

I started to look in earnest for a small house to buy. Rents were outrageous and with an eighty-pound fur-baby, I wasn't exactly a landlord's dream tenant. Besides, I wanted to own my home, with a yard where I could garden and JD could romp (BJ, sadly, had crossed over the rainbow bridge). Cathi is a real estate broker/agent and being a close friend, knew what would be a good fit for me. We looked at many houses, even put an offer on a few, but none of them felt right. It wasn't because the neighborhoods were older or the houses needed work. I was well aware of what my price range would buy. It was just none of them were speaking to me. *I hope I find something soon.*

On another front, I got a call mid-June from my mother's memory care facility. Mom now needed more care than they could provide and had to move to a nursing home. *Now?!* I was beside myself with worry. The few facilities I would even consider all had waiting lists. I had no idea what I was going to do.

Unbelievably (Divine intervention?), my first choice had a bed open up the third week of June. I moved my mom from her comfort zone of the last ten years and into new surroundings with unfamiliar faces. *At least she's in the best place you know and will receive the utmost care. You've worked with these people, you know them, they are kind and loving. She'll be well cared for and safe.* I was only comforting myself. Mom was beyond knowing any one place or face from another. If the touch was kind and the smile genuine, it didn't matter who it came from or where.

At this point, Mom was in a wheelchair and needed to be hand-fed. I would go most days and feed her either lunch or supper. She was Stage 4 and living in the dark blank space Alzheimer's patients dwell in near the end. *I'm so sorry this is happening to you, Mommy, so very sorry.* As difficult as it was to see her unresponsive, I was determined to stay upbeat and chatty in her company. I knew Mom was in there somewhere, feeling my energy and love, and I needed to send her the best I had to give. I touched her all the time, read her stories, sang to her, and relished the times she opened her eyes or squeezed my hand. I made sure to leave all the craziness going on in the rest of my life outside her door.

Come the first week in July, when I hadn't found a house yet, I started getting concerned. My friend Joanne had offered to let JD and me stay with her if the divorce was final before I closed on a place, which I intended to do. But if I didn't find something soon and start the process, it could be months before we moved out. And as the saying goes, fish and overnight company should be thrown out after three days. *Days*, not months.

In early July, I drove by a little ranch for sale and found myself instantly drawn to it. You couldn't see the front or one side of the house because the bushes were so overgrown. I peeked in the backyard and saw that it, too, was overtaken by growth and had no grass. But standing guard amid the mess were two magnificent oak trees, the perfect distance apart for a hammock. *I like it.*

I called Cathi and asked her to set up an appointment, which she got that same day. The minute I walked through the door, I knew I was home. Mind you, it was a very tired 1950s little house. It needed a total update, including the kitchen and bath. I didn't care; it spoke to me, it was home. *There is something about this place.* Cathi felt it too.

"This is the one Cathi," I whispered. "Please tell me it has good bones."

It did. The realtor told us we were the first to see it since it had just gone on the market hours before I drove by. Confirmation it was meant to be. The realtor already had appointments scheduled for the following day but agreed to call Cathi before accepting any offers. Over lunch, I told her I absolutely could not lose that house. It was mine. When he called the next day we made an offer, and it was accepted. I had my home.

A week later, on July 19, 2014, I got the phone call all children dread; my mom had passed. They assured me she wasn't alone, a CNA was with her, telling her she loved her. In the seconds it took a nurse to get to her room, Mom had left her struggle behind. I rushed over to wait with her until the funeral home arrived to take her body. I sat on the side of her bed talking to her, kissing her, and telling her I loved her. I called Debbie, and once again, she was there for me, comforting me, saying all the right things.

After they took Mom's now empty shell from the room, I went home to make the sad calls, missing her already. One person I didn't contact was my brother. I wasn't yet aware my aunts were, at one time, in touch with him and therefore didn't know how to reach him. As final as his departure was ten years earlier, I don't know if he would've cared, but I now regret not having tried.

When Bob returned from a Florida trip a few days later, he once again came flying into the room after reading an email.

One of his golf buddies wanted to pass along his condolences about Mom's passing. Bob was beside himself. "Your mother died? How could you not let me know your mother died?"

"With as nasty as things have gotten between us, personally and legally, why would I?" I asked.

"That's business, Belle. People set that aside when something like this happens." *No, Bob, people do not. Emotionally healthy people with feelings and empathy and moral compasses do not. They can't.*

He asked if he could come to the memorial service, and I said yes.

Mom always said she didn't want a wake or service when she died. "Just cremate me and bury my ashes in the family plot," she'd tell me. I kept the service small and private to stay as close to her wishes as possible, but there was no way I was doing nothing. Her sisters, granddaughter, and people closest to her needed a chance to say goodbye.

There was a short service at the funeral home, and then we each got up and shared a memory of her. It was an intimate touch, a very informal way to honor her, and I knew she loved it from above. After the service, Jean and Jeff hosted a luncheon at a small local restaurant and then took Mom home to stay with them. I had no idea when I'd be settled and didn't want her in a storage unit until we could get to Lincoln, New Hampshire and lay her to rest. She had spent long enough in a cold dark place.

When Bob left on a trip the next day, I went up to his office to give it one final sweep. I smiled when I discovered a copy of my business schedule that I kept in my handbag. *It looks like you're not the only sleuth in the house Nancy Drew.* When I sat down at his desk, I spotted a savings book from a different bank tucked in between two files. It was an account opened in October (the month I filed), in Bob's name only, for a large sum of money. He must've been in a hurry collecting paperwork for his trip and got sloppy. Or maybe it was karma. I called Mr. Lawson, who informed Bob's lawyer of my find, who, in turn, emailed Bob.

Bob got back from his trip two days later and read the email. This time, he calmly came down the stairs, sat in a chair, and looked at me as angry as I'd ever seen him. "How ugly is this going to get?" he asked quietly. Too quietly, I was scared. "You're going through my things now?" *If you only knew.*

Time for me to play dumb. "I was looking for a business card I needed and found the account." Having survived the living arrangements since October, I wasn't about to leave now with the court date only a couple of days away. But I was no longer feeling safe and didn't want to push it. I lied and told him I wouldn't go after it. Divorce brings out the absolute worst in all of us.

Just a week and a half after Mom's service, Bob and I were back in court. When they called our case, the judge tried one more time to get us to reach an agreement. He reminded us if we went to trial, the lawyers' fees would add up quickly, and we would be arguing over much less. He gave us until the end of lunch recess to come to terms.

A short while later, Bob's lawyer announced Bob wanted to talk to me alone. *Anything to end this today.* I agreed. "Don't let yourself get bullied," were Mr. Lawson's parting words.

"I really don't want to do this, Belle," was Bob's opening statement.

"Then don't," I said.

"I'm not paying you that much alimony. I don't make that kind of money." By now, I knew exactly how much he made. But I also knew him, and if I wanted it to end today, I needed to let it go.

"Okay, cut it back to this amount, and I'll still cap it off at four years." He would be seventy years old by then. I didn't want to ruin the man; I just needed to build a nest egg in case I got sick again.

"Why should I pay you any alimony?" he questioned.

"Because you make six times more than I do," I replied.

And because you owe me a marriage.

"Do you honestly think you're entitled to any of my retirement?" he asked, head tilted back and looking down his nose at me for the last time.

"Yes, exactly half. I'll settle for forty percent."

This exchange was so significant because I had held my own with him and not been intimidated. It was an AHA! moment for me. A realization of how far my work with Dr. Leon had brought me.

The lawyers came back in and heard our compromise. They brought up healthcare, and we established I would remain on Bob's for four more years. *Good, that makes up for the reduced alimony payment I agreed to.* Mr. Lawson and I left the room to concur.

The last sticking point was the discovered account. Bob's lawyer approached us, and said Bob wouldn't give half; he was withholding two thousand dollars. "Do with that what you will," she said, and walked away.

"What do you think?" I asked Mr. Lawson.

"I think you're being nickeled and dimed," he said.

"Well, I think two grand is a small price to pay in order to lose two hundred pounds," I said. It took him a second to get it, but when he did, we shared a relieved chuckle. One more trip before the judge and we signed the papers.

Had we gone to trial, I likely would have been awarded more, but I didn't need it. What I needed was for it to be over. As Bob and I walked to our cars, I told him I'd be out the next day. "Okay," he said. And with that, we parted ways.

I sat in my car and took a deep breath. *What a hoorah this has been! But it's over. It's. Finally. Over.* I felt giddy with excitement for my new beginning and saddened over what the marriage could have been; what it should have been. I didn't know whether to laugh or cry, so I did both.

Once I was back in balance, I opened my windows and cranked up the tunes. With a smile a mile wide and butterflies in my belly, I drove off to find my next destination on life's journey.

Yeah, you've got this, Miss Belle.

PART VII

DESTINATION ME

ARE WE THERE YET?

————

TRUE TO MY WORD, I MOVED OUT THE FOLLOWING DAY. I had been packing non-essentials since October and storing them in a friend's basement, so the grande finale didn't take long. I moved the furniture into a storage unit and JD and me into Joanne's.

Joanne and I have been friends for a long time, dating back to the Steven years, and have seen one another through some major stuff over time. Our kids grew up together, and her daughters and granddaughters took dance at my studio. We were close friends until our kids got older, and then, as so often happens, lost touch. We ran into each other years later, the month I filed for divorce, at a neighborhood Halloween parade. We reconnected instantly, our bond as strong as ever. It was wonderful to be supported by a friend I had known since I was sixteen and surrounded by a family I had watched grow up and loved. It was the perfect rest stop for me on my way home.

Joanne lives on a small farm I fondly call the family compound. The property has two houses; Joanne and her dad, Pop, live in one (he's in an upstairs apartment), and Jo's oldest daughter and her family live across the yard in the other. Early mornings, I'd have my coffee on Joanne's back porch watching and listening to the farm wake up. The goats would start their rambunctious play, the hens would cluck, and the rooster would strut around like, well, like a rooster in a hen house. The cows would come in from the field in hopes of some extra hay, and the cats would return from their nightly escapades meowing for their breakfast. It was a peaceful, life-affirming way to start the day.

Before long, nature's peace would become a flurry of human activity. Jo's dad would come down for coffee, the clan from across the yard would come in talking all at once, and Joanne's youngest daughter would drop off her active toddler for the day. It was just what I needed at the time; the perfect combination of nature and loving family chaos. Of course, JD, my Dennis the Menace of dogs, did his part to add to the craziness.

Actually, he started making his contribution before we even moved in, when I took him over to make sure he and Jo's dog would get along. On his way through the door, JD lifted his leg on the doorstop, walked into the kitchen and threw up, then continued into her living room and pooped on the braided rug. In the time it takes to sneeze, the dog had spewed offensive matter from every orifice of his body. He had NEVER done anything like that before, nor has he since. As I was running around cleaning and disinfecting, asking him what the hell he was thinking, I heard Joanne laughing hysterically and looked up. JD was sitting proud as could be with his head cocked to one side and grinning as if to say, "I own this place now. We can stay." He had marked his territory, very efficiently I might add. Thankfully, Joanne is an animal lover AND has a sense of humor. Had it been anyone else, we'd have been living out of my car.

The first night we spent in Jo's guest room, JD rolled over and fell between the wall and the bed. He was quite a sight, wedged between the two on his back, all four paws clawing at the air and whining to beat the band. Once I got him right-side up, he hightailed it out of there and refused to step foot into the room again. We spent the next six weeks sleeping on the couch.

JD was in his glory being a farm hound, albeit one with a lot to learn. He was so excited when he discovered a dog park right in his backyard! He found a break in the electric fence and romped in to play. It didn't take him long to figure out these dogs had horns and hooves and played for keeps. Unable to find the fence break to escape, he howled bloody murder until Jo's son-in-law ran in to save him. He gave the goats a wide berth for the remainder of our stay. JD quickly learned the difference between a chicken and a rooster (you chase one and the other chases you) and discovered not all cats run away when barked at; some stand their ground and hiss and scratch. He learned fast; if you lift your leg on Pop's garden plants, you get tied up, and if you roll in manure, you get hosed down. He finally figured things out, and once he did, it was so much fun to watch him explore the farm. *What a gift this loveable goof is to me.*

When I closed on the house, Joanne suggested I continue to stay with her until the renovations were complete. I thanked her but said I had already stayed longer than expected and didn't want to take advantage. She insisted because, well, because that's the kind of friend she is and the size of her heart.

On Labor Day weekend, 2014, with the major projects completed, I moved into my dollhouse. Joanne rallied her troops, I gathered mine, and by the end of the weekend, it looked like I had lived there for a year. Our collective army painted, scrubbed, built shelves, and hung cabinets. They unpacked my kitchen, went grocery shopping, and set up the furniture. I will never forget the overwhelming feeling of gratitude and love I felt for all of them. *I* don't know what I've ever done to deserve them, but I'm grateful to have these outstanding people be part of my life.

Once my house was in order, I set about cutting back the growth that had overtaken my outdoor space and covered half my house. I hired a company to pull up the larger bushes and trees, but I tackled the rest myself. There were so many scratches on my arms, face, and legs I looked like I had lost a fight with an alley cat. My body ached to the point where I could barely get myself out of the shower and into bed at night. With the growth cut back, I borrowed a power washer and learned how to use it. By the end of a long day, I had restored the vinyl siding to its soft shade of yellow. I was soaking wet, shivering, and would have patted myself on the back but could no longer feel my arms. I loved every minute of it.

My friend B. stopped by with a housewarming gift from our book club, yet more beautiful people who share their friendship with me. It was a gift certificate to a nursery, and together, we picked out plants and bushes to plant along the front of my house in memory of Mom.

Cleanup was done just in time for the leaves to fall, and with two huge trees in the back, I had some major raking to do. Not only didn't I mind, but I enjoyed it. I live in a neighborhood of three-foot, not six-foot fences and friendly neighbors who are always ready to lend a hand for more than just a wave. I worked my tail off those first months, but seeing my property cleaned up wasn't my only reward. I also got to know my neighbors and developed a sense of camaraderie with all of them. I was right where I belonged. I was home.

I vividly remember the Sunday morning in late fall when I woke up and didn't have a single thing to accomplish before the Pats kickoff. *Does this mean I can finally let myself be tired?* And just like that, I was exhausted. Mind-numbing, bone-weary tired. I dragged myself out of bed, threw on a robe, and made a cup of coffee. With my feet up on the coffee table and JD curled up beside me, I reflected on the past year.

I had served my husband with divorce papers, then divided and packed up over twenty years of life and memories we had made together. I lived for nine months in an increasingly unbearable emotional environment. I was diagnosed with my second bout of breast cancer, had a double mastectomy, surgical complications, six weeks of daily treatments, two more surgeries, and weekly trips to get my implants filled. All while continuing to work and keeping the scheduled court dates.

Add in the stress of looking for a house and losing bids on two of them before finding the right one. At the same time, I had only weeks to find a nursing home for my mother and then lost her a month later. Mom's service, the final court date, moving out, moving into Jo's, overseeing renovations, moving into my home, and last but not least, becoming a human weed whacker.

Did all that really take place between October 2013 and October 2014? Yes. Yes, it did. *Forget being tired or even exhausted, lady, you should be in a psych ward.* I poured another cup of coffee and settled back in to go over all the reasons I wasn't residing in a padded room.

Dr. Leon came to mind. We still had work to do, but with the progress we'd already made, I had a better understanding of my childhood and the subsequent effect it had on my life. I also realized I was not imagining nor exaggerating the dynamics of my marriage, and the consequential damage it had caused me was real. I had made great strides towards regaining my self-worth, which had given me my old fight back. Without therapy, I would have never had the confidence to file, much less stay put and stand my ground through the divorce.

Then there was Jeannie. She took incredible care of me, was my emotional rock, and managed everything swirling around my healthcare as well as her Grammy Cracker's memorial luncheon. The circle of life in full motion.

And my friends. Debbie, who talked me down off the ceiling as needed (and it was required often) and was such a support for Jeannie as well as me.

Nancy, who took me to treatments and went to work with me, enabling me to keep my sanity as well as stay financially stable.

Cathi, who helped me find my sanctuary and maneuvered me painlessly through the buying process. We both cried tears of joy when they handed me the keys.

Joanne, who took JD and me in without hesitation, and never made us feel anything less than welcomed and loved. She shared her home, her meals, her family, and her heart.

And, of course, JD, who provided me with unconditional love, no matter what. He was taken from his home, lost his male human (whom he loved), and moved twice in a short amount of time. It took a toll on him, as it did me. But as long as we had each other at the end of the day, all was right in our world, wherever that happened to be. He trusted me, never lost faith in me, and never failed to make me laugh.

It takes a village to survive sometimes, and I realized how lucky I was to have mine.

Yikes, look at the time! The Pats have the one o'clock game this week. I guess I'll be watching it in my robe. Let's hope the team can add a win to my long list of blessings. Life is good.

Y CHROMOSOMES AND ME

"**D**R. LEON, I SUCK AT MEN. I'M NOT GOOD AT PICKING them out or keeping them engaged. And I can't seem to maintain me in a relationship."

He responded with a soft chuckle, and then we set about rectifying the matter. A lengthy process to be sure. I had years of getting it wrong to overcome. Some of it was daddy issues, some learned behavior, some of it was on the men and, drum roll please, some of it on me. Shocking, I know.

As far as boys go, when you get married at sixteen, there's not a lot of history. I've already covered the first crush, first kiss, and my "I wish he was my first." I've said more than enough about both husbands.

It's not that I never had the opportunity to make good choices in men; I just didn't.

When I was nineteen, days after I returned to Seekonk from Buffalo, one of the corner band members knocked on my apartment door. This man was one of the most authentic, genuinely loving people I had ever met. He told me he was crazy about me, would raise Jeannie as his own, and promised to love and take care of us. I turned him down, mostly for his sake. To this day, it is still the most sincere, heartfelt, generous thing a man has ever offered me. *With the chaos my life and I were in at that time, I did you a favor, my friend.* Timing is everything.

When Jeannie was two, I got engaged to Jason, a carpenter who adored my daughter and would've made a great father and husband. I woke up one morning and literally couldn't breathe, I was suffocating. *Is he here again?* I broke it off. After all, who wants a man wholly devoted and attentive to not only you but your daughter? *Geez, Belle.*

Re-enter Dave, the "I wish he was my first" from high school. After running into each other at the racquetball club, we discovered we lived in the same neighborhood, and it didn't take us long to have our, let's call it, belated prom night. We didn't see each other very often because I was twenty-three, working, and raising a daughter, and he was busy being twenty- three. Still, I was shocked when I ran into him and his month-long female house guest at the ice cream stand. Such a disrespectful, unpleasant way to find out he had replaced me. So, of course, I was crazy about him.

Marty entered soon after. He was an ethnic mama's boy whose mother's hatred of me was as intense as his infatuation with me. I was not Catholic, and I was divorced, a double whammy. I swear she wore garlic around her neck to ward me off, and it worked. It took little more than a year for me to have enough of that, and I moved on.

I then started seeing a blue-eyed charmer I met at the racquetball club who played me like a fiddle. I wish I could say I dumped him immediately upon finding out he was married, but I didn't. Being a slow learner, it took me a couple of years—and a marriage proposal. He was afraid Bill was getting a little too close for comfort and told me he would leave his wife if I agreed to marry him. I blurted out, "I can't marry you—you're a cheater!" *Did I say that out loud?* Yes, I did. It caught both of us off guard, but then the truth usually does. Between him and Dave, I decided it was time to find a new sport and stay away from the club.

Bill was the single father of a boy who went to the same kindergarten as Jean. He had custody of his son, was a loving father, and the kids got along great. He was fun, respectful, and we always had a great time together. So naturally, I stopped seeing him after a few months. Who wants a hard-working, handsome guy who's a great father and crazy about you? *Run, Belle, run!*

Re-enter Marty with a much more subdued mother. "If you make my son happy, so be it." There's nothing like a warm welcome into the family fold. Even though her son didn't especially make me happy, I accepted the diamond. Things fell apart when he wanted to move away from Seekonk, and I refused. I was twenty-seven and decided to take a break. *I'm getting too old for this.* I seriously did have that thought. Crazy, I know.

There were casual dates thrown in here and there over the next five years, but nothing noteworthy. I made sure of it.

You've already met nice guy Karl (who lost), and Don Juan (who didn't).

Dr. Leon pointed out the reoccurring theme was I always chose emotionally unavailable men, which initiated me to take a hard look at why. I discovered it was in part because it took less of a commitment from me and gave me an excuse to hold back and protect myself. Nice guys scared the bejesus out of me, and I was afraid to trust them, or me with them.

My father being emotionally unavailable was, unquestionably, a factor. It was less frightening for me to be with a man I already knew would let me down, something I was familiar with and expected. The known was damaging and unhealthy for me but infinitely less scary than the unknown. Their emotional unavailability also gave me a legitimate reason to bail out (that protecting thing again). And I think a little part of me liked the challenge. I discovered it was all of the above and then some. Dr. Leon and I used some serious elbow grease to work on my self-destructive pattern with men. It was not an easy mess to clean up.

———

ONCE I GOT SETTLED INTO THE DOLLHOUSE, I STARTED GOING out on Friday nights with Joanne. Some of the corner guys still had a band, and we'd go to hear them play and dance. Others from the old gang had solo gigs, and we'd grab a bite to eat wherever they were playing. It was fun reconnecting with them after so many years, listening to their music, and running into other familiar faces from school.

On one of these nights I ran into Bernie, who I had dated briefly in school. He introduced me to his wife; we shared some laughs about old times and went our separate ways. A few months later, I ran into him alone and asked about his wife.

"She's leaving me," he said.

"Oh, no, I'm so sorry! What happened?"

"She reconnected with someone from her past online," he said.

"I'm so sorry," I said again. *What else can you say?*

"Nah, don't be, it's all good. These things happen. Want to have dinner sometime?" he asked.

What?! "You just found out your wife of over twenty years is leaving you. Don't you think maybe you need some time to process it?"

"No, I'm fine," he assured me. *He can't be.* "Guys feel differently about this stuff. Seriously, it's no big deal," he added. *Good Lord, I think he is okay.*

"Look, if you need a friend, I'm here, but no, I don't want to go out with you," I said.

When I ran into him again, Bernie tried once more to my very chilly shoulder. Undaunted, he just turned around and introduced himself to the woman sitting behind him. It wasn't long before Bernie's hands were all over her, and she seemed okay with it.

My Achilles' heel also made another appearance. I hadn't seen Dave since the ice cream stand when I was twenty-three years old and honestly hadn't thought about him in decades. Joanne and her friend were with the band one night, and Dave was there. When he found out Jo knew me, he went on about how I was the love of his life, he always had a crush on me, blah, blah, blah. Jo told me he even had to sit down to contain himself. She texted me to make sure it was okay to give him my number, and I said yes. I figured all people grow and mature in thirty-four years. Not so, some remain the same. Dave was a hot mess in high school, a hot mess in my twenties, and a hot mess in my late fifties. He was still here, there, and everywhere all at once, chasing the next shiny object. The big difference this time? I was also a hot mess, made even worse by the fact I thought I was all put together. I was not. Unbeknownst to me at the time, I still had a lot of anger, hurt, and mistrust leftover from my marriage. I wasn't thinking clearly nor acting rationally.

Dave came on strong at first and then fizzled out with no warning, just as he had in my twenties. We discovered our lives had many parallels throughout the years, major life events that happened at the same time for both of us. Add the undeniable draw between us, a physical pull towards one another you could almost see, and it was clear to me something other than coincidence kept putting us in each other's path. He would call and text continuously, but we only went out a couple of times. He said it was work, but I believe it was avoidance. I don't think he quite knew what to make of me. I know I didn't know what to make of him. Thankfully, things didn't get physical this time, so I didn't have to process that.

I found it bizarre when Dave kept bringing up how guilty he felt about dating me (if you could call it that) because his buddy had a thing for me. Immature, to say the least, and baffling since the buddy had never even approached or called me. *I feel like I'm back in high school for Pete's sake.* It soon became apparent to me it was just a lame excuse. When I finally got tired of the broken dates and mixed signals, I told him I wouldn't be put on a back burner like I was in my marriage, and he stopped contacting me. I was devastated. *Why am I so upset?! He's self-centered and has no time for me—I'm supposed to be beyond this kind of unhealthy pattern.*

After I spent some time obsessing about things, I put my big girl panties on and went to get some answers. I needed closure. It was the best thing I could've done. Dave showed me so much in that brief encounter, became so transparent to me. I saw through his bravado and cockiness and realized his puffed-up offense and dizzying behavior was a shield to protect himself—from what I didn't know. I do know I walked away with a much different take on the situation.

I wish I could say that was the end of my hurt, but it was not. It took some time for me to let go of the schoolgirl fantasy I had of Dave. To accept the connection as unhealthy and not magical as I had led myself to believe. To realize that just because two people's paths repeatedly cross in life doesn't mean they were meant to be. To understand that not every powerful connection is a healthy one. Some are incredibly toxic and need to be avoided. Maybe that's why every time our paths intersected, I was somehow saved from the situation. I moved away in school, was unceremoniously replaced in my twenties, and this time hit over the head with a brick called reality. That's what it took for me to finally become aware of the lesson, to learn.

I had dated both Bernie and Dave when they were boys, and here they were again as men. These two man-boys carried a lot of the same character traits as Bob, and I feel they were set back on my path to make me more aware and to reinforce lessons I'd learned in my marriage.

Bernie's situation mirrored mine and Bob's close enough to point something out to me. Both men had been in long-term marriages and managed to move on instantaneously without even blinking an eye. Watching Bernie in action, I realized that for some men, women are interchangeable. It doesn't necessarily matter who it is, only that there is one. Whether it's twenty-five years or twenty-five minutes, moving on is as simple as that. It was an eye-opener for me.

It also brought to mind another telling fact. Bob had always been the one to end his relationships, and he never ended one without already being in another. Those four months without a go-to woman were his first, and my guess is a little scary for him.

I admit I struggled when Bob found a permanent replacement for my seat at the Thanksgiving table within months of being served. But thanks to Bernie, I had insight into how and why, and I felt better about things. I could let it go.

I believe man-boy Dave's reappearance was to make me see my lifelong pattern with men was only broken in theory, not in practice. The hard truth was my work wasn't finished. *Roll up your sleeves, Dr. Leon. We've got some more scrubbing to do.*

All of that was a lot to digest in my first year and a half of being single. I needed to make Dr. Leon and JD the only men in my life for a while. To keep things light and casual, I decided to try online dating. HA.

ALIENS FROM PLANET ONLINE

ONLINE DATING IS A FULL-TIME JOB FOR A MEAGER PAYOUT, at best. I know, I know, I've heard the success stories too. But I've also heard how much time and effort those people spent meeting duds before they found the right one.

In my opinion, dating sites are markets where people shop for a product. That may sound harsh and cynical, but from my experience and the experience of friends, it's the unfortunate truth. You're judging or being judged based on a photo and a paragraph. Scratch that, the picture alone. Anyone who says differently is sugarcoating the reality of it.

In hindsight, since I wasn't looking for a permanent Mr. Right and I was only willing to spend a minimal amount of time on the sites, it was a given I wouldn't find success. It became a standing joke between my friends and me on the odds of a third date happening. I would have an enjoyable time at the first meeting, and on the second one, their façade would crumble. *Bingo, that's why he's been on the site for years.* Here are some of my eye-opening experiences:

Let's begin with the guy who started Jonesing because the diner where we met for an early breakfast didn't serve alcohol. He insisted we go someplace else, and when I refused, he couldn't eat fast enough to get out of there. I almost suggested he start keeping a thermos of Bloody Marys in his car but remembered my manners just in time.

On the flip side of that coin was the gentleman who, when I ordered a glass of wine, started lecturing me on the evils of alcohol. He informed me he couldn't find Jesus until he put the bottle down and promised to help me do the same. *No, thank you, Jesus and I get along just fine.*

Then there was the date who tried to stick his tongue down my throat in a restaurant parking lot. I told him that at my age, I did not make out in parking lots, and he asked if he would ever find out where I lived. When I said not yet (more like never), he inquired why then did he have to keep paying for everything? Because you had six Grey Goose on the rocks and I had two glasses of house wine. *Oh, look, you have nothing to pay for anymore. Bye-bye.*

Enter the self-proclaimed nice guy who wanted to know where the relationship was going because he already had enough women friends. Relationship? It was only the second time we'd met. *I usually like to know a guy's last name before I sleep with him. It's a funny quirk of mine.* Next.

The porno dinner is my most bizarre war story by far. My date informed me over salads that rockin' sex was a must for him, and he needed to know my preferences. *Preferences? Yikes!* When I didn't answer, he proceeded to tell me, in graphic detail, all about the earthshattering sex he'd had with his first and second wives. In VERY graphic detail. *Is this guy for real? Is he trying to turn me on or impress me? Because what he's doing is making me lose my appetite.*

When I commented, "So, how about them Red Sox?" to lightly let him know I was uncomfortable, he said, "Oh, I see, you're one of those women who have a problem with sex."

I put my fork down, my coat on, and money on the table for my uneaten meal. I leaned over on my way out and whispered, "I prefer my men to find out my preferences through exploration." Done.

These were all on the second date. One. Two. *And I'm the one in therapy?*

I'm no quitter, so I gave it one more shot. I decided to reach out this time, figuring if it was my choice, it might have a better outcome. Not so much. His profile picture showed him in a pool holding his grandson. He was average build, had a shaved head (which I find attractive), and, like me, was an avid Pats fan. We emailed a couple of times, and he gave me his number. I called, and Mickey the Mope answered the phone. I tried to start a conversation (keyword: tried) and got only one-word answers.

"Your grandson's adorable, is he your only grandchild?" I asked.

"No."

"How many do you have?" I inquired.

"Three."

"All boys?"

"No."

Okaaay...let's try a new subject. "What do you do for work?"

"I have an engineering degree," he answered.

"So, you're an engineer then?"

"No, didn't like it—quit." Silence. *Well, at least he's working his way up to sentences. The Pats! I'll try that.*

"What do you think of all the changes the Pats are making? I'm afraid some are going to come back to haunt them."

"It doesn't matter what we think; it'll happen anyway," he mumbled. *Wow, this guy's a real charmer.*

"Well, I'll let you go, nice talking to you." *Sort of, I guess.*

Then, unfortunately, he spoke. "What do you think about online dating? I think it sucks," he said.

"No luck, huh?" I asked. *Could it be your engaging personality?*

"None. I met my wife online, and we got divorced after fifteen years. And I recently ended a ten-year relationship with another woman I met on this site."

When I mentioned I didn't see two long-term relationships as an online failure, he replied, "The next relationship needs to be the last one. I hate this dating crap." *I'm sure your dates feel the same way.*

He continued, "Women lie all the time, especially with their pictures. The pictures show young, thin women, and when you meet them, they're ten years older and fifty pounds heavier." *Women lie. I so need to meet you now, sport.*

He sealed the deal with, "We need to meet and see if there's any chemistry because if there isn't, talking and texting is just a waste of time." *Oh, I can already tell you there's zero chemistry, but I'm there. I think you need a little attitude adjustment.*

I got to the restaurant first, and when I saw him enter the bar, I choked on my drink. A red suit, beard, and a couple of ho-ho-ho's, and he could've quit his day job. He was at least fifty pounds heavier and ten years older than his picture.

"Hey, you look just like your picture," he said, making eyes at me. *Hey, you so don't.*

After a half hour of trying to keep the conversation going with his one-word, cranky answers, I looked at him and was as rude as I've ever been.

"I'm trying to have a conversation here, Mickey, wanna help me out?"

End of his making eyes at me, end of the meet and greet, and end of online dating for me. He had never once asked me anything about myself.

I left him sitting at the bar and met friends who were having a post-shopping cocktail. After some great conversation (consisting of full sentences), a few laughs, and a delicious meal, I decided it was a much better way to spend my time.

The above is a sample of my personal experiences, but I have more stories to tell. Online adventures of my single friends shared over a bottle of wine. All of whom know Jesus, by the way, despite their occasional cocktail.

I have a friend who, widowed after many years of marriage, agreed to meet someone at a local coffee shop. Within an hour, the guy told her he would have her in bed in no time. That was bad enough, but then he asked the question, "By the way, how are you groomed?" It took her a minute to realize he wasn't asking about her mani-pedi, and she hightailed it out of there.

Another friend agreed to meet with a guy who had a dazzling smile and a sexy black ponytail. In walked an old geezer with a greasy gray ponytail and no teeth. Not a one. *And women lie?* A lesser person might have asked why he was standing in for his son. She, however, bit her tongue and promptly received a pre-arranged emergency text.

Then there's the friend who met a man who said he wanted to be "right upfront with her." He was living with a woman, but they were no longer a couple, she just stayed to clean and cook for him. He seriously expected my friend to believe this. She informed him that if at the end of the day both their keys unlocked the same front door, they were still together, regardless of whatever he chose to think. *This guy is on a dating site?*

A third friend had a meet and greet where his opening line was, "You look a lot older than your picture."

She responded with, "You didn't mention you were an ass-hole in your profile."

He was profoundly insulted that she could say such a thing. *I'm sorry, what was the first thing out of your mouth?*

And the winner is...the friend who, after a few dates, liked someone enough to go home with him. She woke up the next morning to find him at his computer, trolling the dating sites. I mean, he could have at least waited until he gave her a cup of coffee and a kiss goodbye before he started to hunt for his next prey. *Geez.*

If still waters run deep, these guys are puddles.

If I had to hear, "I never saw it coming," or "I gave her everything, and it wasn't enough," or, "We were happy, and she just left," one more time, I was going to scream. If I had to read one more profile of "I love moonlit walks on the beach and cozy fires on a winter's night," I was going to be ill. It must be a cover profile, or maybe they get it off a Hallmark card. Because guys who talk only about themselves and never ask a single question about you, do not come up with that on their own.

I had someone tell me her friend wasn't having any luck online, changed her profile, and it worked wonders. She suggested I try it. Change it to what? Something I'm not? Or that I want something I don't? I just wanted to find a companion to enjoy an occasional movie or dinner with and let things either take their course or not. I had no interest in joining the ensuing circus.

Craziness. It's all craziness. I'm sure if you talk to men who online date, they have their own set of horror stories just as entertaining.

It takes a certain kind of person to join and travel with that circus. One with thick skin and a lot of extra time on their hands. Either that or a compelling want/need to find a partner. It's not for me; then, now, or ever. Attitude is everything, and on this particular subject, I admit mine is permanently bad.

RENOVATIONS AND

RECONSTRUCTION

I STOPPED SEEING DR. LEON SOMETIME DURING MY SECOND year after the divorce. I didn't have much to say during the last few appointments and felt our four years together had gotten me over the main bumps in the road. The many, muffler-scraping, humungous bumps. It took a lot of hard and painful work. I had to face and resolve my daddy issues and the effect they had on my lifelong failure with men. To own how those and other childhood issues allowed the dynamics of my relationship with Bob to evolve into what it did.

Such as, during my time with Bob, I morphed into someone I hardly knew. Having always been the new kid in school, I learned the quickest way to fit in was to adjust me to accommodate the new norm. A problem short term, but catastrophic over a twenty-five-year period. Belle got lost entirely, and I became only Bob-by-Belle. I lived in Bobby's world, went on Bobby's vacations, played Bobby's sport, did things Bobby's way, and had holidays with Bobby's family. I had also adapted to Bobby's philosophy on life. We lived a lifestyle that was all about the next good time, the next vacation, the next anything to enjoy. In my opinion, a shallow way of life based on what I felt to be a self-serving, self-centered attitude. Facing that it was not entirely Bob's fault (I *did* go along with) it proved to be eye-opening and humbling. *Double*

Ouch. I had to take a look at both Belles and come up with a combination that equaled the real me. A long and confusing process.

At the same time, Dr. Leon's guidance helped me work through the damage inflicted by my marriage through the years and bring me to a healthier place. A place where I could trust that the things said, done, and implied were real and not something I imagined or exaggerated.

I also had to own the baggage I'd brought to the marriage and face the part I played in its demise. A barely passable bridge to find and cross, but I did.

I've heard so many people say therapy didn't help them, that they got nothing out of it. My question to them is this: "Did you show up to work or just to chat?" Because a therapist can only work with you, not do the work for you. You can't just sit and talk for fifty minutes a week and never reflect on what was said or discovered. You can't only hear what you want to hear and disregard the rest. You need to confront and work through some hard truths. Harder still, you need to face your truth and own it. It means breaking some lifelong habits and adjusting the way you view and handle some things. You need to unlearn detrimental lifelong lessons taught to you. None of that can happen in fifty minutes a week. There is homework to do and lots of it. And you will fail sometimes and ace it at times until you finally get it right. Sometimes. Because that's the best you're going to do, and more than most will ever accomplish. Right for you, I mean, because there is no one right way to be or live.

That thought brings to mind my religion, Spiritualism (yet another gift Joanne has given me). You either believe in it or you don't. I never did until Joanne took me to a service one Sunday. Fortunately, the guest speaker/medium was the real deal and not one of the many phonies that are out there. The messages intrigued me, but more importantly, I felt spiritually connected for the first time in years.

Spiritual services are full of humor and upbeat talks from inspiring guest speakers, not sermons or lectures. Music selection covers everything from "Amazing Grace" to Norman Green-baum's "Spirit in the Sky." Impromptu dances have been known to happen in the aisles, and hugs are abundant. We are unconventional, all-forgiving, all-inclusive, and the warmest hearts you will ever meet. We are authentic.

Spiritualism is a religion based on love and acceptance, tolerance, and giving. It encompasses Buddhist, Native American, and Christian beliefs. We believe in and pray to God, Jesus, Mary, Saints, Archangels, all Ascended Masters, and yes, Spirit. We honor Mother Earth, all living things, and practice energy healing and meditation.

There is no guilt, judgment, fear, confessional, or penance in this religion. Spiritualists follow this set of principles, which we recite at the beginning of church service:

Declaration of Principles

We believe in Infinite Intelligence.

We believe that the phenomena of Nature, both physical and spiritual, are the expressions of Infinite Intelligence.

We affirm that the correct understanding of such expression and living in accordance therewith, constitute true religion.

We affirm that the existence and personal identity of the individual continue after the change called death.

We affirm that communication with the so-called dead is a fact, scientifically proven by the phenomena of Spiritualism.

We believe the highest morality is contained in the Golden Rule: "Do unto others as you would have them do unto you."

We affirm the moral responsibility of individuals and that we make our own happiness or unhappiness as we obey or disobey Nature's physical and spiritual laws.

We affirm the doorway to reformation is never closed against any soul here or hereafter.

We affirm the precepts of Prophecy and Healing are Divine attributes proven through Mediumship.

Embracing this religion has given me so much. It has opened my world to infinite possibilities with so much to explore and learn.

Open-mindedness: One of the greatest gifts you can give yourself. I have always had an open mind, but Spiritualism has expanded it to new dimensions. It has allowed me to be introduced to and taught so many things in the last four years. I keep what resonates with me and discard the rest, but I never discount any of it. It has all helped me to learn and therefore grow.

God, Infinite Intelligence, The Universe: Whatever my chosen name is for Him this particular day, I always believed in Him, figured He was around somewhere, but I never felt close to Him. I never felt like we had much of a relationship. Truth be told, I spent a lot of my life pissed off at Him. I know better now. Luckily, He didn't take it personally. I'm sure I'm not the first spoiled brat He's had to wait on to come around.

Archangels, my Guardian Angels and Spirit Guides: My winged posse. I don't know how I managed to go through sixty-two years of life unaware they were with me, but then I was mostly unaware of God being around. I had an intuition, a unique feeling that engulfed me when they put the needed situations or people in my path, but I never knew what it was or why.

For instance, when Bear came to my rescue in kindergarten. Seeing his size and yelling intimidate my tormentors should have made me afraid of him, but I wasn't; I knew he was gentle. Or the mysterious prima ballerina who appeared in Boston and restored my confidence in myself and dance. Being forced to dance at Miss Dana's, where I met Lucy and was compelled to ask her for a Philadelphia phone number for no apparent reason. A phone number that eventually led me to Miss Rose's where I earned my certificate, providing me with a lifelong profession I love. Placing the vision of the astronaut and snakes in my room that fateful night in Erdenheim, preventing me from seeing a horror I wouldn't have recovered from at that age. Having Steven and my paths cross that summer, which saved me from a hole too deep to crawl out of alone. Bringing me the gift of Jean and instantly making me aware when she was conceived, giving me the incentive to change my circumstances. Or Steven's talking so clearly in his sleep, only once, that led me to what I needed to see.

More recently, Joanne and my paths crossing at the parade after all those years when we needed our connection the most. Immediately knowing my home was the one, warts and all. They placed me in the perfect neighborhood and surrounded me with good people, creating a safe haven for me.

At the time of my divorce, I drove a Honda Civic, Stella, that I loved. She was economical and cute, but also small with blind spots, which made for some near misses. I was driving over 350 miles a week at the time and should have been in a larger vehicle, but didn't want the payments. The first winter after the divorce, I pulled out of a side street into an intersection and collided with a van because I couldn't see, or be seen, over a snowbank. The responders had to pry the door open so that I could get out of the car, but I wasn't hurt. Even though the other car was teetering on top of a snowbank, its driver was also unhurt. It was a warning I didn't heed.

Undeterred, I got Stella her facelift, and we sallied forth. Until one day, when I was driving southbound on an interstate and a northbound car's front wheel came off. It bounced over the Jersey barrier and came rolling right at me. I saw it coming, but I was in the middle lane with cars on both sides and nowhere to go. The wheel hit me dead on and rolled up and over Stella. I pulled over to the breakdown lane and got out to call 911, and that's when I saw the damage. The hood, windshield, roof, and trunk were all demolished. Stella was totaled. Between the windshield and sunroof, the entire interior was covered with shards of glass, as was I. Thankfully I had been wearing sunglasses, or chances are I'd be blind. A car's wheel traveling at least 65 mph, going the same speed in the opposite direction as I was, hit me at approximately 130 mph, and there wasn't a scratch on me—not a one. The responding officers couldn't believe I was conscious, much less unharmed. The other driver was also unhurt, and the wheel miraculously didn't hit any other car, nor did we. I finally got the message they were trying to send me and now drive an SUV. I'm also careful to pay better attention to their more subtle hints and my intuition.

There are many other times, too many to list, but I now feel my Angels and Guides around me always and thank them daily for all they do and the love with which they surround me.

Meditation: The gift that keeps on giving. It was a struggle for me to learn to clear my mind, but once I did, it allowed me to gain so much clarity, peace, and self-acceptance. It has taken my self-awareness to new heights and enables me to connect with the universe on a deeper, more profound level. I love sitting quietly and going within, either alone or in a group setting. Once you've learned to be present only in the moment, you can meditate anywhere. One of my favorite times and places to meditate is in nature. I find myself no longer walking through the woods, but walking with the woods. My senses are heightened, allowing me to become more in tune with the natural wonder surrounding me.

Chakras: Here's the bare bones analogy as taught to me; the seven chakras start at the base of your spine and advance up your torso to your crown. They are the Root, Sacral, Solar Plexus, Heart, Throat, Third Eye (intuition), and Crown (connection to the divine). They are the "wheels" where your spiritual and physical energy meets and come together. Keeping them aligned, open, and balanced is challenging but will improve your health and happiness immensely (ask any Buddhist). I find Reiki and meditation help me the most when my chakras are off-kilter. And at times, they're off-kilter a lot.

Spirit: Through meditation, I have learned how to call in and feel my family members come to me from the other side. I recognize them by their different energies and love to feel them around me when they visit.

I was panicked once because a well-meaning but uninformed licensed practical nurse pointed out a nodule under my left arm while I was working. When I meditated that night, BJ, my cuddle buddy during the year, appeared to me, plain as day, and I knew I was okay. After his visit, all my angst disappeared, and I slept like a baby. Dr. Flan examined me the next morning, and it was nothing more than scar tissue. As I've said, you either believe or you don't. I do.

Energy and Spiritual Healing: I'm a true believer. I am a certified Reiki II healer and eventually hope to become a master. I consider the ability to heal an honor and have great respect for the ancient practice. I place my hands on the person or animal I'm treating and ask the Universe to channel its powerful healing energy through me. Once I feel the energy shift, I move my hands about four inches from their body and travel slowly over their chakras and pained area, replacing negative energy with the positive energy being channeled through me to them. I know firsthand (pun intended) the help it provides relieving anxiety, stress, depression, pain, and discomfort.

Drumming Circles: Healing drumming circles are so moving for me. To set intentions with kindred spirits, then collectively drum our healing to the intended is such a feeling of community and solidarity; of hope and purpose. It has an incredibly potent spiritual effect on me. Feeling the rhythm and vibration enter my mind and body until it is my mind and body is raw and primal for me, intoxicating. The Sacred Drums beating in unison, as well as honoring the Native American rituals and chants, nourish my connection to the earth, sky, and water. My drum, which I have named Beating Heart, hangs on my bedroom wall. It is the first thing I see when I open my eyes in the morning and helps me to start my day with a smile in my heart.

Crystals: I still have much to learn about these beautiful healing gems and which one is best used to protect from or help with ailments, but I've seen them provide some relief and comfort to people I know—especially if they are Reiki infused.

I have witnessed the positive effect all these alternative healing methods have had on those of us who are open to them and even some who aren't. Used when receiving medical treatment, they can provide spiritual healing and relief during painful illnesses or procedures. They are also a great way to relieve the stress and anxiety of daily life and to send healing to those who need it.

Mediumship: Buyer beware! There are scam artists peppered in with the gifted. I've seen them work. They start with a general description of someone who is coming through, while closely observing the audience's body language and expressions. They then choose the person with the most visible reaction and go to them. The medium makes a few generic statements, and, based on the continued response of the person, asks a couple of questions. By now, this person is eager to hear from a loved one and starts to feed the medium. They unwittingly provide the information needed for the message. Those so-called mediums are nothing more than expert readers of facial expressions and body language. They prey on vulnerable people who are noticeably hurting from the loss of a loved one.

There are, however, some truly gifted people who can connect with spirit. Here is one of my personal experiences:

I attended a church one Sunday whose guest speaker was from New York. When it came time for him to give messages, his first comment was, "I have a father here, over six feet tall, black curly hair, and his name is John. My lower back hurts, I want to say it's a chronic condition. He is here to see his daughter." *Holy crap!* I raise my hand and keep my expression neutral.

"I smell cigarette smoke, and I'm having trouble breathing. This man died of either lung cancer or COPD in his forties." *This guy is the real deal.*

"Correct," was all I said. I know better than to feed a medium.

"He wants you to know how proud he is of you." Do *not* react, Belle.

"My baby girl, look at my baby girl," he's saying. That's what my father called me before his demons took over.

"He knows he let you down, wasn't there for you, but wants you to know he's here now and watches over you." *You can't cry yet—don't feed the medium!*

"Your father drank too much and took pills," the medium said. This is a statement, not a question.

"Your father knew it was a problem but couldn't stop."

The medium starts to cry. "I was weak, so weak!" *Oh, Daddy...*

"I'm so proud of you! Look what you've accomplished!" He is crying harder now.

The medium sobs and grabs his throat. "I can barely say this, the words come hard, but your father wants me to say it."

The medium becomes inconsolable. "I did horrible things to your brother. Terrible things." With that, my façade crumbled, and I began to cry.

"Your father has left now."

I received this message the day after I spent ten hours writing about my father for the first draft of this book. I had never met this medium, and he knew nothing about me, not even my name.

You either believe or you don't. I do.

A FAST LIFE IN THE SLOW LANE

---

*F*IVE YEARS ALREADY—*YIKES!*
    I've always wanted to tend bar, and now that I was single, I thought it would be a fun way to spend a couple of evenings a week. I took a bartending course and became a card-carrying, tips-certified bartender. I was all set to rock and roll until I shadowed a friend who tends bar one night and got over the fantasy real fast. How they manage to work that hard, remember everything, AND be fun and pleasant is beyond me. I was exhausted by last call and couldn't wait to get home to bed. As I grabbed my keys and she told me we had to break down the bar before we left, I might have growled. When it took the entire next day for me to recover, I decided to move back to the other side of the bar and keep my ten o'clock bedtime. Who am I kidding? It's usually more like nine.

I got a tattoo. Crazy, considering my lifelong opinion of them. I always thought they were over the top and couldn't figure out why anyone would get one. What is the purpose, anyway? Not to mention what they would like when the person got old and saggy—ugh.

Well, I'm already old and saggy, so that was a non-issue, and I soon discovered their purpose. I was missing my mom and still reeling a bit from my second spin with breast cancer. Out of nowhere (well, I now know from where) I got the idea to have the Alzheimer's and Breast Cancer ribbons tattooed on my left inner wrist. When the young artist asked me why that spot, I told him it was on the pulse of the left side, which is the heart side. He got the idea to connect them in the shape of a heart, and just like that, I now have Body Art. A masterpiece if I may say so myself. It hurt more than childbirth. But now, every time I reach for something, I'm reminded of my mom, our bond, and my will to survive—three paramount things to keep at the forefront of my mind.

The first full summer in my dollhouse, I had a deck built, and Pop (Joanne's dad) made Adirondack chairs and a decorative wishing well for me. I bought a birdbath and planters, and Jean and I painted everything in coral, turquoise, lavender, yellow, and tangerine. It looked like the ruins of a Jimmy Buffet tailgating party after the tequila bottles were drained dry. I have no idea what I was thinking. Maybe it was because I was feeling so festive and colorful about my new life, and I wanted to express it. Or perhaps I just took thinking outside the box a little too far. Either way, the look didn't make season two. The following Mother's Day, we painted everything in a more subdued color pallet, making sunglasses optional in my backyard and no longer a necessity.

Our Cape family decided to forgo the Fourth of July trip one year, so I enjoyed a relaxing staycation in my sanctuary. After a week of doing nothing more strenuous than moving from the hammock to the deck, and ordering takeout to be delivered, I was revived and ready to get back to work. On the last night of my hiatus, I awoke around 3:00 a.m. to JD, whining profusely in the hallway. He wouldn't come when I called, so I got out of bed to get him. I found him sitting in front of the living room archway, drooling a river onto my hardwood floor. When I still couldn't get him to budge, I turned the hall light on and found a baby possum, no more than eight inches long, playing, well, possum, on the living room rug.

The two of them must have encountered each other outside, and the little guy went still. Thinking it was dead, my brilliant hound put it in his mouth, brought it through the pet door, and freaked out when he discovered it was alive. He was now more afraid of the possum than it was of him.

As I was yelling at the dog to put it back where he'd found it, and he was cowering behind me for protection, mama possum crossed my mind. The baby couldn't have gotten through the pet door on its own, but mama could if she decided to come looking for her little one. *Okay, calm down! Put the dog in the bathroom, block the pet door, and get a bucket to trap the little guy underneath.*

I turned to put JD away and shut the door, which took two seconds tops. When I turned back around, the critter was gone. *Crap! Okay, think.* In my own state of brilliance, I decided to open all the screen doors, turn out the lights, and stay very quiet so it would leave on its own. After about fifteen minutes, the thought occurred to me it was three thirty in the morning, the dog was locked away, the house in total darkness, and all my doors were wide open. *Ah, duh.* I abandoned that plan. I chose to be optimistic and figuring the critter was gone, let JD out to make sure.

The dog raced directly over to the living room chair and resumed whining and drooling. With that, I realized I most certainly did not have the situation under control. There was no way I was going to bed with a possum in the house, no matter how small, and me whining along with JD wasn't going to help. So, I called the cops.

"East Providence Police Department," he greeted.

"You're gonna love this one," was my opening line.

I explained the situation, and the officer was polite enough not to laugh out loud. He asked for my address, told me animal control wasn't on duty, but he would send a patrol officer over to see what he could do.

I opened the door to a young, strapping cop holding his hands up like a surgeon scrubbed for surgery, wearing black attack gloves. He said, and I quote, "I'm going to do the best I can here, but this a first for me. I know what to do on a shots fired call, but this..."

Once he shined his flashlight under the chair and saw the size of the beast, he felt much better about things. That is until he moved the chair to cover it with the bucket, and the baby took off. The cop was loudly asking if I saw where it went, the dog started howling in the bathroom, and I was standing on the couch, screaming, all of which, thankfully, scared the little guy into playing dead again. My young hero put the bucket over the beast, slid a rake under it to block him in, and carried it out the front door.

As he walked across the street to let it go, I heard him comforting it. "It's okay little guy. You're going to be free in a second. It's all good now." We were both excited when it ran off and we knew it wasn't hurt. *Alright, the cop was excited. I was just glad it was out of my house.*

So much for being rested on my first day back to work. As I headed out the door a few short hours later, I heard JD snoring on the bed. He'd had a tough night and was sleeping in.

I love to sing, so when I found out the community chorus a friend sang with welcomed everyone, without auditions, I joined. On the first night, they handed me a thick packet of sheet music. Seeing the look on my face, my friend asked, "You know how to read music, right?"

"Ah, no. Dancers don't read music, they move to it," I said.

Undeterred, she highlighted the alto sections for me, and that's when I realized there were parts of the song I wouldn't be singing. *Well, that stinks.* I soon discovered I'm an alto only until the sopranos, tenors, et al. join in, and then I become all of the above. I was flat and off-key in all of them but did get to sing the entire song.

Some things just can't be fixed, and my voice is one of them. I quit after four rehearsals and wasn't surprised when no one called to see what had happened to me. I'm sure they shared a collective sigh of relief at my departure, in harmony, of course.

My neighbor has a Harley Sportster, and when I mentioned how much I loved to hear him fire it up, he asked if I wanted to ride. *Hell yeah!* I hadn't been on a bike in thirty-five years and had forgotten how exhilarating the speed was, how vulnerable I felt in the wind and the almost sensual feeling of leaning into the turns. I was giving the down low wave to passing bikers and feeling very cool until we stopped next to another Harley at a red light. The guys started talking pipes, and I mentioned to his lady what a great day it was to ride. She just sized me up and didn't say a word.

"What a witch," I said as we left them in the dust. Then I got a look at myself in the side mirror and cracked up laughing. My earrings dangled under my borrowed helmet and I wore a silk flowered blouse and a pair of ballet loafers. Hardly biker chic. Sitting there in her short denim cutoffs, bra-less Harley tank, and work boots, she was probably wondering what hay wagon I had just fallen off. When my foot got caught on the saddlebag dismounting at the restaurant, and I almost landed on my derrière, I realized just how rusty my biker cool had gotten.

I have since recovered some of it when we ride, but not all. I swapped out the silk blouse for a T-shirt and the ballet flats for sneakers, but I draw the line at work boots—I have fashion limits. And once again, I can get on and off the bike without causing a scene.

When I texted Jean one day to tell her I was going riding, her reply was, "LOL—I'll be home crocheting. Have fun and be careful!" There's that circle of life thing again.

Another full circle example: Holly and I make a point to get together at least once a month now. Having reconnected after many years, we refuse to lose touch again. Our friendship is incredible, as it always was, but there are some changes. It's been over thirty years since we sat in her kitchen, drinking endless cups of tea while Jeannie and Kelly played Barbies. With our kids now grown, pork tenderloin has replaced our tuna sandwiches, and we drink wine instead of tea. By the time Michael picks her up at my house, we're usually pretty silly, whether tipsy or sober. Without the responsibility of parenthood and example setting, we can be as immature in our behavior as we choose. We love it, make no apologies for it and, in reality, are kind of proud of it. I'm sure we leave our adult children shaking their heads at times.

I go to stock car races and the theater and enjoy them equally.

I feel just as beautiful bare-faced and in a ballcap as I do in makeup and dressed to kill.

I go to spiritual sound baths and to hear rock bands and find them both healing.

I love the all-encompassing beat of a native drumming circle, as well as the total peace and quiet of meditation.

I walk in the woods instead of malls and wear flip flops unless there's snow on the ground. My bi-monthly manicures have become special occasions only, but I still get pedicures because of the aforementioned flip flops. I do it as a public service. No one should have to look at my feet straight up for months on end.

I do work that I love, that makes a difference, and I own the business. It would be great if my boss gave me some time off once in a while to regroup. She has promised to address the issue, but I don't hold out much hope.

I love reading, writing, and singing. I've been neglecting the first, I'm working on the second, and the third is a lost cause. It does not, however, stop me.

I am kinder.

I've played golf a handful of times, but only nine holes. I don't miss it. I enjoy going out and slapping the ball around for kicks and giggles with friends, but without my name on the scorecard. That way, I can celebrate the great shots without worrying about how many strokes it'll cost me to recoup from the bad ones. Kind of how I look at life now: celebrate the good, tough your way out of the rough, and don't keep score. Works for me.

I will make only one statement about my politics. I own a pink hat with kitty ears, and I've worn it with pride in two marches. Even better, the cap was my daughter's suggestion, and she knitted it for me with love. I'm proud to say the apple did not fall far from the tree.

The only thing I have zero tolerance left for is intolerance—of any kind. Okay, so maybe that's a second political statement.

I am a Born-Again Virgin. Not a status I'm always content with, but I will remain so until the right one comes along. I date only as friends, emotionally and physically.

The next man in my life will be kind and genuine. He will honor our connection, be open to love and emotionally available. He will be gentle with me. I'll know my prince by the glass flip flop he will hold in his hands. Until, if and when, our paths cross, I will keep the keys to my heart and my chastity belt tucked safely away.

Which brings me to my opinion on being alone. There are people concerned that because I'm alone, I am lonely and therefore must be unhappy. Especially—*Gasp!*—at my age. I assure you I am neither. I love living alone. Let me repeat that: I love living alone. I have my own space and timetable, company when I want it, and privacy when I crave it. Not only do I get to partake in decision making, but my opinion is also respected; me, myself, and I can usually agree. I have complete control of my finances, purchases, and investments. There is less money, of course, but I know exactly where it all is, and the trade-off is well worth it for me.

I blast my music when I want to and have complete quiet when I need it. The TV is only on for Pats games and Nightly News instead of morning, noon, and night. If I need an ear to listen, I have multiple friends on hand; ditto for dining out or catching a movie. My neighbors and I share cocktails, laughs, and BBQ, and are there for each other in a heartbeat if needed.

I have made excellent use of this time alone, exploring and discovering so much about myself. Enough so, I wrote a book.

I am not lonely; I am free. And I'm right where I need to be at this time of my life. As I've said, if the right one comes along, I will review and revise, but for now, I am content.

My home and yard are exactly how I envisioned them that first time I walked through the door. Since the initial renovations, I've opened up a wall between the living room and kitchen, had cabinet doors made, added crown molding, and updated the bathroom. My lawn is lush and green, and my gardens have matured nicely. Those two magnificent oak trees are hosts to a rope hammock that gets plenty of use. I love the little paradise I've created and all it stands for, and the only way I'm ever permanently leaving it is in a body bag.

Things my home does not have: bad memories, negative energy, and a scale. Hence, I have pleasant dreams, positive energy flow, and an extra twenty-five pounds. I'm the biggest Miss Belle there ever was, and I'm good with it. Bobby-Belle spent years worried about her weight and dieting. I've now discovered they make clothes in size twelve and XL in different styles to compliment my body shape. *Who knew?* I do miss being able to rock a pair of high heels all day every day, but such is life. The twins are fifteen years old now and I'm lugging around the extra weight, plus doing yard work. They started to whine a bit but are just fine in flats and kitten heels, so I've adjusted to accommodate them. Speaking of clothes and shoes...

When I moved in five years ago, my closets were packed, tiered, and layered. Three of them had shoe bags hanging on the door, and shoe racks lined their floors. I had shelves full of pocketbooks and more costume jewelry than I could wear in a year.

All of my clothes and shoes now fit into one closet with room to spare, and my coat closet has plenty of space to hang up guests' jackets. I own only four pocketbooks, black, brown/black, summer, and small. The only jewelry I wear is a pair of silver earrings, an angel wing pendant, and my grandma's engagement ring.

I have downsized and simplified everything about my life, and have never felt more sated.

I talk to Infinite Intelligence, strangers, my dog, Angels, myself, my fish, and yes, dead people (I prefer to call them spirits.)

For the most part, all of the above listen, and except for the fish, usually respond.

By all accounts, Bob is a brand new man. My gut and I share a little Mona Lisa smile when we hear this. I don't believe a leopard can change his spots. But on the outside chance my gut and I are wrong, let me point out this brand new construction was built on the backs of his first two wives. Both very fine women, if I may say so myself. That said, I do believe he is happier than he's ever been and, therefore, has adjusted his attitude to maintain his current status quo.

From what I understand, Bob's present woman has plenty of her own money, pays her way, shares his mindset, and enjoys the same type of lifestyle. She owns a beautiful house on the west coast of Florida that Bob calls home, and brings zero responsibility to his table. All this makes her his perfect woman living in his ideal place and climate. Now that I'm finally over any residual anger towards him, I sincerely wish them well and hope Bob gets all the palm trees, rounds of golf, and cold beers it takes to keep him happy. No, you do not detect a note of sarcasm.

My family, friends, and neighbors mean the world to me. I would be nowhere without them; lost. They all provide endless love, support, and laughter from so many different walks of my life. I won't list them for fear of leaving someone out, but I'm confident they all know who they are. I share a unique bond, a connection with each of them that is precious to me, and I'm so blessed to have them along for the ride.

I HAVE RECENTLY LEARNED I'LL NEED TO ADJUST MY SAILS ONCE again. My plastic surgeon has informed me they've recalled my implants. It's rare, but they have caused Large Cell Lymphoma in some women. Evidently, some of the fake ones will try to kill you now too. He's replacing them with non-textured gel-filled implants and some of my belly fat to give them a better shape and keep them in place. It's outpatient surgery and only two weeks out of work if all goes well, which I see no reason why it would not. A virtual walk in the park considering what I've already gone through. When I conveyed that sentiment to friends, one or two said I didn't have to put on a brave face for them. I'm not; that truly is how I look at it. It's unfortunate but much more manageable than some past procedures I've endured, it's a mere squall compared to those hurricanes.

Author William Arthur Ward wrote: "The pessimist complains about the wind; the optimist expects it to change; the realist adjusts the sails." Ultimately, I am, and always have been, a realist, and proud of it. I will weather this storm as I have all the others.

Let me be clear; I AM angry. How is it manufacturers are made to put warning labels on everything under the sun (cough drops, cremes, aspirin) but not on something women are permanently placing in their bodies? Women who have removed cancerous body parts, only to find out they've replaced them with something potentially cancer-causing. Were there warning signs, and we weren't told? Were they put on the market before the proper research was complete? Were doctors informed of potential risks, and if so, when? I have a lot of questions, and I will find the answers sooner rather than later.

The moral of the story is: ask questions and do your research before implanting your new girls, ladies. And have them checked yearly no matter what.

I'VE DONE IT. I'VE DONE THAT CRAZY INSANE IDEA I WAS GUIDED to do: I wrote the book. Parts of it were painful to revisit, more painful, I believe, than living through them the first time. And some memories brought me overwhelming joy and triggered beautiful feelings I had long forgotten. To say it was all eye-opening would be the understatement of the century. It cleansed me, healed old wounds, and brought me tears of sheer happiness. It pointed out my strengths and underlined my weaknesses. It laid bare my character for me to see, to own. I am happy with what that character is today, but now see where it was, at times, flawed. I'm okay with that knowledge. Those flaws help me to become the woman I see in the mirror today, and I like her; she's my friend.

I'm proud of the determination I've shown throughout my life, my tenacity to make it through, make it happen, make it work, make it be. From the time I was a child, I had an instinct to survive, to flourish even, as best I could in whatever situation I found myself. I possessed a can-do attitude and guts born out of necessity. That took a strength, especially as a child, I didn't fully understand until I wrote this book. I was, and still am, the epitome of resilience.

That sound you hear is me patting myself on the back.

One of my favorite comics, Sinbad, says, and I'm paraphrasing, "God takes away our memories as we age, so the older we get, the better we were."

Keeping that in mind, I still only want two do-overs: going to Martha's Vineyard on Jean's birthday and not visiting the dressing room to say goodbye to my students after the last recital. Only two regrets in sixty-two years, but they were doozies. Every other action or reaction I chose, I would do all over again. Life is a chain of events, situations, heartbreaks, and joys. To change one thing, you risk altering them all.

I don't know what the rest of my journey has in store for me or even how many more miles I have left to travel. I wouldn't mind cruising down a paved straightaway for a while, but if not, so be it. I do know who will be driving from here on out: ME, with my winged posse riding shotgun, of course, and the universe lighting the way.

EPILOGUE

THE END. AFTER COUNTLESS SELF-EDITS AND REWRITES, professional edits and revisions, it's finally done. We did it, JD! It took two years, but we did it. I couldn't have made it through parts of my story without you cuddled up next to me, pal. Thank goodness you like the taste of salty tears; you've licked enough of them away. Some of them happy tears, some of them not so much, and some were downright toxic.

Thank you for insisting we go for our walk in the woods when you sensed my frustration or pain when writing. I wasn't always pleasant about going, but once we got there, I knew you were right. I needed to ground myself, and you knew the perfect place for me to do it. The smell of the earth, the sounds of nature, feeling the strength of the trees, and watching your antics as you played. It always cleared my mind and righted my inner compass.

THE END. What an accomplishment! I feel amazing. Renewed, rejuvenated.

"We're proud of you," I hear.

Thank you, I'm proud of me too.

"The hardest part is over," they assure me.

I know. The rest is just the process of self-publishing to research and maneuver. A lot of work but nothing compared to the emotional rollercoaster ride that I've just taken! It might be a lot, but I'm not worried.

I've got this.

ABOUT THE AUTHOR

Belle A. DeCosta is the creator and director of Tap N Time, a seated tap and rhythm class designed for the elderly. When not traveling to nursing homes to share her program, she enjoys being in nature, dining with friends, and writing.

Belle shares a home in East Providence, RI, with her beloved hound, JD, and an aquarium full of assorted fish.

Made in the USA
Middletown, DE
24 June 2020